BRITISH AND IRISH AUTHORS

Introductory critical studies

T. S. ELIOT
the poems

This book is designed to provide a comprehensive and stimulating introduction to T. S. Eliot's poetry for those reading and studying it. The poems, as well as some of the poetic drama (particularly *Sweeney Agonistes*), and relevant sections of the prose criticism, are discussed in detail and placed in relation to the development of Eliot's *œuvre*, and more briefly to his life and a wider context of philosophical and religious enquiry.

In sections devoted to each major poem or group of poems, Martin Scofield examines Eliot's techniques of *personae* or masks; his use of musical effects; the tension between fragmentation and cohesion in *The Waste Land* and other verse; the place in his work of symbolism and imagism, as well as less explored elements such as surrealism and comedy; the relevance to his poetry of concepts worked out in his critical writing; and the criticism of his 'poetic workshop', those essays on other poets which he saw as part of the development of his own verse. One recurring theme in the study is the poetic treatment of the relationship (often conflict) between experience in life and experience in art; another is the relation between Eliot's beliefs and his poetry, and between poetry and belief in general. Eliot in his finest poems is seen above all as a poet of what he called 'the first voice', 'oppressed by a burden which he must bring to birth'. The book concludes with a detailed and helpful study of *Four Quartets*: here as elsewhere Martin Scofield is concerned to look first of all at the texture of the verse and the qualities of the poetic 'surface', while clarifying obscurities and explaining allusions where appropriate. Both students and general readers will find his book informative and his commitment to the poetry infectious.

BRITISH AND IRISH AUTHORS
Introductory critical studies

In the same series:

T. S. ELIOT
the poems

MARTIN SCOFIELD

Lecturer in English and American Literature
The University of Kent at Canterbury

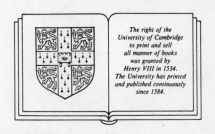

The right of the
University of Cambridge
to print and sell
all manner of books
was granted by
Henry VIII in 1534.
The University has printed
and published continuously
since 1584.

CAMBRIDGE UNIVERSITY PRESS

CAMBRIDGE

NEW YORK   PORT CHESTER

MELBOURNE   SYDNEY

Published by the Press Syndicate of the University of Cambridge
The Pitt Building, Trumpington Street, Cambridge CB2 1RP
32 East 57th Street, New York, NY 10022, USA
10 Stamford Road, Oakleigh, Melbourne 3166, Australia

First published 1988
Reprinted 1989

Printed in Great Britain at
the University Press, Cambridge

British Library cataloguing in publication data
Scofield, Martin
T. S. Eliot: the poems. – (British and
Irish authors).
1. Eliot, T. S. – Criticism and
interpretation
I. Title II. Series
821′.912   PS3509.L43Z/

Library of Congress cataloguing in publication data
Scofield, Martin.
T. S. Eliot: the poems / Martin Scofield.
p.   cm. – (British and Irish authors)
Bibliography.
Includes index.
ISBN 0-521-30147-5. ISBN 0-521-31761-4 (pbk.)
1. Eliot, T. S. (Thomas Stearns), 1888–1965 – Criticism and
interpretation. I. Title. II. Series.
PS3509.L43Z86353 1988
821′.912 – dc19   87-20436 CIP

ISBN 0 521 30147 5 hard covers
ISBN 0 521 31761 4 paperback

To my Mother and Father

GG

Contents

Acknowledgements

I am indebted in more ways than I can easily define to those students and colleagues at the University of Kent with whom I have discussed Eliot over a number of years. Without that activity and the chance it has given me to think about Eliot's poetry and to develop and revise my own ideas this book would not have been possible.

I would also like to thank Dr Michael Halls, the Modern Archivist of the Library of King's College, Cambridge, for permission to read the typescript of Eliot's Clark Lectures of 1926 and other papers, which are a part of the John Hayward Bequest to that Library, and for his kind assistance during my visit.

Finally, I would like to express my gratitude to the secretaries of Rutherford College at the University of Kent, and in particular to Mrs Pamela Hancock, for their invaluable assistance with typing.

Quotations from Eliot's published work are the copyright of the Eliot estate and are taken from the following volumes:

The Complete Poems and Plays, Faber and Faber, London, 1982
Selected Essays, Faber and Faber, London, 1966
The Sacred Wood, Methuen and Co. Ltd., London, 1966
The Use of Poetry and the Use of Criticism, Faber and Faber, London, 1964
On Poetry and Poets, Faber and Faber, London, 1961
To Criticize the Critic, Faber and Faber, London, 1965
After Strange Gods, Faber and Faber, London, 1934
Notes Towards the Definition of Culture, Faber and Faber, London, 1967
The Idea of a Christian Society, Faber and Faber, London, 1939
John Dryden: The Poet, the Dramatist, the Critic, Ann Arbor University, Microfilm 1967, repr. of Holliday, New York, 1932
For Lancelot Andrewes, Faber and Faber, London, 1970

A selective chronology of Eliot's life

(A chronological list of Eliot's major publications will be found in the Select bibliography, p. 257.)

1888	Born on 26 September in St Louis, Missouri
1893–1910	With his family spends summers on the New England coast at Gloucester, Massachusetts
1906–10	Undergraduate at Harvard University
1910	Writes the first two 'Preludes', the first part of 'The Love Song of J. Alfred Prufrock' and 'Portrait of a Lady'
1910–11	Visits Paris to spend a year at the Sorbonne. Attends Bergson's weekly lectures at the Collège de France
1914	Goes to England to study for a doctorate at Merton College, Oxford. Meets Ezra Pound in London
1915	Marries Vivien Haigh-Wood
1916	Begins a series of lectures on Modern French Literature and Modern English Literature, for extension courses at Oxford and London Universities
1917–25	Works with the Colonial and Foreign Department at Lloyds Bank, Queen Victoria Street, London
1917	Assistant Editor of *The Egoist*
1917–19	Gives courses of lectures on Victorian Literature, 'The Makers of Nineteenth Century Ideas' and Elizabethan Literature for the University of London Extension Board
1919	Eliot's father, Henry Ware Eliot, dies
1921	Suffers from ill health, diagnosed as a 'nervous breakdown'. Visits Margate to convalesce, and later Lausanne for treatment. A large part of the first drafts of *The Waste Land* written during this year.
1922–39	Editor of *The Criterion*
1925	Joins Board of Directors of the publishers Faber and Gwyer (later Faber and Faber) and remains active on it throughout his life

1927	Baptized into the Church of England. Becomes a naturalized British citizen
1929	Eliot's mother, Charlotte Champe Eliot, dies
1933	Separation from Vivien Eliot. Visits United States to give the Charles Eliot Norton lectures at Harvard University (published as the *Use of Poetry and the Use of Criticism*)
1938–43	Attends meetings of the 'Moot' group (together with Karl Mannheim, Middleton Murry and others) to discuss political and social problems in relation to Christianity
1939	Vivien Eliot suffers a final breakdown after many years of mental illness, and dies in 1947
1948	Eliot receives the Order of Merit
1957	Marries Valerie Fletcher
1965	Dies in London on 4 January

Introduction

This study attempts to approach Eliot's poetry in the spirit of his own remarks about his first reading of Dante, in his essay of 1929. He says there that he has always found an elaborate preparation of scholarly knowledge a barrier in approaching a poet's work; or that at least 'it is better to be spurred to acquire scholarship because you enjoy the poetry, than to suppose that you enjoy the poetry because you have acquired the scholarship' (*Selected Essays*, p. 237).[1] Nevertheless he goes on to say that an initial response to the poetry will lead the reader naturally to want to know more and penetrate deeper: 'if from your first deciphering of it there comes now and then some direct shock of poetic intensity, nothing but laziness can deaden the desire for fuller and fuller knowledge' (p. 238). So the present study assumes that the reader will have read at least some of Eliot's poetry and that his or her interest has been sufficiently stimulated to want to look into it more deeply, to find some account of how the poems work on the reader, and to gain a more conscious understanding of the poems. It tries to give an account, that is, of what it is we enjoy in the poems, and of the significance of that enjoyment. At the same time it recognizes that Eliot's poetry is often complex and erudite, and that appreciation can be increased by 'fuller knowledge'; so it will seek to provide whatever elucidation of Eliot's literary echoes and allusions will contribute directly to an understanding of the poems, or guide the reader towards fuller exploration.

It could be said that there are two stages in an approach to Eliot's poetry. Neither is in the end separable from the other, and finally there is only one 'way of reading' the poems, which is the same as for all other poems. We immerse ourselves in their flow, attending with as much receptiveness as we can muster to the varied play of rhythm, imagery, tone and meaning, allowing the poems to register in us their moments of greater and lesser intensity, their guiding ideas, their appeal to our senses and to our intellect. But one can distinguish, if not separate, two kinds of attention we may give to them. The first and most important is

1

the reading as I have described it; the second, ancillary to this, is the study of the poems that may involve, as well as close readings, the reading of Eliot's own notes and the reading of the 'sources' to which he directs us (in the case of *The Waste Land*), the reading of his own criticism, and finally others' criticism of his poetry. Needless to say this second kind of attention will only attract us if we have responded with enough interest to our first readings: in Eliot's words, 'if there comes now and then some direct shock of poetic intensity'. And the pursuit of more elusive 'meanings' is only worth while if it in turn leads back to that primary experience of the poems.

It may be worth beginning with these truisms because two kinds of reaction to the poems are not uncommon. The first, and possibly less harmful, one says that one should look at nothing but the poems, and that all exegetical commentary and explanation of allusions (including those in Eliot's own notes) is pedantic and obfuscatory. The second says that it is mainly (or even only) through an explanation of allusions and a tracing of sources that we can get at what a particular poem is 'about', can understand it. Both these reactions are misguided: the first because it is, to begin with, impossible as well as undesirable to read any poem without bringing to it one's knowledge of past literature and history of the world in general; and since this is so it is illogical to deny the usefulness of increasing our relevant knowledge. The second is misguided because it replaces the poem, and the effects which the poem achieves, by a tissue of references and meanings which may be constructed out of many of the materials which the poet himself used, but which loses sight of the poet's unique act of selection and creation. It also loses sight of the famous axiom that Eliot laid down in his 1929 essay on Dante: 'It is a test (a positive test, I do not assert that it is always valid negatively) that genuine poetry can communicate before it is understood' (*Selected Essays*, p. 238). He did not of course say that poetry was not *better* for being understood; indeed he goes on: 'The impression can be verified on fuller knowledge.' But just as the poet may begin (as Eliot himself said) with a rhythm or an image which precedes any conscious meaning or intention, so the reader may begin by responding to the rhythm or the image before being aware of anything that could strictly be called meaning.

On the question of meaning and of the supposed 'difficulty' of modern poetry, Eliot later wrote that this difficulty may be due to several reasons: there may be 'personal causes' which force the poet to express himself obscurely; the difficulty may be due to novelty; or it may be caused by the reader's apprehension that the poem is going to be difficult, his desire to be clever or his fear of being taken in. 'There is such a thing as stage fright, but what such readers have is pit or gallery fright' (*The Use of Poetry and the Use of Criticism*, p. 151).[2] Or, finally, 'the difficulty is caused by the author's having left out something which the reader is used to finding; so that the reader, bewildered, gropes about for what is absent, and puzzles his head for a kind of 'meaning' which is not there and is not meant to be there' (p. 151).

All these causes of difficulty or supposed difficulty are at work in much of Eliot's poetry. The question of 'personal causes' we shall return to later; but for the moment the last two are worth bearing in mind. A reader should approach many of the poems without expecting too much readily graspable 'meaning' of the usual kind. This is still worth saying even today when we may be more used to obscurity in poetry, since there have also been various poetic reactions against Eliotic obscurity, and few poets have followed very closely Eliot's method. The reader should also be ready for a technique of fragmentation, hiatus, lacunae, 'the author's having left out something'. The obscurity is not wilful, but is a means, among other things, of getting the reader to see reality from new angles and its elements in new juxtapositions. Above all, perhaps, there will often be surprising and initially baffling transitions. Leonard Woolf recorded in his autobiography that Virginia Woolf 'once tackled [Eliot] about his poetry, and told him that "he wilfully concealed his transitions". He admitted this but said it was unnecessary to explain, explanation diluted facts . . . What he wanted was "to disturb externals".'[3]

It follows from what I have said that the way to begin with Eliot's poetry is with its 'surface', with the succession of images and dramatic scenes, with the musical rhythms, and what has been called the 'musical organization' of many of the longer poems, the pattern of recurring phrases and motifs that establishes a series of echoes and correspondences and begins to impress on the reader their connections and significances. What Eliot said about Tennyson in his essay of 1936 on *In Memoriam* is, in one aspect, remarkably suggestive and appropriate (more so than the view of Eliot as essentially an anti-romantic and 'impersonal' poet would lead one to believe) when applied to Eliot himself:

Tennyson's surface, his technical accomplishment, is intimate with his depths: what we most quickly see about him is that which moves between the surface and the depths, that which is of slight importance. By looking innocently at the surface we are most likely to come to the depths, to the abyss of sorrow. (*Selected Essays*, p. 337)

It is perhaps not true that what moves in Eliot between the surface and the depths (if by that we mean his ideas, theories, beliefs) is of slight importance. Tennyson, for Eliot, was 'a mind almost wholly encrusted by parasitic opinion' and we cannot say that of Eliot. But still it is true in an important way that 'his surface, his technical accomplishment, is intimate with his depths'.

So I have tried in this study to concentrate always on the poetry itself with its wealth of immediate human suggestiveness as well as its more complex or hidden meanings. Eliot has perhaps sometimes suffered from being seen as one of the great progenitors of something called 'Modernism', which usually connotes a poetry which is especially abstruse, self-reflective, 'theoretical' and in various ways quite unlike any of the poetry that preceded it. 'Modernism' is not a term which Eliot uses in his own criticism, and I doubt if he would have approved of it. He would, of course, have agreed with Pound that modern poetry had to 'make it new'. 'The language which is more important to us,' he wrote in his essay on Swinburne (1920), 'is that which is struggling to digest and express new objects, new groups of objects, new feelings, and aspects . . .' (*Selected Essays*, p. 327). And in 'The Metaphysical Poets' (1921) he asserted that, because of the complexity of modern civilization, modern poetry must be 'difficult': 'The poet must become more and more comprehensive, more allusive, more indirect, in order to force, to dislocate if necessary, language into his meaning' (p. 289). But he did not see modern poetry doing anything essentially different from what poetry had always done. And some of his theories, like that of poetic 'impersonality', although still, I suggest, important, have sometimes obscured the way in which his poetry can still be seen in a significant sense as 'personal', the expression of personal feeling. However much he is also a kind of conduit for the broad river (and the streams and tributaries) of the European tradition, and to some extent of traditions further afield, it is his personal experience and his poetic genius which direct them into new channels. It is the intimate contact with a unique human voice which is at the heart of the reader's experience of Eliot's poetry. What the voice says may be

4

compounded of many elements – the poet is himself a kind of 'compound ghost' – but this does not abate that shock of recognition with which we encounter the distinctive note.

Eliot is first and foremost a great poet and after that a great critic, and he himself was fond of pointing out how closely (and perhaps indistinguishably) the 'creative' and the 'critical' interact. So although this is primarily a study of the poems, I have also tried to draw on Eliot's criticism to illuminate his own poetry. This will involve looking both at his general ideas about poetry and at his criticism of individual poets, which latter he himself judged to contain the most valuable of his critical writing. As well as showing us the poets who most influenced his own poetry, examples from the particular criticism will also, I hope, give some idea of how Eliot changed and revitalized an understanding of the English poetic tradition, and can still provide unexpected insights into past poets. In his time Eliot revolutionized readers' perceptions of Donne, Marvell, and the Metaphysical poets. That revolution has now long since been completed, but his criticism can still refresh, often unpredictably, our sense of poets as different as Johnson, Shelley, Tennyson and Kipling. He can challenge conventionally accepted valuations ('There is more essential poetry in Turgenev's "Sportsman's Sketches", even in translation, than in the whole of Thomas Browne or Walter Pater') or make us think again about writers we had perhaps not taken seriously enough (like Poe, more intelligent 'than Browne, than Pater, or even Ruskin').[4] There will only be room for some of this achievement to emerge in this study, and it will arise particularly in relation to what Eliot wrote about early influences on his poetry (where poets like Edward Fitzgerald, James Thomson and John Davidson are cast for us in a new light). But the poetry itself has also, as well as its other powers and attractions, the power to make us re-read earlier poetry in a new way. The poetic style of the speech of the 'familiar compound ghost' in Little Gidding II with its powerful generalizations can, in conjunction with Eliot's essay on Johnson, give us an awareness of the possibilities of a Johnsonian poetry; and the verse of 'Gerontion', as much as the critical essays, has enabled us to see the qualities of the verse of Middleton and Tourneur.

I have chosen to focus on the poems, and to make only passing mention of the plays, because it seems to me (as to many others) that Eliot's essential achievement is contained in the former. The complete poems also form a remarkably coherent whole. They have that 'continuous development from first to last' which Eliot found in Shakespeare, and are 'united by one significant, consistent and developing personality' (*Selected Essays*, pp. 193 and 203). They are bound together by recurring motifs and preoccupations, images that echo earlier images and in that echo achieve a resonance and significance they would not entirely have on their own. The poems, for example, begin and end with a journey. 'Let us go then, you and I', are the opening words of the first poem of Eliot's first volume, 'The Love Song of J. Alfred Prufrock'; and the last of *Four Quartets* begins its closing verse-paragraph:

> We shall not cease from exploration
> And the end of all our exploring
> Will be to arrive where we started
> And know the place for the first time.[5]

There is a sense in which those lines are true of a reading of Eliot's poems: the experiences which are the subject of 'Prufrock', 'Portrait of a Lady' and other early poems are being continually revised in the later poems, and placed in a new perspective. The journey also proceeds through the intervening poems: from the walk in 'Rhapsody on a Windy Night' and the 'old man driven by the Trades' in 'Gerontion', through the road to the chapel and the 'hordes swarming / Over the endless plains' in Part V of *The Waste Land*, to 'Journey of the Magi', the sea voyage in 'Marina', the return 'down the passage which we did not take / . . . Into the rose garden' in 'Burnt Norton', and the pilgrimage to Little Gidding. Ending as it does in 'the middle way' of 'East Coker' and the pilgrimage, the ghostly 'patrol', and the continued 'exploration' in 'Little Gidding', it can not unjustly be compared (though there are no exact correspondences) with Dante's journey in *The Divine Comedy*.

In this pattern the plays have only a lesser part. Perhaps only *Sweeney Agonistes* (1932), *Murder in the Cathedral* (1935) and *The Family Reunion* (1938) are really a part of it at all; and it is significant that several passages and images from the latter two find a more vivid life in *Four Quartets*. What makes the three plays a potential part of the 'continuous development' is above all their preoccupation with guilt and purgation through suffering. But the effort of projecting this subject into a medium which requires plot structure and the creation of characters independent of the author puts a strain on Eliot's artistic resources. For all the virtues of the plays, we feel for instance that Becket's martyrdom is partly a rather uneasy (artistically and morally perilous) analogy for processes going on inside the author; and the projection of personal problems and solutions into the character of Harry in *The Family Reunion* ends up by making him, as Eliot later said, 'an insufferable prig'.[6] The verse too, for all its accomplishments, particularly those of the choruses in *Murder in the Cathedral*, lacks the life and variety that Eliot found it possible to achieve in a form like that of *Four Quartets*. I have, however, included some discussion of the dramatic fragment *Sweeney Agonistes*, perhaps Eliot's best poetic drama. That does have a varied rhythmic life, and extraordinary accommodation of speech rhythms to those of verse without the rather flat intonations of the three- or four-stress lines of the later plays. It also has an urgency, and a touch of the melodramatic and the macabre, which give it some of the excitement of the poems before 1925. And in the figure of Sweeney, Eliot has created a character who has a distinct individuality quite different from that of the author, which yet seems to articulate some of the author's deepest fears and obsessions.[7] On the whole, however, this study will suggest that for all his dramatic powers, Eliot is essentially a poet of what he called 'the first voice', the voice of the poet himself (however disguised at times); a poet not primarily concerned with an audience (as Eliot thought the verse playwright must be) but one concerned to get something said, 'haunted by a demon', 'oppressed by a burden which he must bring to birth in order to obtain rellief' (*On Poetry and Poets*, p. 98).

I have said that Eliot can be seen as a 'compound ghost', a writer compounded out of many elements of the European tradition. But how far is he also, for us today, a 'master' as the ghost in 'Little Gidding' was for him? He is no longer the great eminence, *the* predominant presence in English poetry and culture, that he was in the middle years of this century. His politics have been much attacked,[8] his religious orthodoxy has not, it would seem, commanded any great following in the literary world. The influence of his poetry on other poets has always been rather elusive: after the first impact of his poetry in the twenties (when, it has been said, it was impossible to pick up a manuscript submitted by a young poet without finding the words 'dry', 'dust', 'desert' and the like on the first page) his deeper influence on outstanding poets is very often a matter of general professional example than of a direct stylistic kind. William Empson wrote: 'I do not know for certain how much of my own mind he invented, let alone how much of it is a reaction against him or indeed a consequence of misreading him. He has a very penetrating influence, perhaps not unlike an east wind.'[9] And more recently Donald Davie has written of the profound general influence of Eliot on his own literary life.[10] Stylistically one can see traces in the early Auden, and most recently (and of a different kind) in Geoffrey Hill. But his poetic influence is more like Shakespeare's than Milton's, to the extent that his influence has been powerful but subterranean: there is no tradition of Eliotic verse as there was a tradition of Miltonic verse in the eighteenth century.

Finally, does his poetry have — and was it ever its most important function to have — a moral message for modern civilization: is Eliot a master in that sense? Or should we (and can we) detach Eliot's poetry from its 'philosophy' in the way that Arnold detached Wordsworth's twenty-nine years after the poet's death. The question of the part Eliot's beliefs play in his poetry, and the question of how much our response to his poetry depends on our response to his beliefs will be examined in the course of this study. But whatever our conclusions on this question, it seems certain that Eliot will retain his place, with W. B. Yeats, as one of the two greatest poets of the first half of this century, because of both the quality of his art and the predicament (and effort to overcome it) that his art presents.

1

Aspects of the life of the poet

I

In the sketch of the poet's life which follows, I have tried to select aspects which have some bearing on the poems. But in thinking about the connections between the life and the work (to use a convenient but not always sustainable distinction) it is worth bearing in mind the words of G. Wilson Knight, writing on Shakespeare's literary 'sources', and applying what he says broadly to biographical matters. The arguments from 'sources' and also 'intentions'

> try to explain art in terms of causality, the most natural implement of intellect. Both fail empirically to explain anything essential whatever . . . the word 'source', that is, the origin whence the poetic reality flows, is a false metaphor . . . The 'source' of *Anthony and Cleopatra*, if we must indeed have a 'source' at all, is the transcendent erotic imagination of the poet. (*The Wheel of Fire*, p. 8)

If we apply these words to biographical matters, we may say similarly that we cannot trace any clear causal connection between particular circumstances and particular poems. There is always the element of imagination. Short of a complete knowledge of the psychic history of the poet (which would also presuppose a set of scientific psychological laws) we must be always moving in a world of speculation. And of course the question of biographical, and also literary, influences is only a secondary matter if what we are mainly seeking is a sharper impression and a clearer understanding of the poems. This chapter and the next, then, will seek simply to provide a brief context for the poems in the life of the poet which may here and there throw some light on the major poems or suggest certain intellectual connections and affiliations. Readers who are not especially interested in biographical matters and literary and intellectual influences, and who want to begin where the *Collected Poems* begin, with *Prufrock and Other Observations* in 1917, can pass over this chapter and the next and begin with Chapter 3. Others, particularly if they are to some extent familiar with

9

the poems already, may find moments of insight into the poems through a selective turning over of the soil out of which they grew.[1]

Thomas Stearns Eliot was born in St Louis, Missouri, on 26 September 1888. His father, Henry Ware Eliot, was a successful businessman, President of the Hydraulic-Press Brick Company. His mother, Charlotte Champe Eliot (*née* Stearns), had been a teacher before her marriage, and was the author of a number of moral and didactic poems, many of them on religious subjects, such as *Savonarola*, a long poem about the fifteenth-century Florentine preacher. Eliot's paternal grandfather, William Greenleaf Eliot, had gone from Harvard Divinity School to St Louis, where he had founded the Unitarian Church and where he also helped to found Washington University and the Academy of Sciences. Further back among Eliot's ancestors was the Reverend Andrew Eliot from East Coker in Somerset, who emigrated to Salem, Massachusetts in the second half of the seventeenth century, and who is also believed to have officiated at the Salem witch trials, and, according to one source, to have 'had great mental affliction on that account in the residue of life'. But perhaps the most distinguished of the poet's early ancestors was Sir Thomas Elyot, writer and diplomat under Henry VIII, friend of Sir Thomas More, and the author of several works including *The Boke Named the Governour* (1531), a treatise on kingship. East Coker is, of course, the starting point for the second of *Four Quartets*; and in that same poem Eliot quotes the words of Sir Thomas Elyot in the passage on the vision of the rural marriage dance.

Eliot's ancestry, then, seems to have been characterized mainly by figures in public and ecclesiastical life, figures with a strong sense of public moral duty. Edmund Wilson has described Eliot as 'the Puritan turned artist',[2] and this element of puritan tradition does seem to have been particularly important in the formation of the man and the poet. Eliot once described himself as combining 'a Catholic cast of mind, a Calvinistic heritage, and a Puritanical temperament' (*On Poetry and Poets*, p. 209). The Puritan tradition, in its older form, may have contributed to the sense of sin and guilt which is so notable a feature of many of his poems, to the moral and religious integrity of his work, and also to the sense of public responsibility which much of his writing on culture and society manifests. Eliot's great intellectual effort as a young man was to make himself a European poet, and in his criticism (in 'Tradition and the Individual Talent' and in his essays on Dante, Virgil, Baudelaire and many others) he repeatedly stresses the idea of the unity of European culture. However, the American puritan strain of his sensibility should not be underestimated. In this, as in so many other ways, he makes one think of Henry James, or at least of one of the main preoccupations of James's novels: the conflict between the relative austerity and simplicity of one element of the nineteenth-century American consciousness, and the cultural sophistication of Europe.

But Eliot's reaction to the immediate particular form of religion to which his family adhered, Unitarianism, was one of antagonism. The English Unitarians trace their descent from mainly Presbyterian congregations in the seventeenth century. In America, Unitarianism is said to have arisen in the middle of the eighteenth century 'in opposition to the old Puritan conviction of man's innate sinfulness'.[3] Unitarianism denied the godhead of Christ, and stressed the social, moral and rationalistic aspects of religion. Emerson had resigned his pulpit in the 1830s because of his dislike of 'corpse-cold Unitarianism'; and later in his life, Eliot wrote of how he himself disliked 'the intellectual and puritanical rationalism' of his early environment. He also once spoke of how his parents did not talk of good and evil, but of what was 'done' and 'not done'; whereas he himself wrote, 'So far as we are human, what we do must be either evil or good' ('Baudelaire', 1930, in *Selected Essays*). What the religion of his family lacked was a sense of passion, mystery and suffering, qualities which were to be so marked a feature of his own poetry.

One aspect of his father's moral attitude was, it appears, the distaste with which he regarded sex, which he described as 'nastiness'.[4] How far Eliot himself was influenced by this view, or how far he reacted against it, is perhaps impossible to establish. Certainly one can see that in his poems the treatment of sexuality is frequently accompanied by a sense of disgust. In his essay on Baudelaire Eliot quoted with approval Baudelaire's aphorism: 'the unique and supreme pleasure of love lies in the certainty of doing evil', and commented: 'Having an imperfect, vague romantic conception of Good, he was at least able to understand that the sexual act as evil is more dignified, less boring, than as the "life-giving" cheery automatism of the modern world.'[5] The question of Eliot's attitudes to sexuality are not to be summed up in an introductory paragraph, and what matters most is the way they impinge on, and are worked out in, the poetry, and placed in relation to other things. But it will become apparent that the matter is of central importance, and closely bound up with the question of religion.

It is important that Eliot should have been born in a big city like St Louis. In an address reprinted as 'The Influence of Landscape upon the Poet' (in *Daedalus*, Spring 1960) he spoke of the dual influence of the urban landscape and the rural and coastal landscape of New England, where, at Gloucester, Massachusetts, his family would spend each summer from June to October. He recalled how the area of St Louis in which his family lived 'had become shabby to a degree approaching slumminess', and that this was the source of his urban imagery, on which that of Paris and London 'had been superimposed'. The memory of the yellow fog from the factory chimneys of St Louis was to re-emerge, mingled with images of Boston, in 'The Love Song of J. Alfred Prufrock'.[6] And throughout his life Eliot retained an attraction towards scenes of urban dinginess and decay, an attraction which he found echoed in some of the poets he most admired, like Laforgue, Baudelaire and John Davidson. The other influence from St Louis was the Mississippi. 'I feel,' he wrote later in life, 'that there is something in having passed one's childhood beside the big river which is incommunicable to those who have not.'[7] Incommunicable except, perhaps, in poetry: for the memory of the Mississippi lies behind the 'strong brown god' at the beginning of 'The Dry Salvages'.

The sea, that other great source of imagery for 'The Dry Salvages', is recalled from the other half of Eliot's American landscape, the New England coast. The Dry Salvages are a group of rocks on the north-east coast of Cape Ann, north of Gloucester, Massachusetts. The young Eliot went sailing, and later in life, we are told, 'he remembered those days with great joy, and the presence of the sea always instilled in him feelings of serenity and well-being'[8]; though one might point out that these were not the only emotions associated for him with the sea, as the imagery of 'The Dry Salvages' with its 'drifting wreckage', 'drifting boat with slow leakage' 'an ocean . . . littered with wastage' and its solemn tolling bell-buoy which 'measures time not our time, rung by the unhurried / Ground swell', makes clear. The sea also recurs in the imagery of 'Death by Water' in *The Waste Land*; and in *Ash-Wednesday* and

'Marina' it provides powerful and nostalgic images of the return of past memories.

Eliot as a boy was also a keen bird-watcher. He was given a *Handbook of Birds of Eastern North America*, and many of the birds he noted seeing reappear as part of the processes of memory in the later poems in which he was rediscovering his early life: in 'the cry of the quail and the whirling plover' in *Ash-Wednesday*, and the sweet, excited 'palaver' of birdsong in the delightful poem 'Cape Ann' (1936). Eliot's sharp sensitivity to the natural world is sometimes forgotten in accounts of his poetry but it is pervasive, even though he rarely makes it the main subject of individual poems. (The sequence *Landscapes*, in which Cape Ann appears, and which he subsequently published among his *Minor Poems*, is an exception.) It is more obviously present in later works like *Four Quartets*, but it emerges poignantly from time to time in the early poems, often in the form of images which are 'correlatives' for certain states of mind, as in the passage in 'What the Thunder said' in *The Waste Land*, where for a moment of speculation amid the drought of the desert there is 'the sound of water over a rock / Where the hermit-thrush sings in the pine trees'. This derives from a New England memory, and so, one imagines, does the example of mindless 'automatic' animal life in 'Rhapsody on a Windy Night':

> And a crab one afternoon in a pool,
> An old crab with barnacles on his back,
> Gripped the end of a stick which I held him.

The process by which a poet selects material which will be of use to him later was once illustrated by Eliot with an example in which he must surely have been thinking of his own boyhood:

There might be the experience of a child of ten, a small boy peering through sea-water in a rock-pool, and finding a sea-anemone for the first time: the simple experience (not so simple, for an exceptional child, as it looks) might lie dormant in his mind for twenty years, and re-appear transformed in some verse-context charged with great imaginative pressure. (*The Use of Poetry and the Use of Criticism*, pp. 78–9)

And it must surely be that memory itself which surfaces in 'The Dry Salvages' in the description of the sea and

> The pools where it offers to our curiosity
> The more delicate algae and the sea anemone.

13

In an account of a poet's life it is unwise to give primacy to any one area of his experience over others, since the sources of poetry are so various, and it is characteristic of the poet to draw on the experience of the whole man. But some account of his formal education is important, particularly in the case of Eliot, whose poetry draws so readily and widely on his learning. His wider and more independent reading (particularly in poetry) will play a more important part, but that will be the subject of the next chapter.

At Smith Academy in St Louis, where Eliot was a pupil between the ages of ten and seventeen, he studied Greek, Latin, French, German, Ancient History and English (which was taught as rhetoric). The reading was wide: in his final year he is reported to have studied Hill's Principles of Rhetoric, *Othello*, *The Golden Treasury*, Milton, Macaulay, Addison, Burke's *Conciliation with America*, Virgil's *Aeneid* books III and IV, Ovid, Cicero, Homer's *Iliad*, Racine's *Andromaque* and *Horace*, Hugo's *Les Misérables*, Molière's *Le Misanthrope*, La Fontaines's *Fables*, and physics and chemistry.[9] (One notices the weight given to classical and French texts.) It was, one imagines, a solid preparation for Harvard, to which he went in 1906.

In his first year at Harvard, Eliot studied German Grammar, Constitutional Government, Greek Literature, Medieval History and English History: a typically American syllabus on the 'free elective' system in which students choose freely from a range of widely different courses. In the next two years of his Bachelor's course he studied, among others, French Literature, Ancient Philosophy, Modern Philosophy and Comparative Literature. But the study that was most important to him at this stage was his reading of Baudelaire and Dante. In Baudelaire he found a poet of the city, colourful, pungent and sensuous; and one, moreover, who took evil and despair as his central subjects. In Dante he was struck, as his later essays testify, by an extraordinary ease, vividness and clarity of language, with a particular power of visual imagery, and also by the way in which this acute perception was ordered into a total vision. He also began his studies of Donne in his first year; this interest was to have a profound effect on his own poetry and to emerge also in one of his most important critical essays, 'The Metaphysical Poets', in 1919.

In his M.A. studies at Harvard, from 1909–10, Eliot took a

course under Irving Babbitt, 'Literary Criticism in France with Special Reference to the Nineteenth Century', and the influence of Babbitt was to be an important one on his general intellectual development. Babbitt's *Literature and the American College* (1908) propounded a theory of tradition and the relation of tradition to originality which must have played some part, at least, in the process of Eliot's thinking which led to views such as those expressed in his essay of 1919, 'Tradition and the Individual Talent'. Babbitt's *Rousseau and Romanticism* (1919) was published after the years formative of Eliot's counter-romantic reaction, but one imagines that some of those ideas were already being expounded by Babbitt while Eliot was at Harvard. Babbitt criticized the emotional indulgence of Rousseau, his stress on individualism, and his 'war against the two great traditions, Classical and Christian'. And this too has its counterparts in Eliot's thinking, in his avoidance of the autobiographical expression of emotion in his poetry, his stress on impersonality and tradition, his later interest in classicism and his commitment to Christianity. But Babbitt's influence should not be overstressed: with his moral strenuousness, his talk of always 'struggling forward' and never 'sinking back' into child-like wonder (something of which he accused Coleridge, for example),[10] and above all his rationalistic humanism, which tried to draw eclectically on all the great religions to form a composite wisdom of its own, Babbitt can never have provided more than half-truths for Eliot. In his essay of 1938, 'The Humanism of Irving Babbitt', Eliot expresses his ultimate dissatisfaction with Babbitt's position in terms which suggest that it reminded him too uncomfortably of the Unitarianism of his background. 'His humanism is really something quite different from that of his exemplars, but (to my mind) alarmingly like very liberal Protestant theology of the nineteenth century: it is, in fact, a product – a by-product – of Protestant theology in its last agonies' (*Selected Essays*, p. 475).

The next important thinker Eliot encountered was Henri Bergson, whose lectures he attended during his year in Paris, 1910–11. In 1923 Eliot spoke of the influence of Bergson's *Matière et Mémoire* on his own philosophic thinking, rather than on his poetry;[11] but it does also seem to be the case that Bergson's theory runs parallel in many ways to what was soon to be Eliot's poetic practice. He emphasized the individual 'datum' of consciousness as opposed to mental systems or sets of ideas, and stressed the importance of what was open and fluid in mental life, as opposed to what was closed and fixed. This seems to be in tune with the spirit of Eliot's 'fragmentary' poems like *Prufrock*, 'Rhapsody on a Windy Night', 'Gerontion' and '*The Waste Land*'. He also examined the workings of memory and the ways in which memories mingle in the consciousness with direct immediate impressions, in a way that recalls Eliot's poetic procedures.[12] In the paper on Bergson, Eliot wrote that the most important thing about Bergson's ideas had to do with 'the heterogeneous qualities which succeed each other in our concrete perception', and the difference between these and the underlying harmony which one should be able to deduce.[13] Bergson's ideas about time and consciousness, and about the 'real duration' of time in the consciousness as opposed to fixed or measured time, are also comparable in a distant way with Eliot's much later preoccupation with the perception of time in *Four Quartets*. The modes of thinking of the poet and the philosopher are so different that the effort of comparing Eliot's poetry with Bergson's philosophy would perhaps be misguided; but at least one can say that Bergson's ideas were part of the intellectual atmosphere of the time, and that Eliot drew on them in that alchemy of the poet which he describes in 'The Metaphysical Poets', in which the mind of the poet 'is constantly amalgamating disparate experience' and combining the reading of Spinoza with the smell of cooking (*Selected Essays*, p. 287).

The culmination of Eliot's philosophical studies was his doctoral dissertation, 'Knowledge and Experience in the Philosophy of F. H. Bradley', which he prepared and wrote between 1913 and 1916. It is beyond the bounds of a study of his poetry to try to sum up adequately the complexities of Bradley's thought and Eliot's reaction to it, but from our particular perspective we can say, perhaps, that what interested Eliot in Bradley was his preoccupation with the relation between surface appearances and absolute truth, and the relation between subjective, private knowledge and objective, public knowledge. Is the universe 'concealed behind appearances', or can we, through common objects, 'discover the main nature of reality'? Eliot's poems up to and including *The Waste Land* are full of the shifting and perplexing details of the surface, but there is often too the sense of a half-glimpsed reality behind appearances, as in 'Preludes' IV (written two years before he began his serious study of Bradley).

> I am moved by fancies that are curled
> Around these images, and cling:
> The notion of some infinitely gentle
> Infinitely suffering thing.

But equally strong in Bradley and in Eliot's response to him is a scepticism about how far anything can be known beyond appearances and the closed circle of individual perception; and Eliot, at this stage, went further than Bradley in the direction of subjectivism: Bradley asserted that 'My experience is not the whole world', but Eliot replied in his thesis that 'What is subjective is the whole world', and 'All significant truths are private truths'.[14] And in the note to line 411 of *The Waste Land* Eliot quotes a passage of Bradley that seems to assert a kind of solipsism: 'My external sensations are no less private to myself than are my thoughts and feelings . . . Regarded as an existence which appears in a soul, the whole world for each is peculiar and private to that soul.' In the same way the protagonists in Eliot's early poems are almost invariably locked in a private world of mental impressions, 'each in a prison', and unable, like Prufrock, or the narrator in 'Portrait of a Lady', or Sweeney in *Sweeney Agonistes*, to communicate to others, to 'say just what I mean'.

II

In 1915 Eliot married Vivien Haigh-Wood. It soon became apparent that the marriage was to be an unhappy one. Vivien Eliot suffered from ill health from at least as early as 1915, ill health compounded of both physical and mental elements. Eliot himself by 1921 had begun to suffer from acute anxiety and depression, and in October of that year he took a leave of absence from his position at Lloyd's Bank (which he held between 1917 and 1925) on account of an illness described as 'nervous breakdown'. He spent some weeks convalescing at Margate on the Kentish coast, and later visited a specialist in nervous disorders in Lausanne.

The consequences of his unhappy marriage for Eliot's life and poetry are incalculable. It would be too much to say that his marriage alone made Eliot a poet of unhappiness and failed relationships – the theme is already there in 'The Love Song of J. Alfred Prufrock' and 'Portrait of a Lady', both written around 1910–11 – but its influence on *The Waste Land* (1922) and

Eliot's poetic development thereafter can hardly be overestimated. There can be no simple equation between the experiences of the life and the poetry. The pressure of personal experiences combined with an artistic need to break out of the romantic mould of direct personal expression in poetry led Eliot, as we shall see, to choose oblique forms of expression, the use of fragmentation, myth, echoes of other literature and *personae* (figures who act as masks for the poet). But it becomes clear both from the nature of the poetry itself and from the biographical evidence, that Eliot is frequently drawing on personal experience in a more direct way. The scene with the middle-class couple in Part II of *The Waste Land*, 'A Game of Chess', stands out from the other episodes in that Part with an intensity which by itself signals its probably personal nature. And the taciturn man is clearly part of the central voice of the poem, and the neurotic, insistent lady cannot but recall something of what we have learned about Eliot and his wife at this time from biographical sources.

At the same time, however, there would seem to be no mere transposition of the life, and it is not true that at the time of the writing of the poem Eliot's marriage had entirely broken down. Vivien Eliot went with her husband to Margate, and in the first typescript draft of 'A Game of Chess' she wrote in the margin, beside the episode with the middle-class couple, 'Wonderful!' She also suggested (with slightly different wording) the line (164) 'What you get married for if you don't want children?'[15] If there is an element of biography in this episode, Vivien Eliot's reaction suggests that she was as perceptive about the problem of their relationship as her husband, and ready to recognize and appreciate an objectification of it.

After 1922 Vivien Eliot's health and mental condition deteriorated further. Their life together began to be intolerable and in 1925 Eliot first spoke to friends of the possibility of their separation.[16] In 1933 he left for America to give the Charles Eliot Norton lectures at Harvard, and instructed his solicitors to inform his wife that he desired a separation. It appears that thereafter they met only once, in 1935. In 1938 Vivien Eliot entered a private mental hospital in London, and she died in 1947.

This is not the place to offer an analysis of the tragedy of Eliot's first marriage, nor to try and establish in any detail its effects on his poetry, even assuming this kind of undertaking to be possible. But one cannot help being aware that there must be some kind of relation between the poetry of failed love (in

'Gerontion', *The Waste Land*, *The Hollow Men*) and the experience of the life. Furthermore, the renunciation that is the theme of so much of the poetry after 1925 would seem to have been one that was forced on the poet because of 'the vanished power of the usual reign' rather than one freely chosen. And the sense of marriage expressed in 'East Coker', and still more the disenchanted view of *The Cocktail Party*, where marriage is seen as mutual exploitation or at best as a dreary compromise, have an obvious connection with the life. The second line here, from *Ash-Wednesday* II:

> Terminate torment
> Of love unsatisfied
> The greater torment
> Of love satisfied

is an extraordinary one: but according to William Empson, who reported that around 1930 Eliot would welcome the news of any breakdown in his friends' marriages (for their sake), he meant it literally.[17] By contrast, Eliot's second marriage, to Valerie Fletcher in 1957, brought him a happiness which he had not known before. But it came too late to have a profound effect on his writing. The little poem 'A Dedication to my Wife' (1959) is a touching biographical record, but as a poem it is undistinguished.

III

In 1922 Eliot took on the editorship of *The New Criterion* (soon to resume its old title *The Criterion*), and began a long engagement with this quarterly periodical which lasted until 1939. In its early years the magazine published new work by some outstanding contributors, including Pirandello, Virginia Woolf, E. M. Forster, D. H. Lawrence, Herman Hesse and Yeats. And Eliot himself contributed poetry, a large number of reviews and frequent editorial commentaries. In relation to his own poetry and criticism one can discern in these writings a tendency that is a part of a general shift in his thinking about literature after 1922. In his preface of 1928 to the second edition of *The Sacred Wood* (first published in 1920) Eliot asserted that

The problem appearing in these essays, which gives them what coherence they have, is the problem of the integrity of poetry, with the repeated assertion that when we are considering poetry we must consider it primarily as poetry and not another thing.

(*The Sacred Wood*, p. viii)

But since 1920 he had noted in his own mind 'not so much a change of reversal of opinion, as an expansion or development of interests', particularly in the connection of poetry with morality, religion and politics. Already in 1922, at the end of the first volume of *The Criterion*, he had stated that

It is the function of a literary review to maintain the autonomy and disinterestedness of literature, and at the same time to exhibit the relations of literature — not to 'life', as something contrasted to literature, but to all the other activities, which, together with literature, are the components of life. (p. 421)

And this development of interest is important not only in relation to his own critical writing (which one can see in the increasing appearance of titles like 'A Note on Belief' (1927), 'Literature and Propaganda' (1930), *The Use of Poetry and the Use of Criticism* (1933), and 'The Social Function of Poetry' (1954)), but also in relation to his poetry. Sometimes the development was in an unpromising direction, as with the attempt at a socially didactic art in *The Rock* (1934). And there is even something suspect about some of Eliot's reasons for turning to writing for the theatre, a desire for 'social utility' and the ability to reach a wider audience; if not suspect in itself, then certainly in relation to its effects on the poet's methods of composition. 'The problem of communication presents itself immediately'; the writer has to aim at an 'immediate effect',[18] which tends to mean in practice a watering down of the poetry to make it as unobtrusive as possible. But the wider concern with the social ramifications of literature, its connection with religion and politics, is also reflected in poetry which directly incorporates questions of belief, as in 'Journey of the Magi' and *Ash-Wednesday*, or politics, as in the *Coriolan* poems, or questions of religious life, history and tradition, as in *Four Quartets*. I shall argue below that this poetry is still at its best when it is closest to the poetry of the 'first voice' (as Eliot called it in 'The Three Voices of Poetry'), when it maintains its primary obligation to the most intimate springs of personal feeling.[19] But in his best poetry Eliot's most personal feelings are themselves inextricably connected with issues of belief, history and society.

As well as his poetry, plays and literary criticism, Eliot wrote a substantial amount on 'non-literary' subjects. In *The Criterion* and elsewhere he reviewed books on religion, humanism, history, politics, philosophy and psychology. In 1939 he published three lectures on *The Idea of a Christian Society*, and in 1948 *Notes Towards the Definition of Culture*, a book which among other things has much to say on the role of art within a society, and the relation of culture to religion. Regarding the latter, his remarks on religion as 'the whole *way of life* of a people' (p. 31) and his observation that from a certain point of view 'behaviour is also belief' (p. 32) have a direct relevance to some of the questions of poetry and belief which I shall examine in Chapter 8, in particular to the idea that poetry can show a belief's 'possibility for being lived' — the way it integrates with other experience at the most fundamental levels.

Having settled in England in 1915, when he virtually made a final decision to abandon an academic career and dedicate himself to poetry and criticism, Eliot continued to live mainly in London, and became a British citizen in 1927 in the same year as his baptism and confirmation into the Anglican Church. The important question of his 'conversion' will be looked at more fully below, in relation to his poetry. It seems to have been a gradual process, growing out of the early experience of his family's religion, tempered by a reaction against that, complicated by his studies of Dante and Catholicism on one hand and his interest in Eastern religion on the other, and finally precipitated by the psychological crisis of his marriage and his 'breakdown' in 1921–2. His conversion (if it can be called that) sprang from a deep emotional need for moral and spiritual order. As regards intellectual assent, he described how he discovered the least incredible belief and grew slowly to accept it (*The Criterion*, April 1933).[20] And his faith always co-existed with scepticism. Talking of Marxism, he once said: 'They seem so certain of what they believe. My own beliefs are held with a scepticism I never even hope to be rid of.'[21]

Like his religious beliefs, Eliot's political leanings were in the direction of traditionalism and conservatism. He once said that his readings of Charles Maurras, the French political writer, a Royalist, traditionalist and reactionary, though not a Catholic believer, helped to convince him of the need for religion.[22] Eliot's politics always tended towards the right, and in *Notes Towards the Definition of Culture* he argues against social egalitarianism and asserts the need for 'élites'. But the accusation of fascism which has sometimes been brought against him cannot be sustained. In 1923 he congratulated the *Daily Mail* on a series of admiring articles about Mussolini; but by 1928 his attitude towards Italian fascism had become deeply sceptical, as a review of several books on the subject in *The Criterion* shows.[23] He never expressed any admiration for Hitler, and his writings on politics just before the outbreak of the Second World War show his deep fear of the forces that Hitler represented.[24] Anti-Jewish feelings, undeniably there at least twice in his writing before 1939, disappear entirely from them after the terrible events of the war. He never republished the book in which he expressed the view that for the sake of homogeneity in a society 'any large number of free-thinking Jews' is 'undesirable' (*After Strange Gods*, 1934, p. 20), and later (in connection with the book's discussion of Lawrence) said he was a sick man when he wrote it.[25] His attitude towards democracy was highly sceptical; but in 1930 he wrote in a letter to Bonamy Dobrée: 'I think we are in agreement that "Order" and "Authority" are more dangerous catchwords now, than "Liberty" and "Reform" were fifty or seventy-five years ago . . . I am terrified of the modern contempt of "democracy" . . . I am as scary of Order as of Disorder.'[26]

IV

When Eliot settled in England in 1915 he set about becoming as English as he could. He lost virtually all traces of an American accent, and his dress was generally that of the conventional English business or professional man. This was partly no doubt the result of his deep feeling and admiration for English traditions and conventions, but it was also a kind of protective covering, a conventional exterior ('a face to meet the faces that you meet') which disguised the deep divisions and intensities of the inner man, a kind of playing 'Possum' (Pound's favourite nickname for Eliot). He liked to cultivate a lighter and more humorous side to his character (which he nevertheless tended to do rather ponderously) by writing a letter to *The Times* on Stilton cheese (November 1935), or, more significantly, by publishing a book of verses for children, *Old Possum's Book of Practical Cats* (1939). (He always had a taste for nonsense verse, and once called Edward Lear a great poet, and compared him with Mallarmé.)[27] After 1945 he had achieved the position of leading writer of the English-speaking world, a literary 'dictator' (to use the common though somewhat misleading term) who was to his time what Dryden or Johnson or Coleridge or Matthew

Arnold were to theirs. But the great period of his own creative work had come to an end with *Four Quartets*, despite the appearance of three more plays (*The Cocktail Party*, 1949, *The Confidential Clerk*, 1954, and *The Elder Statesman*, 1958). In his social role as 'great writer' and intellectual leader he became increasingly the representative of orthodoxy and the 'Establishment': he sat on ecclesiastical committees and delivered addresses at literary conventions and prize-givings – sometimes reluctantly, as with his address on 'Goethe as the Sage' in May 1955, in which he gave a conventional eulogy of Goethe's greatness, despite his fundamental lack of sympathy for the subject (he had once said of Goethe's poetry 'I can't stand his stuff').[28]

The details of the life and the opinions are not the important things, however. They may give us clues to understanding, but what matters in the end is the completed work, that body of writing over which Eliot took such extreme care, and by which he wished to be remembered. It is the work which (to apply Eliot's words about certain Elizabethan dramatists) gives us 'the pattern, or we may say the undertone, of the personal emotion, the personal drama and struggle, which no biography, however full and intimate, could give us; which nothing can give us but our experience of [the works] themselves.'[29] Of these works it is (I suggest) the poems that give us the essential pattern expressed at the level of greatest intensity. The works are not merely personal; they also give us an insight into more than the poet himself, an insight into areas of experience which lie outside the poet's conscious control and awareness and speak to quite other times and conditions than his own. 'The great poet, in writing himself, writes his time,' Eliot once said.[30] And in writing his time he can also speak to ours.

2

Early poetic influences and criticism, and *Poems Written in Early Youth*

We do not imitate, we are changed; and our work is the work of the changed man; we have not borrowed, we have been quickened, and we become bearers of a tradition.

(T. S. Eliot, *The Egoist*, July 1919, p. 3)

I

Eliot once wrote that one of the best ways of increasing one's understanding of Dante, after reading the poems themselves, is to read the authors he read and admired;[1] and this is true also of Eliot, so long as we are able to read his authors with some element of direct interest and response, as well as the interest derived from the study of Eliot himself. And in looking at some of the poets who particularly influenced him we are given invaluable assistance by the criticism which he himself wrote. In many cases this transformed contemporary awareness of these poets (independently of its interest in connection with his own poetry) and it still exerts its influence today, and helps to make a 'direct interest' possible for us. Eliot himself put a high valuation on his criticism of individual authors who had influenced his own work, and felt that the best of his literary criticism ('apart from a few notorious phrases which have had a truly embarrassing success in the world') was contained in those essays. He called them the 'by-product of my private poetry workshop' and felt that they were part of his own poetic activity. (See 'The Frontiers of Criticism', *On Poetry and Poets*, p. 106.) In the case of Eliot, therefore, looking at 'influences' is not a mere indulgence in academic speculation but an opportunity, virtually unrivalled in the history of English literature, to look inside the 'poetry workshop' of a great poet at some of the reading and thinking which quickened his imagination and made him the bearer of a tradition.

The most striking and perhaps unexpected quality of Eliot's earliest tastes in poetry is their romanticism. In *The Use of*

Poetry and the Use of Criticism (p. 33) he records how at
of fourteen he picked up a copy of Fitzgerald's *Omar*, an
overwhelmed by the experience of 'a new world of feeling' wh
the poem gave him. 'It was like a sudden conversion; the wor
appeared anew, painted with bright, delicious and painful
colours.' The religious simile is suggestive and characteristic of
the interpenetration of artistic and religious language in Eliot.
But the 'delicious and painful colours' also remind us of Eliot's
less often noticed visual sensitivity. Afterwards, he records, he
took 'the usual adolescent course' with Byron, Shelley, Keats,
Rossetti, Swinburne.

Nor was this early romantic taste something which Eliot entirely rejected in his own poetry. We tend to think of him as
essentially counter-romantic, with his stress in well-known early
essays like 'Tradition and the Individual Talent' (1919) on the
impersonality of the poet and his need to 'escape from emotion'.[2] But Prufrock (as I shall suggest below) is a would-be
romantic hero, and there is much colour and vigour comparable
to *Omar* in Eliot's early verse.

> Wake! For the sun who scattered into flight
> The Stars before him from the Field of Night,
> Drives night along with them from Heav'n, and strikes
> The Sultan's Turret with a Shaft of Light.
>
> (*The Rubáiyát of Omar Khayyám*, stanza 1)

The exotic trumpet call of that is very different from Eliot's kind
of urgency. But is it too paradoxical to suggest that those lines
must have struck the Victorian ear, accustomed to the language
and calendar-maxims of much mid-Victorian verse, with
something of the same pleasurable shock with which the im-
perative of Eliot's opening to 'Prufrock' struck the ears of many
readers tired of a diet of Georgian verse?

> Let us go then, you and I,
> When the evening is spread out against the sky
> Like a patient etherised upon a table;
> Let us go, through certain half-deserted streets,
> The muttering retreats
> Of restless nights in one-night cheap hotels
> And sawdust restaurants with oyster-shells:

This too is a love song, though in a different key: the time is
somnolent evening rather than bracing morning, and the sky is
like an etherised patient rather than a striking shaft of light.

But the rhythm in Eliot's lines, as in Fitzgerald's, is the life of the thing: urgent, rousing and calling to activity. Fitzgerald's is a trumpet call; and Eliot's, with its syncopated rhythm, is another kind of trumpet, the instrument of jazz. I am not, of course, suggesting an influence of Fitzgerald's on Eliot's particular lines – the mode is so utterly different. But at a deeper level, where the response is to a certain freshness, a new accent, which prompts the poet to catch the same excitement in a totally different way, there is a kind of affinity.

The dramatic quality (the 'éclat' of the curtain-raiser) is also common to both passages, and this is a quality which the adolescent Eliot admired in Byron, and one which is there in much of the verse of his early manhood. It is true that Eliot wrote in his essay on Byron:

a return, after many years to the poetry of Byron is accompanied by . . . gloom: images come before the mind, and the recollection of some verses in the manner of *Don Juan*, tinged with disillusion and cynicism only possible at the age of sixteen, which appeared in a school periodical. (On *Poetry and Poets*, p. 193)

But he affirms in the same essay that although he approached Byron's earlier narrative poems with apprehension he found them highly readable and expert in narrative, with 'a torrential fluency in verse and a skill in varying its form from time to time to avoid monotony', 'a genius for divagation' (or digression), a sense of drama (or perhaps melodrama). 'It is that same gift which Byron was to turn to better account in *Don Juan*.' Narrative is rarely, of course, a feature of Eliot's own verse; though it is there to some extent in the plays, in 'Portrait of a Lady' and in 'Journey of The Magi'. But one quality which Eliot learned, in a subterranean way, partly from Byron, was a quality of melodrama, or caricature.

> Who thundering comes on blackest steed,
> With slackened bit and hoof of speed?
> Though young and pale, that sallow front
> Is soothed by passion's fiery brunt . . .

Eliot enjoyed that, in a humorous way, as something 'which is enough to tell us that the Giaour is an interesting person, because he is Lord Byron himself, perhaps' (p. 197). Byron may have meant it as heroic, but Eliot, I think, responds to it as a kind of mock-heroic. And this gives us a clue to a significant feature of Eliot's poems up to and including *The Waste Land*.

Just as Dryden and Pope took the heroic strai
Virgil and Milton and used them for mock-heroi
poses, so Eliot frequently takes the modes of the
and nineteenth-century (and also earlier) poets a
the purposes of mock-heroic caricature. T'
whereby the romantic element is not of itse..
brought into relation with the actual failings of the pro...

> There will be time to murder and create,
> And time for all the works of days and hands
> That lift and drop a question on your plate;
> Time for you and time for me,
> And time yet for a hundred indecisions,
> And for a hundred visions and revisions,
> Before the taking of a toast and tea.

> > ('The Love Song of J. Alfred Prufrock')

Whether or not we register the echoes of Ecclesiastes ('To
everything there is a reason, and a time for every purpose under
heaven: A time to be born, and a time to die; a time to plant,
and a time to pluck down that which is planted; a time to kill,
and a time to heal . . .' etc; or, in the context of other references
in the poem, the reminiscence of Hamlet in 'time to murder and
create' set close by 'time for a hundred indecisions'), we take
immediately the general effect of the grand and heroic in combination with the mundane and trivial. Byron himself began to
do the same kind of thing with his own romantic and heroic
impulses when he wrote *Beppo, The Vision of Judgement* and
Don Juan: that is to say, he brought to bear on them the comic,
satiric and commonsensical parts of his mind, with the purpose
of criticizing and tempering them. Eliot's early poetry, like
'Prufrock' and 'Portrait of a Lady', does not, of course, have
the genial man-of-the-world ease of *Don Juan*, and was written
by a young man rather than one who is looking back on life. It
is concentrated, fragmentary, intense, where Byron discourses
and expatiates. But both share a brilliant variety of tone, a play
of wit, sometimes even buffoonery. And above all they show a
similar conflict of romantic feeling and an Augustan satiric
impulse, a conflict between the passions of the heart and
deflating analyses of the intellect. 'The only cure for Romanticism is to analyse it,' wrote Eliot.[3] Byron might have said
rather: 'To grow order.' But in their poetry romanticism is not
easily disposed of, and remains throughout an energizing and in
Eliot's case often disruptive force.

The effect, both positive and negative, of Byron and the other Romantic poets was a general one which persisted and was continually modified thoughout Eliot's life. More immediate influences on Eliot, while he was an undergraduate at Harvard, were Laforgue, Baudelaire and the French Symbolist poets; Dante (whose influence again was to persist and ramify to a unique degree, as will be seen below); and in a more limited but still stimulating way, two Scots poets (who lived mainly in London), James Thomson (1834–82) and John Davidson (1857–1909). These latter, in different ways, caught a note of urban pessimism and despair which, combined with that of Baudelaire and Laforgue, was to sound, in a renewed form, in Eliot's poetry up to and including *The Waste Land*. Thomson's 'City of Dreadful Night' is a long phantasmagoric poem about a dark, mythic city set on a river, lagoon and marshes, a 'Venice of the Black Sea', in which the protagonist wanders declaiming his despair and encountering other shadowy figures and visions – a 'Lady of the Images' prayed to by a 'young man wan and worn who seemed to pray'; a nihilistic preacher; an old tramp crawling on all fours in search of a way back to a lost childhood happiness; a combat between angel and sphinx. The high and portentous rhetoric of the style is very unlike Eliot (though two lines perhaps find an echo in 'East Coker': 'O Melancholy Brothers, dark, dark, dark, /. . . Oh dark, dark, dark, withdrawn from joy and light'). But the poem, if turgid, achieves a kind of authenticity by its very relentlessness; and its use of varying verse forms in different sections (including a kind of modified *terza rima*), its echoes and use of quotations from Dante, and the semi-allegorical use of the City as a kind of Inferno, must all have played their part in its strong impression on Eliot.

'What exactly is my debt to John Davidson I cannot tell, any more than I can describe the nature of my debt to James Thomson: I only know that the two debts differ from each other.'[4] The difference that Eliot found in Davidson must have lain partly in the difference of verse technique, for Eliot admired Davidson in his best-known poem 'Thirty Bob a Week', for having 'freed himself completely from the poetic diction of English verse of his time'. But he was also inspired by the content of the poem, and 'the complete fitness of content and idiom'. The poem is a powerful ballad, a dramatic monologue, with a rhythmic force not unlike that of Kipling's 'Danny Deever', which was also a favourite of Eliot's (and which he knew by heart at the age of twelve). In authentic accents of bitterness and black humour a London clerk ponders his fate.

> I couldn't touch a stop and turn a screw,
> And set the blooming world a-work for me,
> Like such as cut their teeth − I hope, like you −
> On the handle of a skeleton gold key;
> I cut mine on a leek, which I eat it every week:
> I'm a clerk at thirty bob as you can see.

But what makes the poem particularly distinctive is the penetration, the finality, of the clerk's despair. He is not primarily, perhaps, complaining about the inequalities of the social system; he seems to see his case as representative of human life in general, a baffling combination of determinism and free will. The meaning is difficult to grasp; the poem is more elusive than at first it looks; but the vision seems to be one of a man who sees his life as determined and yet chosen: he is trapped and yet responsible. The poem can be read as one about social injustice, but it seems also to be about something else − despair at the injustices of life itself. Eliot also admired other of Davidson's poems: ' "The Runnable Stag" has run in my head for a good many years now; and I have a fellow feeling with the poet who can look with a poet's eye on the Isle of Dogs and Millwall Dock.' But of 'Thirty Bob a Week' Eliot wrote: 'The personage that Davidson created in this poem, has haunted me all my life, and the poem is to me a great poem for ever.'

In 1908 Eliot discovered Arthur Symons's book *The Symbolist Movement in Literature* (1899), and this introduction to the work of Gautier, Baudelaire, Mallarmé, Laforgue and several other modern French poets was to be of great significance for him. Symons drew attention to the way in which Baudelaire's work is made out of 'his whole intellect and all his nerves', and to the ability 'to "cultivate one's hysteria" so calmly, and to affront the reader (*Hyprocite lecteur, mon semblable, mon frère*) as a judge rather than as a penitent . . . to be so much a moralist, with so keen a sense of the ecstasy of evil'.[5] In Mallarmé he saw a priest-like dedication to his art, and an intensely refined endeavour to capture a spiritual reality beyond the objects of the world. He quoted several of Mallarmé's famous formulations about his own poetry: 'I say: a flower! and out of the oblivion to which my voice consigns every contour . . . musically arrives, idea, and exquisite, the one flower absent from all bouquets', and (more specifically relevant to Eliot): 'The pure work implies the elocutionary disappearance of the poet, who yields place to the words . . . they take light from mutual reflection, like an actual trail of fire over precious stones, replacing the old lyric afflatus or the enthusiastic personal direction of the phrase.' The detachment of the poetry from the direct treatment of the world of things, and the 'elocutionary disappearance of the poet', were to find a kind of counterpart in Eliot's stress (particularly in 'Tradition and the Individual Talent') on the difference between experience in life and experience in the poem, and in his technique of 'disappearing' (he approved of the title 'The Invisible Poet')[6] behind a number of different masks or *personae*. Eliot was never a Symbolist poet in the full sense, like Mallarmé, but certain Symbolist tendencies and sometimes passages recur throughout his work, mingled with more discursive and referential elements.

It was in Laforgue, however, that Eliot was to find the most immediate source of stimulation for his own poetry. Symons identified many of the elements that were to appeal to Eliot. 'The verse is alert, troubled, swaying, deliberately uncertain, hating rhetoric so piously that it prefers, and finds its piquancy in, the ridiculously obvious' (p. 297); 'He sees the possibilities for art which come from the sickly modern being, his clothes, his nerves.' Laforgue, says Symons, 'has invented a new manner of being René or Werther: an inflexible politeness . . . He will not permit himself, at any moment, the luxury of dropping the masks' (p. 304). What Eliot found in Laforgue was a way of combining his loftier aspirations with his sense of irony, his romantic and even heroic feelings with his satiric perception of absurdity and pretension. Symons quotes one of Laforgue's poems in full, the 'Autre Complainte de Lord Pierrot': in it we see the confrontation between an ardent and romantic woman whose feelings are utterly unmasked in her effusive speech and a bored, witty, disillusioned man, whose replies to her are politely inconsequential or else deflationary:

> Et si ce cri lui part: 'Dieu de Dieux! que je t'aime!'
> — 'Dieu reconnaîtra les siens.' Ou piquée au vif:
> — 'Mes claviers ont du cœur, tu sera mon seul thème.'
> Moi: 'Tout est relatif.'[7]

('And if this cry breaks from her: "God how I love you!" / — "God will acknowledge his own." Or stung to the quick: / —

"My keyboards have heart, you will be my sole theme." / I: "Everything's relative." ') It is a forerunner, as are other of Laforgue's poems, of the situation in Eliot's 'Portrait of a Lady', where, however, the moral and emotional complexity is much greater. Its last stanza has other anticipations:

> Enfin, si, par un soir, elle meurt dans mes livres,
> Douce; feignant de ne pas croire encore mes yeux,
> J'aurai un: 'Ah ca, mais, nous avions De Quoi vivre!
> C'était donc sérieux?'

('At last, if, one evening, she dies in my books, / Sweet, pretending not yet to believe my eyes, / I will utter a: "Now then; but we had enough to live on! / Was it serious then?" '). There is a premonition of the ending of 'Portrait of a Lady' and in the last a foretaste of 'Conversation Galante' in the volume of 1917 (with its appropriately French title), though there it is the woman who is bored and ironic in the last line:

> And — 'Are we then so serious?'

The uneasy, discordant confrontation of man and woman in Laforgue is there in new modes in several of the 1917 poems, including 'The Love Song of J. Alfred Prufrock' itself. So is the dingy urban scenery of 'one night cheap hotels', 'broken blinds and chimney-pots' and 'the trampled edges of the street'. Laforgue's 'L'Hiver Qui Vient' (translated by Martin Bell) is a good example of the kind of thing, in which urban squalor is heightened by the contrast of romantic touches:

> Halloween, Christmas, New Year's Day
> Sodden is drizzle — all my tall chimneys —
> Industrial smoke through the rain!
> No sitting down, all the park benches are wet.
> It's finished, I tell you, till next season.
> Park benches wet and all the leaves rust-eaten,
> Horns and their echoes — dying, dying . . .[8]

But what a translation is less likely to catch is the particular music of the original, and it was this as much as any other element which inspired Eliot. The last two lines of the above, in the original,

> Tant les bancs sont mouillés, tant les bois sont rouillés,
> Et tant les cors ont fait ton ton, on fait ton taine! . . .

(with their satisfying sound effects and puns — 'ton' also means 'tone' and 'taine' recalls 'tain', 'silvering'); or something like this (from 'Dimanches'),

> Hier l'orchestre attaqua
> Sa dernière polka

helped to prompt the music of 'Prufrock':

> And indeed there will be time
> To wonder, 'Do I dare?' and, 'Do I dare?'
> Time to turn back and descend the stair,
> With a bald spot in the middle of my hair –

or that of 'Portrait of a Lady':

> Among the windings of the violins
> And the ariettes
> Of cracked cornets
> Inside my head a dull tom-tom begins
> Absurdly hammering a prelude of its own,
> Capricious monotone

It is a verse which is both free and controlled, fluctuating and exact in its register of each particular effect: as Symons said of Laforgue, 'It is really *vers libre*, but at the same time correct verse, before *vers libre* had been invented' (*The Symbolist Movement*, p. 297); or as Eliot himself wrote in 1917 in 'Reflection on *Vers Libre*': 'the so-called *vers libre* which is good is anything but free' (*To Criticize the Critic*, p. 184).

Reading Laforgue, then, acted as a catalyst for Eliot's own writing, and the result was immediately seen in the poems published in the *Harvard Advocate* in November 1909 and January 1910, 'Nocturne' and 'Humouresque' (discussed more fully below); but the final results were not to be seen until the *Prufrock* volume of 1917. Another important ingredient which went into the making of that volume was Eliot's encounter with the Metaphysical Poets. A vivid, early poetic impression was once recalled by Eliot in a B.B.C. talk,[9] when he described how once, as a boy, waiting in a dentist's waiting-room, he picked up a volume of the works of Edgar Allan Poe, and read these lines, quoted as an epigraph to the story 'The Assignation':

> Stay for me there; I will not fail
> To meet thee in that hollow vail . . .

The poem from which they were taken was Henry King's 'The Exequy', and Eliot records how he was compelled to find it and read it through. He must have been struck by the urgency of the lines, their mysterious suggestion of death (which would have been accentuated by the story), and above all by the chilling effect of sound in the word 'hollow', those hollow vowels suddenly opening an aural chasm amid the predominant sounds in 'stay', 'vail', 'meet' and 'thee'. Later, in his essay 'The Metaphysical Poets' (1919), he quoted the lines in a longer passage to illustrate King's use of the extended comparison of dying to a journey. And he closes the quotation with the lines:

> But heark! My pulse, like a soft Drum
> Beats my approach, tells *Thee* I come;
> And slow how ere my marches be,
> I shall at last sit down by *Thee*.

in which he noted 'that effect of terror which is several times attained by one of the Bishop King's admirers, Edgar Poe' (*Selected Essays*, p. 284). The early impression and the later recollections are a good illustration of the powerful and often chance effects of individual poetic lines or couplets on Eliot's mind, as well as being an interesting indication of how early the accents of Metaphysical poetry began to impress themselves on him.

Eliot's essays 'The Metaphysical Poets' and 'Andrew Marvell' were not written and published until 1921, but his reading of Donne began at Harvard and the influence of the Metaphysicals is most clearly seen in the volumes of poetry of 1917 and 1920. On the evidence of the essays, what most appealed to Eliot in terms of his own poetic practice were the Metaphysicals' heterogeneous imagery 'compelled into unity', their complexity, their employment of the element of 'surprise', and above all − in a term which virtually incorporates all the other qualities − their wit. Eliot enlarges the scope of the term 'wit' to an inclusiveness and centrality which it had lost since the seventeenth century. (Matthew Arnold's notorious pronouncement on Dryden and Pope had been that 'their poetry is composed in their wits, genuine poetry is composed in the soul' − 'Thomas Gray', in *Essays in Criticism*.) Wit in the Metaphysical poets means a fusion of thought and feeling, the intellect 'at the tips of the senses' (from the essay on Massinger, *Selected Essays*, p. 210). It also involves the 'alliance of levity and seriousness (by which the seriousness is intensified)' (p. 296), and this quality is particularly relevant to Eliot's own early poems of 1917 and 1920. 'It implies a constant inspection and criticism of experience. It involves, probably, a recognition, implicit in the expression of every experience, of other kinds of experience which are possible' (p. 303). This latter formulation would seem to be a way of describing irony, and it is highly relevant to the procedures of 'The Love Song of J. Alfred Prufrock' or 'Portrait of a Lady' or the poems of 1920, which keep alive a sense of the romantic in the midst of the banal – and *vice versa* – looking forward (however vainly) to 'a time to murder and create', or merely 'Recalling things that other people have desired'.

One element of metaphysical wit which Eliot's own poetry does not often correspond to, on the other hand, is its frequently severe logical argument, and its frequent use of extended 'conceits' or comparisons, and one should not overemphasize the influence of this poetry on his own. When Eliot finds similarities between the Metaphysicals and a passage from Laforgue, beginning 'O géraniums diaphanes, guerroyeurs sortilèges, / Sacrilèges monomanes' ('O diaphanous geraniums, warrior spells / Monomaniac sacrileges'; *Selected Essays*, p. 289), we may feel that the differences are overwhelmingly greater, and that the comparison tells us little about the precise quality of Donne or Marvell. But there is a kind of connection in the sheer surrealism and heterogeneity of imagery, if nothing else: and the connection was obviously an important one for Eliot's own 'poetic workshop'. The passage preceding the above gives us a general clue to the importance of both the modern French school and the Metaphysical poets for Eliot:

It appears likely that poets in our civilization, as it exists at present, must be *difficult*. Our civilization comprehends great variety and complexity, and this variety and complexity, playing upon a refined sensibility, must produce various and complex results. The poet must become more and more comprehensive, more allusive, more indirect, in order to force, to dislocate if necessary, language to his meaning.

(Selected Essays, p. 289)

The complexity of the modern world also called for a sense of order with which to manage it, and the search for this order was at least part of the reason that drew Eliot to Dante. The full influence of Dante upon Eliot is not seen until the later poems, particularly *Ash-Wednesday* (1930) and *Four Quartets* (1936–42), and the essay of 1929 in *Selected Essays*. But Eliot began his reading of Dante at Harvard, and the influence of the thirteenth-century Italian poet upon him is so pervasive, from the first, that some discussion of it is called for here. Eliot's essay of 1929 suggests that he first read Dante without any great historical or linguistic preparation, and was struck first of all by the 'peculiar lucidity' of his style, his 'visual imagination', and the force and clarity of individual images, particularly the similes, and especially the type in which the purpose is 'solely to make us *see more definitely* the scene which Dante has put before us' (p. 244). And this visual gift is at the service of a power that has been lost by modern civilization, the power to see visions. 'We take it for granted that our dreams spring from below: possibly the quality of our dreams suffers in consequence' (p. 243).

Eliot may have been exaggerating the matter as a general principle (and even in relation to himself) when he affirmed that 'more can be learned about how to write poetry from Dante than from any English poet' (p. 252); but the statement points to the intense significance that Dante held for him in a certain direction, in 1929, but also earlier. In his essay of 1920 in *The Sacred Wood* he stresses the importance of Dante's philosophy, not for its own sake or 'as a matter for argument', but for the part it plays in the poetry 'as a matter for inspection', where the poet is trying to '*realize* ideas' (p. 162) — presumably in some more physical or dramatic form — rather than discuss them as ideas. Above all, Eliot is impressed (in this essay) by Dante's ability to create the structure of 'an ordered scale of human emotions': 'Dante's is the most comprehensive, and most *ordered* presentation of emotions that has ever been made' (p. 168). This idea of ordering the emotions by means of some kind of system is one that was to be especially important to Eliot in the years between *The Waste Land* (1922) and *Ash-Wednesday* (1930), and we shall return to it in a later chapter. More important, perhaps, in the years up to 1932 was the visual vividness of Dante, particularly the Dante of the *Inferno*, and the dramatic presentation of states of passion, despair and suffering, though always with the promise, if as yet only glimpsed, of a larger perspective in which to view these. The states of Prufrock, Gerontion, Sweeney and still more that of the various figures of *The Waste Land* are, in differing degrees, the states of hell or limbo; and Eliot, in the years from about 1911 to 1925 was, in actuality and imagination, traversing these states, and had not yet achieved for himself that perspective. For these earlier years, a statement from the Dante essay of 1920 is perhaps most pertinent. Eliot concurs with Landor's description of Dante as 'the great master of the disgusting', and adds:

The contemplation of the horrid or sordid or disgusting, by an artist, is the necessary and negative aspect of the impulse toward the pursuit of beauty. But not all succeed as Dante did in expressing the complete scale from negative to positive. The negative is the more importunate.

(*The Sacred Wood*, p. 169)

The importunacy of the negative, and its fascination, were doubtless reasons for Eliot's being attracted towards another group of writers to whom he brought penetrating critical insights and whose writing had a stimulating influence on his own: the Elizabethan and Jacobean dramatists. Other reasons were their power of metaphoric concentration, their frequent power of melodrama, and the fluency and conversational vitality of their blank verse. To begin with metaphor: in his essay on Massinger (1920) Eliot drew a contrast with Massinger's 'elder contemporaries', Middleton, Webster and Tourneur. Those writers had 'a gift for combining, for fusing into a single phrase, two or more diverse impressions. ". . . in her strong toil of grace" of Shakespeare is such a fusion; the metaphor identifies itself with what suggests it' (*Selected Essays*, p. 209). Quoting lines of Tourneur and Middleton, he spoke also of 'words perpetually juxtaposed in new and sudden combinations, meanings perpetually *eingeschachtelt* [literally, 'encapsulated'] into meanings, which evidences a very high development of the senses, a development of the English language which we have never perhaps equalled'. It is a power that one finds rarely in nineteenth-century English verse; but one finds it frequently in Eliot's poetic phrases: 'Webster was much possessed by death', 'the fever of the bone' ('Whispers of Immortality'); 'These with a thousand small deliberations / Protract the profit of their chill delirium' ('Gerontion'); 'fear in a handful of dust', 'the heart of light' (*The Waste Land*, I).

Fluency and vitality of verse, and a capacity for expressing the deepest moral dilemmas, Eliot found in several places in Jacobean drama, but particularly in Middleton. De Flores in *The Changeling* has a language of masterly 'directness and precision'. Middleton 'has no message; he is merely a great recorder. Incidentally, and in flashes and when the dramatic need comes, he is a great poet, a great master of versification' (*Selected Essays*, p. 169). Eliot then quotes Beatrice's speech from *The Changeling* (V. iii. 150ff.):

> I that am of your blood was taken from you
> For your better health; look no more upon't,

> But cast it to the ground regardlessly,
> Let the common sewer take it from distinction.
> Beneath the stars, upon yon meteor
> Ever hung my fate, 'mongst things corruptible;
> I ne'er could pluck it from him; my loathing
> Was prophet to the rest, but ne'er believed.

The direct limpid dignity and despair of this passage is indeed remarkable. And the lines have an echo, as we shall see, in the passage in 'Gerontion' that begins 'I that was near your heart was removed therefrom'. In all, the Jacobean dramatists exemplified variously for Eliot a verse which was at once colloquial, concentrated in metaphoric intensity, moving easily from casual to elevated, and excitingly varied in pace. Of Tourneur: 'His phrases seem to contract images in his effort to say everything in the least space, the shortest time' (p. 191). And this is combined, in *The Revenger's Tragedy*, with 'peculiar abruptness' and 'frequent changes of tempo'. There is perhaps no other verse in English literature which we can describe in terms such as these – unless it be the verse of *The Waste Land*.

Finally, the power of caricature, and of 'negative' vision: Eliot found the former in Marlowe, in Barabas in *The Jew of Malta* and in *Dido, Queen of Carthage* ('We saw Cassandra sprawling in the streets'), or at least 'an intense and serious and indubitably great poetry, which, like some great painting and sculpture, attains its effect by something not unlike caricature' (pp. 124–5). He also found it in Ben Jonson: the simplification of his characters 'consists largely in reduction of detail, in the seizing of aspects relevant to the relief of an emotional impulse . . . This stripping is essential to the art, to which is also essential a flat distortion in the drawing; it is an art of caricature, of great caricature, like Marlowe's' (p. 159). Jonson's characterization is of the surface, but 'the superficies . . . is solid'. By its means, and by means of farce, Jonson, like Marlowe, achieves 'the terribly serious, even savage comic humour, the humour which spent its last breath in the decadent genius of Dickens' (p. 123). And this power of caricature and farce also has an essential place in Eliot's poetry up to *The Hollow Men*. The grotesque and comic images of Prufrock's mind ('Though I have seen my head, grown slightly bald / brought in upon a platter'), the prostitute's eye which 'Twists like a crooked pin', ('Rhapsody on a Windy Night'), 'The damp souls of housemaids / Sprouting despondently at area gates' ('Morning at the Window'), 'the young man carbuncular' ('The Fire Sermon') and 'The supplication of a dead man's hand / Under the twinkle of a fading star' all have, in different ways, that element of heightened emphasis or grotesque that we can include under the term caricature. And farce is an essential ingredient of *Sweeney Agonistes*, and of 'Prufrock'. It is also no accident that this power most often accompanies a vision which is either partly satiric or 'negative' in the sense that it is inspired in particular by the ugly, grotesque or despairing. And behind it lies very often that 'hatred of life' which Eliot found in Tourneur. Eliot's poetic creativity is also fed by other impulses; but it is arguable that his most *vivid* verse is fuelled above all by this, which is 'an important phase, even if you like, a mystical experience, in life itself' (*Selected Essays*, p. 190).

This account of Eliot's response to other poets before 1922 would be seriously lacking if it did not consider Ezra Pound. Eliot met his fellow American (also a mid-Westerner) in 1914, by which time Pound had already been in England for over five years. Apart from what would appear to be Pound's general influence on Eliot's decision to stay in England and devote himself more fully to poetry (rather than to philosophy and academic life), the question of Pound's influence on Eliot is in these early years something of a puzzle (whereas the effect of Pound's criticisms of the first draft of *The Waste Land* was clear and radical). Eliot wrote early on that 'His verse is touchingly incompetent'[10] and complained that his poems were old-fashioned. But in his essay of 1917, 'Ezra Pound: His Metric and his Poetry' (reprinted in *To Criticize the Critic*, 1965) – although a great deal of it consists of quotations from the reviews of other critics – he praises Pound's verse technique, and in particular defends his *vers libre* from charges of looseness, describing it as 'only possible for a poet who has worked tirelessly with rigid forms and different systems of metric' (p. 168):

The freedom of Pound's verse is rather a state of tension due to constant opposition between free and strict. There are not, as a matter of fact, two kinds of verse, the strict and the free; there is only a mastery which comes of being so well trained that form is an instinct and can be adapted to the purpose in hand.   (p. 172)

Whether or not Pound's verse practice actually influenced Eliot's own, it is clear that the two poets were thinking and experimenting often along the same metrical lines, particularly in relation to 'free verse', and that description of Pound's free verse could be applied directly to Eliot's experiments in 'Prufrock' or 'Portrait of a Lady'.

Pound's doctrines of 'Imagism' (to be found in 'a Retrospect', in *Literary Essays of Ezra Pound*, edited by Eliot, 1954) appear to have been less directly influential on Eliot, although in his essay of 1917 he quoted several of Pound's 'Don'ts for Imagists'. But he later dissociated himself from the Imagist movement proper, which he located around 1910 ('I was not there').[11] Something of the Imagist clarity and concentration can be seen in Eliot's first two volumes and in *The Waste Land* (accentuated by Pound's revisions). In the 1917 volume single concentrated images stay in the mind ('I have measured out my life with coffee spoons'), and the description of the fog as a cat in 'Prufrock' is virtually a little self-contained Imagist poem which has something in common with the more fanciful and playful Imagist descriptive poems (T. E. Hulme's 'The Sunset' would be an example). Some time around 1917 Pound encouraged Eliot to read Gautier's *Émaux et Camées*, and the tight precision of Gautier's quatrain forms, and the emphasis in the poems on hard, sculptural qualities, had a strong influence, as Eliot later recalled,[12] on Eliot's quatrain poems in his 1920 volume. But the dogmatic prescriptions of the Imagists, and their limited practice, can never have had more than a partial influence on Eliot: the music of his verse is infinitely more varied than their short 'sculpted' lines, and from the first he incorporates 'abstractions' (vetoed by Pound) as well as concrete images in his verse.

As well as Pound's commitment to the art of verse, his erudition and his exploration of the past and poetic tradition appealed to Eliot. His defence of Pound's erudition in 1917 looks forward to his own use of a wide and selective learning in *The Waste Land*, and should be borne in mind when talking about the 'problem' of Eliot's alleged obscurity: 'To display knowledge is not the same thing as to expect it on the part of the reader; and of this sort of pedantry Pound is quite free' (*To Criticize the Critic*, p. 166). But more important is Pound's use of the past to explore the present. Looking back on Pound's early poetry in 1928, in his Introduction to Pound's *Selected Poems*, he felt that Pound's use of former literature (for imitation or translation) and his exploration of history were the sign of a genuine 'originality' rather than derivativeness. 'The poet who is "derivative" is the poet who *mistakes* literature for life, and very often the reason why he makes this mistake is that – he has not read enough.' 'One is not modern by writing about chimney-pots, or archaic by writing about oriflammes . . . If one can really penetrate the life of another age, one is penetrating the life of one's own' (p. 11). Now we may feel, I think, that all the same Pound *is* often archaic while writing about oriflammes; and that a kind of antiquarianism often imbues his early poetry. Eliot may sometimes, we feel, be generously taking the will for the deed with Pound's poetry, though he was quite right about 'Hugh Selwyn Mauberley': 'a great poem', 'a positive document of sensibility . . . also a document of an epoch . . . genuine tragedy and comedy' (p. 20); one would expect him to be, for 'Mauberley' is Pound's equivalent of *The Waste Land*. But it is the direction of his interest in this aspect of Pound which is important, for it reflects his own poetic experiments in drawing on the literature of the past, and past culture in general, as a way both of searching for his own poetic identity and of creating a poetic criticism of his age – experiments which were to bear fruit most obviously in *The Waste Land*, but to a greater or lesser degree throughout his poetic career.

II

The poems now printed as *Poems Written in Early Youth* in *The Complete Poems and Plays* are mainly interesting for the ways in which they contain both echoes of earlier traditional styles which Eliot was soon to abandon completely, and tentative and uncertain experiments in new modes which he was to develop with much more striking success in the volume of 1917. 'A Fable for the Feasters', for instance, may have been those 'verses in the manner of *Don Juan*' to which we have seen him referring. It shows a skilful handling of rhyme and metre and a certain feeling for buffoonery and farce, but it is mainly mere pastiche, with none of the genuinely creative response to Byron which I have suggested above, or that creative use of allusion which Eliot develops in 'The Love Song of J. Alfred Prufrock' or *The Waste Land*. As Eliot said in his essay on Massinger: 'Immature poets imitate; mature poets steal' (*Selected Essays*, p. 206). It is the same with many of the poems in this group. There are two versons of 'Song' ('If time and space the sages say') written in the verse form of Ben Jonson's 'Drink to me only with thine eyes'; a solemn public-occasion poem written for a graduation ceremony at Smith Academy in 1905, touched very faintly by the shades of Tennyson and Arnold; and 'Song' ('When we come home across the hill') which reads almost like two discarded stanzas from Tennyson's *In Memoriam*.

However, the more interesting poems are those in which Eliot begins to find that note of witty irony and disenchantment which is so resonant in the poems of 1917. 'On a Portrait' describes the portrait of a Rossettian woman, but in a very un-Rossettian quatrain which looks forward to the poems of 1920. and the concluding couplet breaks the mood of dreamy Pre-Raphaelite beauty with a surprising hint of irony, as if the world of the animal or the physical were symbolized, looking askance at the spiritual:

> The parrot on his bar, a silent spy,
> Regards her with a patient curious eye.

'Nocturne' is the first poem to take up the full Laforgueian manner: one might say it is too Laforgueian, too close to pastiche. It has a 'Romeo, grand sérieux' and Juliet, and a 'bored but courteous moon', and a murder (which echoes the ending of Laforgue's *Hamlet*). But it is noticeable that the irony is directed mainly against the woman − and women in general − in contrast, on the whole, to the more self-critical ironies of the later *Prufrock* volume. The whole poem also raises the question (accentuated by the precisely formal rhyme and metre) of the relation between life and literary convention, which is to preoccupy Eliot throughout his literary career. Firstly, for the reader as well as for the writer, how far do the conventions of literature, through which we partly learn, and learn to express, many of our deepest feelings, assist, and how far do they impede, the realization of authentic feeling? For the writer in particular, how far do these conventions distort authentic expression by encouraging an aesthetic 'effectiveness' which will distort the realities of feeling? 'Blood looks effective on the moonlit ground' says the narrator in this poem; and the whole poem is an elegant mockery of the way in which romantic passion can become merely material for the picturesque.

There is also in 'Nocturne' a hint of the merging of the narrator and the hero which takes us in the direction of 'Prufrock' and 'Portrait of a Lady':

> The hero smiles: in *my* best mode oblique
> Rolls toward the moon a frenzied eye profound,

(my italics). The hero rolls his eye in the narrator's best mode: the narrator as his inventor causes him to do so; but there is also a sense that the narrator himself does this, and the hero copies him. It is an incomplete example of the 'dédoublement' (doubling or splitting) of the personality which Eliot saw in Laforgue,[13] where the speaker in the poem is aware of another part of himself, an *alter ego* or *egos*. In the next poem, 'Humouresque', he similarly creates a 'marionette' who acts out the narrator's imaginary role. But the technique is not as developed or as searching as in later poems, where the protagonist himself often *becomes* the narrator and hence more directly a mask for the poet himself – a technique which allows for less detachment on the part of the poet and enforces more self-confrontation.

There is a faint suggestion of a 'doubling' of the personality in 'Spleen' (written in 1910), in the poet's addressing someone who is most probably himself; but it is more notable as the first of the poems in which one of the elements is a light satire of bourgeois life ('Evening, lights, and tea! . . . this dull conspiracy'). And another significant element is the way in which his dull surroundings act on the person addressed:

> Bonnets, silk hats, and conscious graces
> In repetition that displaces
> Your mental self-possession
> By this unwarranted digression.

The 'digression' is that of the Sunday *flâneurs*, the wandering townspeople themselves; but it is also the poem itself, 'unwarranted' because it upsets the bourgeois proprieties with its note of mockery. 'Digression' will recur in the later poems either as one of the ways in which the protagonists try to escape the banalities of their surroundings into a richer inner life (Prufrock will say 'Is it perfume from a dress / That makes me so digress?'); or as a way of avoiding their own too painful inner feelings (as in 'Conversation Galante': 'She then: "How you digress!" '). 'Self-possession' and its displacement will also recur: in 'Portrait of a Lady' the narrator, in the midst of the Lady's emotional assaults, says, 'I keep my countenance / I remain self-possessed'. Finally, in the last stanza of the present poem, 'Life' is personified by a figure who anticipates Prufrock and his concern with the Absolute, the 'overwhelming question':

And Life, a little bald and gray,
Languid, fastidious, and bland,
Waits, hat and gloves in hand,
Punctilious of tie and suit
(Somewhat impatient of delay)
On the doorstep of the Absolute.

The poem aims at the lightly witty treatment of a serious predicament (the stifling of the serious by the trivia of life), but compared with the later poems on this subject it strikes one as a little self-conscious and primly clever in its pretensions: the personification of Life and of the Absolute do little more than sketch an idea, and the details of social life do not have the sharpness of those in the *Prufrock* volume: the subject needs the expansion of fuller characterization and more detailed presentation; above all it needs the varying tones which we get so richly in that volume.

'Early work' is often too easy a critical reflex; but on the whole it is an apt reaction to most of the poems in this volume. Some of them repay scrutiny; but even then it is mostly in the ways that they show early sketches of themes and images developed later that they are interesting. The Harvard graduation 'Ode' need not detain us, except to say that its metre is used, with more success, in 'Bustopher Jones: the Cat About Town', and that its presence among the witty disenchanted Laforgueian poems suggests, if nothing else, Eliot's willingness to assume for a moment the role of 'public' or official poet in a way that anticipates (perhaps rather ominously) one of his later roles as spokesman for orthodoxy and (more positively) the element of detachment in his craftsmanship, the ability to move between stylistic extremes. But the last poem in this collection of early pieces, 'The Death of Saint Narcissus', is worth looking at in more detail.

This poem (written in 1914) is the earliest of Eliot's published poems in which a religious element is predominant. The Greek myth of Narcissus is combined with the story of St Narcissus (a Bishop of Jerusalem in the second century) to present a composite figure who moves from self-absorption to absorption in God, by way of various metamorphoses. The tone is solemn, the verse is unrhymed (except in the form of repeated words), and the rhythm has no very marked life. There are one or two nicer touches to suggest the self-absorption of the figure: 'His eyes were aware of the pointed corners of his eyes / And his hands were aware of the pointed tips of his fingers'; or the curiously auto-erotic image, 'That he knew he had been a fish / With slippery white belly held tight in his own fingers'. But the transition from Narcissism to being 'a dancer before God' is, initially, abrupt and unexplained; and the various 'metamorphoses' do not really help to explain it, or even to show any kind of poetic logic.

It has been suggested that 'the turning point in Eliot's life came not at the time of his baptism in 1927, but in 1914 when he was circling, in moments of agitation, on the edge of conversion'.[14] 'The Death of Saint Narcissus' is the only collected poem of a group written in 1914–15, which also includes poems beginning 'After the turning . . .', 'I am the Resurrection!' 'So through the evening . . .', and poems entitled 'The Burnt Dancer' and 'The Love Song of St Sebastian'. The first three of these, together with 'The Death of Saint Narcissus', have been printed in their uncorrected typescript form in the Facsimile edition of *The Waste Land*, edited by Valerie Eliot (1971). Since these poems were never completed or revised and do not form part of *The Collected Poems and Plays*, I do not propose to discuss them here. Like 'The Death of Saint Narcissus' they contain frequent anticipations of parts of *The Waste Land*, which is made up of many fragments written over different periods from as early as 1914.

It certainly appears that Eliot was deeply preoccupied with the subject of religion and with various religious images around 1914. But 'The Death of Saint Narcissus' is not one of his major poems, and any serious religious element is compromised (as Lyndall Gordon points out) by the curious tone of the poem, the suggestion of a sensuous masochism at the end (which is not the sensuous passion of a poem of genuine martyrdom like, say, Crashaw's 'Hymn to St Teresa'), and the aftermath of aridity and the taint of the shadow of death.

> Because his flesh was in love with the burning arrows
> He danced on the hot sand
> Until the arrows came.
> As he embraced them his white skin surrendered itself to the
>   redness of blood, and satisfied him.
> Now he is grey, dry and stained
> With the shadow in his mouth.

There is more of the Narcissus than of the saint in the poem, one might say, more perversity than sanctity. (There is an interesting comparison to be made here with Tennyson's more successful poem 'St Simeon Stylites', where we feel both the perversity and the sanctity more powerfully.) It is an experiment with a poetry of sanctity, but, if Eliot was at this time deliberating seriously about religion, he was too honest a poet to force the issue beyond this strangely grotesque and ambivalent presentation. It is a mark of this honesty and also of a slow deliberateness of composition, that when the first stanza of 'The Death of Saint Narcissus' was recast into its final form in the first paragraph of 'The Burial of the Dead' in *The Waste Land*, it ended not with the ambivalent image of the saint's body as in the earlier poem —

> I will show you his bloody cloth and limbs
> And the gray shadow on his lips

— but simply with an unequivocal image of emptiness and horror,

> I will show you fear in a handful of dust.

3

Prufrock and Other Observations (1917)

The volume of 1917 was Eliot's first published volume of poems: the individual poems were written at various times from 1910 and some of them had been published in magazines,[1] but the 1917 volume appears to have been carefully put together, and should be seen as a whole. The volume is dedicated to Jean Verdenal, a young Frenchman whom Eliot met in Paris during his year there from 1910–11. He was a medical student with literary interests, who shared Eliot's enthusiasm for Laforgue and other modern French writers including Charles Maurras (the political thinker and leader of the Action Française). The epigraph from Dante (*Purgatorio* XXI, 133–6) suggests the strength of Eliot's feeling for Verdenal, who was killed in the French expedition to the Dardanelles in 1915, but it also gives some clue to Eliot's attitude to his poems: 'Now can you understand the quality of love which warms me towards you, so that I forget our vanity, and treat the shadows like the solid thing' (Eliot's own translation in his essay on Dante, 1929). In Dante the Roman poet Statius is talking to his fellow-poet, Virgil, whom he has tried to embrace, forgetting that they are both mere spirits or shades. Eliot's use of the lines suggests, perhaps, that his friendship with Verdenal helped him to believe in the reality, the substantiality of the poetic shadows which inhabit his verse, the haunting figures and images which seem to come as often from a rich inner world of imagination as from things observed outside the mind.

And yet the title of the volume is *Prufrock and Other Observations*: Prufrock, as well as being a mask for the poet, is an 'observation', something noted in the external world. And this element in the title suggests one of the qualities of the volume, that of detached (and frequent ironic) social observation. At times it comes close to satire, although the poems do not have the strong moral and critical standpoint of proper satire: the poetic protagonists, whether Prufrock or the narrator in

'Portrait of a Lady' or the observer in 'Preludes', are too uncertain of their own perceptions and their own worth to take the firm antagonistic stance of the satirist, and the poems are an exploration of the minds of the speakers in the poems as much as, or more than, an exploration of an external social milieu.

The volume is unified by certain preoccupations, and has a certain shape. It begins (and it is an appropriate beginning too for Eliot's poetic work as a whole) with the invitation of a Love Song,

> Let us go then, you and I,

and ends with 'La Figlia Che Piange', which describes a parting between two lovers. And of the ten poems in between, the first, and most important, 'Portrait of a Lady', and the last two, 'Hysteria' and 'Conversation Galante', are concerned with relationships between men and women. In between we have what can be described primarily as 'observations' of urban scenes or characters. The volume begins and ends with groups of more inward or 'subjective' poems (which also contain the most significant poems in the volume); and these groups encapsulate or surround the poems of social observation. It is as if the external, social world were contained within an enveloping subjectivity, a process that is also enacted within individual poems: the social world of Prufrock is perceived as images which inhabit his mind.

There is also a certain unity of place and time in the volume. The settings are almost entirely urban, and made up of the more dingy corners of cities: back streets, sawdust restaurants, passageways, vacant lots, gutters, area gates. And the time is generally late afternoon, evening, or night, as at the beginning and middle of 'Prufrock', the beginning and end of 'Portrait of a Lady', 'Preludes' I, III and IV, 'Rhapsody on a Windy Night' and 'The Boston Evening Transcript'. Evening in Eliot's poetry is often a time when the pulses of life quicken, as in the rhythms at the beginning of 'Prufrock', or in 'The Fire Sermon' in *The Waste Land*, 'the violet hour'

> when the eyes and back
> Turn upward from the desk, when the human engine waits
> Like a taxi throbbing waiting,

Evening is a time when the pressures of the social and workaday world are eased, and the individual may be prompted to search for a deeper and intenser life within himself (if he does not just read the *Boston Evening Transcript*). But even the gestures of rebellion and escape may amount to very little. As Prufrock muses:

> Shall I say, I have gone at dusk through narrow streets
> And watched the smoke that rises from the pipes
> Of lonely men in shirt-sleeves, leaning out of windows? . . .

Evening and night are times when, potentially at any rate, the mind can turn inwards towards its inner images, towards an unconscious life.

Eliot does not talk *about* the 'unconscious' in these poems, but he frequently presents its workings. It has been pointed out that he would have found a suggestive idea of the unconscious, and an example of its poetic workings, in Laforgue, who spoke of 'the rage of wanting to know oneself — to plunge beneath conscious culture towards the "interior Africa" of our conscious domain. I feel myself so poor, when known as I know myself, Laforgue, in relation to the exterior world. And I have rich mines, submarine strata, which ferment unknown.'[2] And the images of both the submarine and Africa find their equivalents in Eliot's poetic practice, in 'I should have been a pair of ragged claws / Scuttling across the floors of silent seas' and the mermaids and the 'chambers of the sea' at the end of 'Prufrock'; and in that startling outburst of unconscious life in the third section of 'Portrait of a Lady':

> And I must borrow every changing shape
> To find expression . . . dance, dance
> Like a dancing bear,
> Cry like a parrot, chatter like an ape.

(There was a disconcerting parrot, too, at the end of 'A Portrait'.) And in 'Mr Apollinax', the strange vitality of the eponymous figure, so disruptive of polite social conventions and afternoon tea, is conveyed in an underwater image:

> His laughter was submarine and profound
> Like the old man of the sea's
> Hidden under coral islands
> Where worried bodies of drowned men drift down in the green silence,
> Dropping from fingers of surf.

(which in turn is to be echoed in Part IV of *The Waste Land*, 'Death by Water').

Many of the stylistic and other elements which give a certain common tone to the poems in this volume will emerge in the discussion of individual poems; but one recurring feature might be picked out here since it has certain larger reverberations. This is the quality of fragmentariness and the concern, within the poems, with fragments. Eliot's characteristic poetic practice at this time – and to some extent throughout his poetic career – was to write either very short poems, or fragments of poems which he then worked up later into longer poetic wholes. This is particularly important in relation to longer poems like *The Waste Land* (1922) or *Ash-Wednesday* (1930), but it is also relevant to the poems published in 1917. The 'Preludes' appear to have been written at various times over a period between 1910 and 1912, and the first part of 'Prufrock' was written in 1910; the poem was completed in 1911 and then added to in 1912, though the additions were later removed (see note 1). And this fragmentary method of composition is echoed in the fragmentary nature of some of the poems themselves. 'Prufrock' in particular moves abruptly from paragraph to paragraph, often with sudden inconsequentialities and changes of direction. 'Portrait of a Lady' has a narrative coherence, but it too contains surprising and abrupt transitions, like the 'changing shape' passage quoted above.

This technique of the fragmentary is related to, is perhaps a reflection of, a concern with the fragmentary in the subject matter of the poetry. The mind of Prufrock is unable to cohere into a single train of thought, unable to squeeze 'the universe into a ball / To roll it towards some overwhelming question'. He is always inclined 'to digress'. The narrator in 'Portrait of a Lady' is distracted by the 'dull tom-tom inside his brain'. In 'La Figlia Che Piange' we are given merely a glimpse of the scene of parting which is the starting point of the poem. And these fragments and partial glimpses are often imaged by means of a kind of synecdoche, where a part is made to stand for the whole; sometimes, indeed, it takes the place of the whole, so that we are mainly aware of a disembodied part.

There are many variations of this technique. Sometimes a whole way of life is caught by a detail, or by the detail of a detail:

> I have measured out my life with coffee spoons;

When Prufrock thinks of people he thinks of parts of them, most often of 'eyes' (a feature which recurs throughout Eliot's poetry), or of arms ('And I have known the eyes already, known them all − / . . . And I have known the arms already'). And when he suddenly breaks off one train of thought to call up one of those submarine images of life free of the monotonous social round, he thinks he should have not been even a whole creature but only 'a pair of ragged claws'. In 'Preludes' II the 'consciousness' registers 'muddy feet that press / To early coffee stands'; and

> One thinks of all the hands
> That are raising dingy shades
> In a thousand furnished rooms.

And in IV we see 'short square fingers stuffing pipes', and, once again, 'eyes / Assured of certain certainties'. In 'Morning at the Window' the fog tosses up 'Twisted faces from the bottom of the street'; and, in a touch reminiscent of Carroll's Cheshire Cat,

> An aimless smile that hovers in the air
> And vanishes along the level of the roofs.

The technique of disembodiment becomes most surreal in the image of 'Mr Apollinax', whose cerebral activity ('his dry and passionate talk') is so intense a part of him that it is perhaps not surprising that

> I looked for the head of Mr Apollinax rolling under a chair
> Or grinning over a screen
> With seaweed in its hair.

And finally, in the same poem, the process of synechdoche is at work in the way Mrs Phlaccus and Professor and Mrs Channing-Cheetah, those bastions of bourgeois propriety, are remembered, exquisitely, only by 'a slice of lemon, and a bitten macaroon'.

That image of Mr Apollinax's disembodied head exemplifies a strain of surrealistic imagery which runs throughout this first volume, and indeed persists in varying forms throughout Eliot's poetry. It is a symptom of the desire to escape from the constricting round of social life into a richer and more vivid world of the imagination (as Prufrock does, in perhaps the most notable example, with the mermaids and the 'chambers of the sea' at the end of his Love Song). But the image is also an example of a characteristic element of Eliot's wit, the delight in surprising or fantastic or extreme images partly for their comic value. These often take the form of outlandish metaphors or similes. Prufrock's evening 'spread out against the sky / Like a patient etherized upon a table' is the best known (and will be examined more fully below): comedy might be disputed here, but the element of shock or surprise is undeniable. It serves to disconcert the reader, and to widen his sense of the possibilities of language and alert him to the way in which language is likely to be stretched in the poem. The extended 'conceit' (or little Imagist poem) of the yellow fog seen as a cat, which follows shortly afterwards, is less wayward and surprising, but we are still very conscious of its art or elaboration, and the effect here, I would suggest, is essentially light and playful, and adds to the sense of the detached amusement which is important to the poem. Also in Prufrock, the hands 'That lift and drop a question on your plate' are more than a little disconcerting and bizarre; and Prufrock 'sprawling on a pin', or seen as 'a pair of ragged claws', or his head 'brought in upon a platter' all raise a smile as well as a sense of pathos in the reader, and are part of that comic tone which is of the essence of the poem.

'Portrait of a Lady', which proceeds with more formal narrative realism than 'Prufrock', is characteristically less marked by extreme or surprising images (except in that one explosion of the unconscious into the bear, the parrot and the ape). 'Preludes', too, is generally more simply descriptive in its concentration on external details, and more straightforwardly conceptual in its reaching after some reality that lies behind them (the 'notion' of IV). But it ends with another surprising conceit, which helps to repudiate (it would seem) the rarified near-whimsicality of the previous stanza. It is as if in his gesture of repudiation, or at least self-mockery, the poet detonates a flash of 'wit', a kind of joke which confirms the new attitude in the gesture and the laugh:

> Wipe your hand across your mouth, and laugh;
> The worlds revolve like ancient women
> Gathering fuel in vacant lots.

This kind of 'surprising' image succeeds best when one feels behind it the pressure either of some intense unconscious impulse trying to break out into expression, or of some poetic playfulness and high spirits in the process of creation itself. In 'Rhapsody on a Windy Night', the prostitute's eye which 'Twists like a crooked pin' has a remarkable vividness and point; but the simile of midnight shaking the memory as 'A madman shakes a dead geranium' seems more 'stock', as does the extended metaphor of the moon as a senile old woman, who with her 'paper rose' seems to come from the dusty stage of some old French theatre (and who was perhaps to resurface many years later in Giraudoux).[3] Those images have a period flavour which makes them evocative but limited. In 'Morning at the Window', on the other hand, there is a metaphor which has the comic surrealism of Dickens, and something more:

> I am aware of the damp souls of housemaids
> Sprouting despondently at area gates.

The housemaids as bedraggled urban plants are Dickensian; but the Eliotic touch is in the 'souls', that faint suggestion of the spiritual that hovers over Eliot's cityscapes. Also Eliotic and 'metaphysical', in its use of unexpected erudition as an element of surprise, is the simile in 'The Boston Evening Transcript' of the speaker turning

> Wearily, as one would turn to nod good-bye to Rochefoucauld,
> If the street were time and he at the end of the street,

(though the first line seems amusingly effective by itself – listening to La Rochefoucauld's jaundiced maxims would pall after a while – and the second, made slightly obscure by its added element of abstraction, perhaps blurs the effect). And there is the extraordinary simile for Mr Apollinax's laugh, almost nonsensical, teasing the reader with the impossibility of visualization, but capturing that strange combination of glee and grotesque half-humanity in the protagonist:

> In the palace of Mrs Phlaccus, at Professor Channing-Cheetah's
> He laughed like an irresponsible fœtus.

The element of comedy, or humour (one perhaps needs the broader, non-generic term) which plays over that last image and several others in the above paragraphs, will emerge more fully in the discussion of 'Prufrock' and 'Portrait of a Lady', but it is so pervasive and essential in this volume as a whole that it deserves more general discussion. Since the wit of the Metaphysicals and the comic satire of the Augustan poets and later Byron, it is broadly true to say that the comic element had disappeared from the mainstream of English poetry. Browning is an exception to this in some of his best poems (for instance 'Fra Lippo Lippi'): but the other Victorian poets generally only managed humour in minor poems (Tennyson's 'Northern

Farmer' poems, or Christina Rossetti's 'A Frog's Fate'); and in the poets of the 1890s (Johnson, Dowson, AE, the early Yeats) and the Georgian poets it disappeared almost entirely. This must have been one of the reasons that Davidson's 'Thirty Bob a Week' stood out so sharply for Eliot from most recent poetry during his time as an undergraduate at Harvard (1906–10). The Victorian ethos, on the whole, required solemnity and 'soul' (the two things went together) from major poetry: Matthew Arnold could be simultaneously witty and serious in his prose, but in his poetry and in the touchstone of 'high seriousness' by which he measured the possibilities of poetry of the European tradition, there was no place for comic poetry (the eighteenth century was relegated to 'an age of prose'). A fundamental part of Eliot's genius was, if not satiric, at least quizzical, ironic and humorous. And a large part of the poetic revolution he effected in English poetry lay in his reintroduction of that quality which he admired in Andrew Marvell, the 'alliance of levity and seriousness (by which the seriousness is intensified)', (*Selected Essays*, p. 296).

A light but intense and searching mockery of conventional middle-class life (with the New England that Eliot knew most intimately taken as the chosen territory) runs through most of the poems in the 1917 volume. One might call it 'satiric', were it not for the fact that the scrutiny, and the revelation, are as much of the mind or the consciousness behind the observations as of the external realities themselves (or more); the firm moral (or at least formal) stance of the satirist is absent, and the wavering and self-doubting observer often mocks himself as much as others (and invariably so in the most important poems). The figures in the poems are among other things, a gallery of observed comic types: J. Alfred Prufrock, the 'dame précieuse' and the repressed bachelor in 'Portrait of a Lady', the weary Bostonian who returns to Cousin Harriet with the evening paper, Miss Helen Slingsby ('Aunt Helen'), Miss Nancy Ellicott ('Cousin Nancy'), Mrs Phlaccus, and Professor and Mrs Channing-Cheetah (a touch of fantasy in those names), the elderly waiter with the difficult clients ('Hysteria'). The strokes that characterize them are generous or abbreviated depending on the context: Prufrock's portrait is full of details of his clothes, his stature, the 'bald spot in the middle of (his) hair'; somewhat less is remembered (as we have seen) of the New England society people in 'Mr Apollinax'. Places, too, are often suggested vividly in a few strokes ('smells of steaks in passageways'), but they gain their final tone and significance as much from the whole poem to which they contribute. Eliot admired Henry James for his ability to 'make a place real not descriptively but by something happening there':[4] Eliot's places are made real not so much by external actions but by the inner drama of consciousness which takes place within their settings — or within which they themselves are located.

But to return to the question of comedy: a great deal of the comic tone arises from the bathos of setting the drab realities of everyday life ('Ah! Que la vie est quotidienne,' Laforgue had said) against some kind of ideal life or the aspiration after a fuller existence. In some poems the world divides into two classes:

> . . . evening quickens faintly in the street,
> Wakening the appetites of life in some
> And to others bringing the *Boston Evening Transcript*,

— though even those readers 'Sway in the wind like a field of ripe corn': a wistful and incongruous touch of nature and romanticism. In 'Aunt Helen' the banal style of the narration mirrors the trivialities undermining the serious standards at which, we gather, Aunt Helen aimed. In 'Preludes', 'One thinks of all the hands / That are raising dingy shades' — how much of the observer's fastidious detachment from the scene there is in that 'One thinks'! And the woman in the third section had 'such a vision of the street / As the street scarcely understands', but in a setting of comic pathos and self-cherishing loneliness where

> You curled the papers from your hair,
> Or clasped the yellow soles of feet
> In the palms of both soiled hands.

In 'Cousin Nancy', on the other hand, the conflict is external, between the vigorous Miss Nancy Ellicott (surely with an echo in the name here) who 'Strode across the hills and broke them' and who 'smoked / and danced all the modern dances', and her conservative aunts, and behind them, the bastions of the nineteenth-century tradition, the ranged books of Matthew Arnold and Ralph Waldo Emerson.

> Matthew and Waldo, guardians of the faith,
> The army of unalterable law.

In 'Mr Apollinax', the contrast between passionate vitality

and dull propriety is dramatically distinct; in 'Conversation Galante', a totally different kind of poem more in the Laforgueian mould, there is a dialogue between two sophisticated lovers: a man who, however ironically, tries at least to talk about romance, passion and seriousness, and a woman who laconically deflates these aspirations. The little social comedy arises from the way the man tries to deflect indifference or ridicule by being witty and ironic as well as romantic, playfully teasing the woman in the last stanza, 'You, madam, are the eternal humorist, / The eternal enemy of the absolute', but meeting only with the woman's literalism, her refusal to play the game of irony: 'And — "Are we then so serious?" '.

As with any good poetry, however, it is difficult if not impossible to detach these elements of 'subject-matter' (here of comedy — perhaps one might call it the comedy of thwarted idealism) from the texture and music of the verse: the effect is so much a result of the poetry as a whole. And this is no less true of the comic effects than of other kinds.

> In the room the women come and go
> Talking of Michelangelo.

The fact that these lines are unmistakably tinged with comedy depends a great deal on the quality of the rhyme and the couplet effect of the whole (whether it suggests cocktail party chatter or — giving weight to a possible sense of relentlessness in the rhythm — a rather intensely serious conversation). And how much of the effect of a kind of mock-heroic incongruity in

> Should I, after tea and cakes and ices,
> Have the strength to force the moment to its crisis?

lies in the choice of the rhyme-words? Rhyme can provoke amusement by incongruity or extravagance (as frequently in Byron): in 'Mr Apollinax' much of the comic surprise of the simile for the protagonist (described above) comes from the outrageous rhyme of 'Professor Channing-Cheetah's' with 'irresponsible foetus'. Or it can clinch an irony by confirming the sense of an inevitable progression, as in the man's inescapable reponse to the lady's words in 'Portrait of a Lady':

> 'And youth is cruel and has no more remorse
> And smiles at situations which it cannot see.'
> I smile, of course,
> And go on drinking tea.

Eliot's protean brilliance in the handling of rhyme, even simply of comic rhyme, cannot be dealt with fully at this point; but one might also notice the masterly use of what may be called 'flat rhyme', or rhyme which is merely the repetition of the same word, or of non-rhyme. In 'The Boston Evening Transcript' the only 'rhymes' are 'street' with itself, and *Boston Evening Transcript* which recurs three times with a marvellous flat regularity at the beginning, middle and end of the poem, each time with a duller thud. And in 'Aunt Helen' the few banal and random rhymes ('four/before/for' and 'street/feet') only accentuate the general absence of music and deliberate prosaic flatness of the tone.

II

So far I have been discussing general features of the 1917 volume, and elements of style and subject common to different poems. But the ultimate test of the volume is the achievement of individual pieces, and I want now to turn to the three poems which seem to me to deserve the most extended scrutiny, which together also constitute an exploration of some of Eliot's deepest concerns, and which look forward to his development in later volumes. These three are 'The Love Song of J. Alfred Prufrock', 'Portrait of a Lady' and 'La Figlia Che Piange'. They are, as we noticed earlier (together perhaps with 'Rhapsody on a Windy Night'), the most inward-turning poems of the volume; they are related by similarities of form and music; and they have a common central subject, the relations between men and women. Romantic aspiration and bafflement, heroism and triviality, assertion and timidity, cerebral analysis and the dreams of the unconscious – these and other oppositions of the emotional and mental life jostle against each other in the poems, and all end in uncertainty and irresolution, in disenchantment or unanswered questions.

'The Love Song of J. Alfred Prufrock': the title itself, the first title in Eliot's first volume of poems, captures the paradox. It is a love song; but then there is the name – prosaic, awkward, with hints of primness or effeminacy, and with its suggestion of modern American business in the initial and first-name form. The epigraph (from Dante's *Inferno* XXVII, 61–6) perhaps need not detain us long. Translated, it runs: 'If I thought that my reply would be made to someone who would ever return to the world, this flame would move no longer. But since no-one has ever returned alive from this abyss, if what I hear is true, I reply to you without fear of infamy.' Its use suggests that Prufrock is in a kind of hell and that he is addressing someone who is there too; but Prufrock's 'hell' (if it can be called that) is a very different and much less solemn and august one than Dante's; the solemnity of the passage is out of key with Eliot's poem, and not with any discernible ironic intent; and Dante's speaker (Montefeltro, a corrupt friar) does not seem to throw any light on Eliot's figure. Eliot had been reading Dante avidly for some time, and the passage may doubtless have carried some personal significance: but for the reader of the poem it seems an example of how Eliot's erudition may sometimes intrude on his material.

> Let us go then, you and I,

with its lilt and its reminiscence of traditional love-song openings – 'Come live with me and be my love' or 'Come into the garden, Maud' – and the expansiveness of the next line:

> When the evening is spread out against the sky

are abruptly brought up short by the third:

> Like a patient etherised upon a table;

In the third line of his first volume, Eliot throws down a squib in the path of convention. For there is no simile to compare to it in previous poetry, or not in English poetry – certainly not since the Metaphysicals (and it is not quite characteristic of them either). It is surely intended to surprise and even shock: it is *outré*, even though it is not quite arbitrary and has its points of aptness – we have a general sense of a horizontal evening sky (above housetops, when we re-read the poem) and the sense of a world deadened or anaesthetized – but the shock to romantic expectation is uppermost. Paradoxically, it wakes us up, alerts us to a new urgency and restlessness, which the syncopated rhythms of the following lines ('Of restless nights in one-night cheap hotels') increase. The rhythms, like the streets, lead us with a certain relentlessness to an 'overwhelming question'. But

> . . . do not ask, 'What is it?'
> Let us go and make our visit.

It is, among other things, a piece of advice to the reader: we are not to press too insistently for meaning, for a formulation of the question; first we must visit the terrain, enter into the poem.

And what we are also entering is a mind, a consciousness. 'the 'room' of the next couplet disconcerts us again, at first: what room? Are we inside it, or outside in the 'half-deserted streets'? The answer, it becomes apparent as we read, is that these locations are all fragments of Prufrock's world, within his consciousness. There is no narrative progression in the poem, and no organized geography of its town houses and streets. The women who at two moments in the poem 'come and go / Talking of Michelangelo' do so in a room at the back of Prufrock's mind, a room which is part of a theatre of consciousness in which are performed the insistent scenes of Prufrock's embarrassment, anxiety or shame. The poem is as much Prufrock's interior monologue as his love song to another (the equivocation between these two modes is important and we shall return to it), and the scenes flicker before his mind's eye.

The women talking of Michelangelo are made to sound trivializing, or perhaps just relentlessly intellectual (either way they contribute to an impression which is disturbing for Prufrock), but perhaps the latter tone fits better with the cold poise of the woman who rebuffs Prufrock in a later glimpse. But the 'yellow fog' of the next verse-paragraph is playful, and allows a moment of escape. It would be a mistake to dwell too much on the gloom and 'alienation' (to take a fashionable critical word) of Prufrock's condition, or at any rate on that of the poem. Eliot's whole art here consists in his ability simultaneously to render and to control, to order, the negative experiences (embarrassment, failure, absurdity) which Prufrock embodies. The wit and comedy of the poem, whimsical (as here with the fog) or mordant, the detached creative play, are the means of effecting this rendering and this control, of allowing the author to enter into Prufrock's experience and yet to remain detached. The fog seen as a cat is a little 'Imagist' poem, a little flourish of fancy which demonstrates for a moment the artist's freedom (and the falling into the historic past tense from the third line to the end of the passage, the only instance of this in the poem, helps suggest almost a moment of detachment from Prufrock himself, as if this is the poet rather than Prufrock speaking). After it, we can return to more insistent matters. 'And indeed there will be time . . .'

The paragraph that follows gives us Prufrock's aspirations. The echoes of the Psalms have a sonority which consorts ironically with the fog–cat, 'the hands that drop a question on your plate' and the 'toast and tea', as have the 'hundred indecisions' (shades of Hamlet when one rereads these lines) and the 'hundred visions and revisions' (which itself contains its little internal bathos, 'revisions' being much more prosaic things than 'visions'). The aspirations build up with the cumulative rhythm, swelling from 'time' to 'time' to be deflated at last with 'Before the taking of a toast and tea'; and then (in a lower voice) the Michelangelo women again. The music is perfect and the mock-heroic deflation is exact, but the Augustan element is like nothing in Dryden and like only a little in Pope (the 'Prologue to the Satires'?), because the satiric butt is the protagonist and speaker himself. Prufrock is acutely conscious of his exits and re-entrances (or *vice versa*: is he breaking free of the social gathering or re-entering it with some daring revelation? At any rate it is for some such possibly trivial gesture that there will be time); his looks, and his clothes, with the solidity of which he comforts himself against his own lack of substance:

> My necktie rich and modest, but asserted by a simple pin –

the assertion of sartorial propriety (together with that of the pedantically precise choice of the word 'asserted', a fine touch) being the only kind of assertion that he can manage.

'For I have known them all already . . .': Prufrock's thoughts move from the future tense to the past, back to the future ('Shall I say . . .?') and to the conditional ('Should I . . .?') and to the past conditional ('And would it have been worth it . . .?'). The tenses are the proper medium for memory, deliberation, indecision, speculation. Very rarely does Prufrock's mind come to rest in the present, the time of statement, assertion, command or action; when it does briefly, it is merely to question his own mental processes ('Is it perfume from a dress / That makes me so digress?') or to describe a circumstantial detail ('And the afternoon, evening, sleeps so peacefully!'). So when he says, finally coming to some conclusion,

> No! I am not Prince Hamlet, nor was meant to be;

part of his meaning is that he was not meant *to be*, in the present tense, but only to inhabit the twilight tenses of the past, the future and the conditional.

That line also recalls that, for Hamlet, 'To be or not to be' was 'the question'; so is it also Prufrock's 'overwhelming question'? We cannot know, because Prufrock does not even formulate his 'question'. Prufrock does seem to aspire to 'being' of a Hamlet-like kind — being which is also acting: 'to murder and create' (but which?) — or perhaps to putting a particular question to a particular person. The lines

> To have squeezed the universe into a ball
> To roll it towards some overwhelming question,

have for many readers recalled Marvell's 'To His Coy Mistress':

> Let us roll all our strength, and all
> Our sweetness up into one ball

(as have the earlier lines about time). And Prufrock's social (and other) unease also focuses on women talking persistently, the

> Arms that are braceleted and white and bare
> (But in the lamplight, downed with light brown hair!)

the 'perfume from a dress' and the 'skirts that trail along the floor'; and on one woman in particular, and the possibility that she

> settling a pillow by her head,
> Should say: 'That is not what I meant at all.
> That is not it, at all.'

There is more than a faint suggestion, therefore, that if Prufrock's question was not going to be a metaphysical, Hamlet-like one, it was to be an amorous one. At any rate it is upon the rack of the eternal feminine that he is broken. He has had prophetic ambitions (as well as heroic and amorous ones) and 'I have seen my head (grown slightly bald) brought in upon a platter' — but again we may remember that it was Salome who asked for the head of John the Baptist.

The poem is a 'Love Song' — and that gives the clue to the source and direction of feeling (however thwarted) — but a love song of a peculiar kind. For (to come back to the question) who is the 'you' of the first line? One's first sense is that it is the person (presumably a woman) to whom Prufrock is addressing his love song; and, secondly, because of the way we generally read poems, that it is (also) the reader, who is put in the place of the recipient of the song, and who is invited (as I have suggested) to 'go and make our visit'. The effect is to draw us into a more intimate imaginary relation to Prufrock. But after the first paragraph this addressee, the 'you', only reappears two, or possibly three, times: in 'Time for you and time for me', in 'among some talk of you and me', and possibly in the last line

60

of the poem. And it is the second instance that creates the problem. There are 'you and me' and then, at the end of the paragraph, there is the 'one, settling a pillow by her head', who cuts short whatever revelation Prufrock was trying to make. Is this, then, the woman who is important to Prufrock? And where does that leave the recipient of the 'Song'?

This opens the way, I think, for the interpretation that sees Prufrock as addressing himself in his song, addressing a kind of *alter ego*. This would be in line with the ideas of the '*dédoublement* of the personality against which the subject struggles' of which Eliot spoke in relation to Laforgueian irony (*The Criterion*, 12, 469). One half of Prufrock (broadly, his idealism and aspiration) is heroic and romantic; the other is timid, calculating and self-deflating. In the poem, then, Prufrock is talking primarily to his recalcitrant half. It would also make the poem a kind of development from 'The Death of Saint Narcissus', in which self-love and self-absorption are central subjects: in that poem the 'narrative' is done from the outside, and Saint Narcissus is seen moving from self-worship to worship of God, but with an outcome that is chillingly sterile. In 'Prufrock' the problem of self-absorption is looked at from the inside, in a dramatic interior monologue by one half of the self to the other.

'Prufrock', then, is a love song which is half-addressed to the self, though there still, I think, lingers the ambiguity that it is *as if* directed outward to another, and that this is part of its aspiration. The *dédoublement* against which Prufrock struggles is almost resolved at the end when he comes to rest in a confession of his limitations ('Am an attendant lord . . . almost, at times, the Fool'), and this allows him the indulgence of a whimsically satisfying melancholy and self-cosseting, even a kind of self-assertion:

> I grow old . . . I grow old . . .
> I shall wear the bottoms of my trousers rolled.
>
> Shall I part my hair behind? Do I dare to eat a peach?
> I shall wear white flannel trousers, and walk upon the beach.

But the self-assertion does not last long, and in a poignant cadence:

> I have heard the mermaids singing, each to each.
>
> I do not think that they will sing to me.

Prufrock's love song has not been reciprocated. But still the poem ends with the beautiful lines of lyrical and romantic fantasy, the memory of the vision of mermaids which returns in the last line. It is a fitting close to the love song, a close in which Prufrock's thwarted and self-mocked romanticism is allowed a final momentary flowering, a vision which is at once whimsical (it is essentially nostalgic and fanciful — we do not feel it could portend any future realization or achievement) and beautiful.

It is also a perfect close in its catching of two important motifs in the poem as a whole: the music of the 'Song' and the 'voices dying with a dying fall / Beneath the music of a farther room', and the 'ragged claws / Scuttling across the floors of silent seas', which was one of Prufrock's earlier fantasies of escape. And it is a fittingly romantic ending to what is in many ways a romantic (as well as counter-romantic) poem: 'mock-romantic' might be a good term for it, by analogy with 'mock-heroic' — if we remember that in Augustan mock-heroic poetry, the positive or heroic elements are there not simply to be undermined, but to provide a standard of value against which contemporary triviality is to be judged. The paradox of waking in the last line,

> Till human voices wake us, *and we drown*

(my italics) is like that at the end of Keats's Nightingale *Ode*:

> Fled is that music: — Do I wake or sleep?

— in both, the 'reality' of the waking state may be less vital and real than that of the dream.

The poem is a shifting succession of images, dream-like, protean in its variety of image, music and tone, in a way that it is difficult to do justice to in description. There is an element of pyrotechnic display, but one does not feel that this compromises the sincerity of the poem. The movements from urgency to playfulness, from declamation to deflation, from precise observation to moments close to caricature ('And I have seen the eternal Footman hold my coat and snicker'), are dazzlingly done. The poem maintains a light touch, but the moments of genuine disgust are powerful ('Then how should I begin / To spit out all the butt-ends of my days and ways'). In some ways it is the end of the Laforgueian tradition; in others it looks forward to the preoccupations (in particular, with love) in Eliot's later poems. It was (to use a metaphor of which Eliot might not have disapproved) a resounding number with which to ring up the curtain on a poetic career.

III

'Portrait of a Lady' examines the Prufrockian world, and to some extent the Prufrockian type (in the narrator), but in a completely different way: with an additional point of view, a narrative rather than a 'stream of consciousness' mode, a quieter tone, a more dramatic sense of conflict, and perhaps in the end with greater penetration. The portrait is of the lady, but we gradually become aware that it is the man, too, who is being revealed. The music of the poem (the verbal music which complements and is complemented by the 'music', which is one of the poem's recurring motifs) is, if anything, subtler than in 'Prufrock'. And in general the poem is perhaps the finest achievement of this volume because of its direct and delicate rendering of experience.

My last phrase perhaps needs some explanation. We do not know on what particular experience, if any, the poem is based. (The lady is said to have been modelled on a well-known Boston *précieuse* or society lady whom Eliot and his circle knew at Harvard; but, of course, even if this is so, the historical lady may have given the merest hint to the poet; nothing more would be needed for one who must have admired and cultivated the Jamesian ambition to be 'one of those on whom nothing is lost'.) But the important thing is the effect of the poem − the effect of authenticity. We know that Eliot wrote a poetry of masks or *personae*, but the masks are (surely more than was ever the case with Browning or the early 'medieval' Pound) masks for himself, versions or projections of aspects of his own personality. And one can infer from the quality of the poem that the 'experience' dealt with is in some essential (though not necessarily biographical) way a reorganization of the experience of the poet himself. We feel that Eliot in this poem renders his own experience in a way that is remarkably full and intense, and orders it (which involves moral judgement) in a way which is remarkably precise.

A great deal of the achievement of the poem is due to the gift for dramatic verse by which Eliot is able to render the exact tones and nuances of the lady's speech, anxious and effusive in its appeals for sympathy. The verse form, 'free' and yet entirely controlled in its effect of rhythm and rhyme, helps at all points to effect this. Rhyme in particular helps to point the exact stresses, and the line-lengths and -endings (open and wistfully expansive or closed and suggesting a desperate attempt to drive a point home) gives us the expansion and contraction of the lady's confidence:

'You do not know how much they mean to me, my friends,
And how, how rare and strange it is, to find
In a life composed so much, so much of odds and ends,
(For indeed I do not love it . . . you knew? you are not blind!
How keen you are!)
To find a friend who has these qualities,
Who has, and gives
Those qualities upon which friendship lives.
How much it means that I say this to you —
Without these friendships — life, what *cauchemar*!'

(One might also notice how the lady's plangent repetitive syntax slyly betrays her with its hidden ambiguities: it is, for instance, one of the problems of the lady's life that it is 'composed so much'.)

The poem is so unobtrusively full of subtle touches of verse, tone and language that to do it justice one would have to quote it all. One or two examples must suffice: 'an atmosphere of Juliet's tomb' (the prepared romantic setting suddenly and comically laden with doom); 'And so the conversation slips . . . / And begins' (and *really* begins). But comment is otiose for

'Ah, my friend, you do not know, you do not know
What life is, you who hold it in your hands';
(Slowly twisting the lilac stalks)

or

I feel like one who smiles, and turning shall remark
Suddenly, his expression in a glass.
My self-possession gutters; we are really in the dark.

— though one might notice how that last line and the earlier 'My self-possession flares up for a second' 'takes up' in metaphor the literal 'four wax candles' of the opening scene-setting. This blending of the literal and the metaphorical is in fact particularly characteristic of the poem, which is much concerned with the way the details of an external scene become the elements of a state of mind.

It might be objected that the art of the poem *is* obtrusive, with all these calculated effects (though of course to pick them out makes them seem more calculated). But one dominant preoccupation of the poem is precisely the way in which art relates to the rest of life, and in particular the different ways in which the protagonists react to art and draw upon it to make sense of experience, or to express themselves, or to further their ends. The lady prepared the room's romantic atmosphere with a conscious artfulness, and the narrator thinks of 'Juliet's tomb'. They have been to hear Chopin, who is then used to steer the conversation towards intimacy (and whose wistful or passionate music finds a remarkable equivalent in the poem as a whole). The lady recalling her 'buried life' echoes Arnold's poem of that title with its Victorian melancholy, its soul-weariness, but also its romantic belief that there *is* a 'buried life', 'a central stream' beneath the distracting surface; in the lady's conversation it sounds as if it may be merely the figment of a literary imagination, though there is always the possibility that it *is* there, even for her. The man is genuinely disturbed by the sound of the street-piano, and in one of his moments of mental escape he thinks of the wild movements of a dance to image his frustration and his need.

This preoccupation with art has a large significance for the poem as a whole. The revelation of the poem lies in the way we move from being acutely aware of the embarrassingness of the lady and of the man's false position, to an equal awareness (which is also the narrator's own) of the narrator's responsibility for the situation. The epigraph to the poem ('Thou hast committed − / Fornication: but that was in another country, / And besides, the wench is dead.' − *The Jew of Malta*) comes to seem apt in this case, as a brutal overstatement of what is nevertheless a truth about the narrator's relationship and responsibility to the lady. At the end of the first section (or 'act' − the dramatic term would be appropriate) the man is distracted by an internal music 'That is at least one definite "false note" ' (wittily placing the indefinite false notes of the music of the conversation), but escapes into the 'bachelor' world, the 'tobacco trance'. By the end of the second he has focused more clearly on his responsibility − 'how can I make a cowardly amends / For what she has said to me?' the street-piano and the smell of hyacinths make him aware of his own emptiness, 'Recalling things that other people have desired'. By the end of the third section he is entirely doubtful of his feelings (which in Part I had been so wittily composed so as to put the lady in the wrong) and of his 'right to smile'. And his final paragraph contains an awareness of the possible distortions effected by a composed and ironic position, which reflects on the whole undertaking of the poem.

The scene of the last paragraph, imagined by the narrator, fits the mood of sympathetic but somewhat casual melancholy and speculation:

> Well! and what if she should die some afternoon,

and is a very 'composed' one, a picture from the brush of an Impressionist:

> Afternoon grey and smoky, evening yellow and rose;

The narrator also imagines himself 'pen in hand', as if in the act of composing. And the last lines contain more than one irony.

> Would she not have the advantage, after all?
> This music is successful with a 'dying fall'
> Now that we talk of dying —
> And should I have the right to smile?

Would she not have the advantage because she has secured sympathy by dying? Because she is *au-dessus de la mêlée*? Because, when one looks back on the story, she, at least, committed herself, tried to achieve friendship (or even love), tried to live? And because it is she who commands, who calls up the final music of the poem, who is and was the life of the poem, indeed its muse? The narrator, on the other hand, is left merely as the 'successful' composer. He is, virtually, the poet, who has shaped the music of the poem, with its final, satisfying, 'successful' close, but out of the failure in life. 'This music is successful': there is a world of irony and regret, and even bitterness, in that.

'Portrait of a Lady', then, is conscious of its own construction and of the processes of art, in a way that cannot be discerned in 'The Love Song of J. Alfred Prufrock'. And this is not just a matter of self-regarding self-consciousness, because this awareness is intimately connected to the narrator's (and poet's) moral self-evaluation. The very detachment of the artist (in this particular case), his necessary detachment, may be related to an inhibiting detachment in his human relationships. Whether one causes the other (and if so, which causes which) it is not necessary for us to speculate. What is of immense importance, for this poem and for Eliot's future development as a poet, is that he has discovered his central subject: the sense of lack, of emptiness in his human relationships (which is also an awareness of this possibility in human relationships in general), and of the way in which art can serve either to disguise or distort this fact, or to express it and overcome it by placing it in a new perspective, a new pattern.

Before looking at 'La Figlia Che Piange', which continues this theme of the relationship of love and art in a different mode, one might pause here to mention as a stark contrast what is perhaps the most curious and, in certain ways, disturbing poem in the 1917 volume – disturbing not because of its success but because of a violence and hardening of tone – the prose-poem 'Hysteria'. It was first published after all the other poems in the volume (in Pound's *Catholic Anthology*, November 1915), and given the order of composition and publication of the other poems so far as we know it, this may suggest that it was the most recently written. It is a description of a woman's attack of hysteria, written in the first person as if by her companion, and, despite the element of wit, in a style of cold, even brutal detachment. The detachment would seem to be the result of a reaction against a sense of personal threat, the threat of being engulfed in the hysteria until it becomes almost cosmic in its scope, yet seen with a kind of mad clarity:

. . . until her teeth were only accidental stars with a talent for squad-drill. I was drawn in by short gasps, inhaled at each momentary recovery, lost finally in the dark caverns of her throat, bruised by the ripple of unseen muscles.

The image is also, of course, of an engulfing sexuality, and the concentrated detachment of the prose (which is far from being a genuine artistic detachment, since one feels the note of desperate stratagem) is an attempt to escape this encroachment.

I decided that if the shaking of her breasts could be stopped, some of the fragments of the afternoon might be collected, and I concentrated my attention with careful subtlety to this end.

What is unpleasant in the poem is the complete withdrawal of compassion for the woman, and her fragmentation into physical items: the teeth, the throat, the 'shaking of her breasts'. It is the fragmentation we have seen in 'Prufrock' and elsewhere, but here turned deliberately into a defensive (and offensive) weapon. The scrupulous balance of self-criticism which is maintained, in the matter of relations between men and women, in 'Prufrock' and 'Portrait of a Lady', is here abandoned in favour of one-sided irony and distaste, compounded by the chillingly clinical prose.

IV

In 'La Figlia Che Piange', the third most important poem in the volume, there is a return to a subtle music and a compassionate speculativeness which makes this an entirely fitting conclusion to the collection, in that it looks back, and forward. It has been described as a love poem, its subject 'love in the lyrical sense, with no irony in the tone or context';[5] but although it is a love poem, I do not think we can exclude irony from its tone, even if it is only the irony of uncertainty, in which statements must mean potentially more than they seem to do at first glance because the speaker is in so much doubt about how to evaluate his experience and his loss. But because of its precise and careful progression, and of certain difficulties in its syntax, a brief 'reading' of the poem will be the best way to proceed.

The Italian title, 'La Figlia Che Piange' ('The Weeping Girl'), is reported to have been taken from the title of a marble tablet, which Eliot was told of and tried to find in a museum in northern Italy during a visit there in 1911. One presumes that its lyric suggestiveness caught his imagination, and its provenance is not otherwise important. The epigraph is also mainly evocative in itself – in English, 'O maiden how may I remember you' or 'What name shall I give you?' Its source in Virgil's *Aeneid*, I, 327, where Aeneas is questioning Venus, may carry some associations of divinity into the poem, but these would seem to be very secondary. Once again, the important elements for our impression lie on the surface. It is a poem about a memory: the epigraph has no question-mark, but it says both 'how may I remember?' and potentially 'how shall I remember?' – what form is memory to take? It is a poem about a memory, but also about the recreation of a memory in the poem. So the poet begins with a series of commands (an analogy might be with a portrait-painter or a theatre-director) – 'Stand on the highest pavement of the stair' – which 'compose' a beautiful scene and a fragile moment of parting, before him. (There might also be an analogy with techniques of religious meditation which begin with 'composition of place', a technique of conjuring a scene in the imagination to induce the proper frame of mind). The movement is lyrical, but the action described is, perhaps deliberately, a shade theatrical.

The second stanza reflects on the scene, and we have again, most probably, that 'doubling' of the personality that we have

encountered before. 'I' and 'him' are both the speaker: this is
how he would have liked himself to have parted from the girl,
and also how he would have left,

> As the soul leaves the body torn and bruised,
> As the mind deserts the body it has used.

Those lines of course imply a criticism of himself – his parting
would have been violent and cruel – and they also imply a
criticism of the first stanza (which has not *seemed* to be violent
or particularly cruel). In addition they reflect in a highly significant way on a passage in the essay 'Tradition and the Individual
Talent' which I shall examine in the next chapter, the passage
about the separation in the artist between 'the man who suffers
and the mind which creates'. For the danger of the notion of
'impersonality' is that it will lead to a cold or irresponsible
attitude in the artist towards the experience which provides his
subject-matter, like a violence towards or a betrayal of the
'body' by the 'mind' or the 'soul'. This poem indeed constitutes,
among other things, a radical critique of that essay (the fact that
the poem precedes the essay in time is immaterial to the point
here). Instead of this violent betrayal, 'I should find' (now, in
the present moment of composition) 'Some way incomparably
light and deft', a way, one might note, which is still tinged with
irony – 'Simple and faithless as a smile and shake of the hand'.

In the last stanza the pulsing rhythms render the insistence of
the original memory in the imagination –

> Compelled my imagination many days,
> Many days and many hours:
> Her hair over her arms and her arms full of flowers.

And the reflection that follows catches a play of irony and various
meanings: 'I wonder how they should have been together' could
mean 'I wonder how they would have been had they stayed
together' or even 'I wonder how they were *ever* together'; and 'I
should have lost a gesture and a pose' suggests either 'I should
have lost a precious memory of a gesture and a pose' or 'I should
have lost merely a gesture and a pose'.[6] The opposing possibilities
are hinted at in the infinitely speculative tone. But the last lines are
unequivocal. The speaker tries to preserve an irony by using the
slightly deprecating, slightly pedantic term 'cogitations'; but the
genuine amazement and disturbance are still there:

Sometimes these cogitations still amaze
The troubled midnight and the noon's repose.

The poem is a criticism both of the memory and of the way the memory can be recreated. In his creation, his posing, of the idealized beauty of the first stanza, does the poet (the poem asks) betray experience? Would the alternative of the end of the second stanza be less cruel and more honest? Just as in 'Portrait of a Lady', the poem creates a beautiful artefact, but asks, 'Is the aesthetic result achieved at the cost of some distortion, evasion or betrayal?' A failure of love has once again been examined, and rendered in a form at once lyrical, romantic and sceptical. How can memory be best recreated and ordered in art? Whatever the answer in this particular case, the scene of the girl with the flowers remains to compel imagination at the end of the poem, and its metamorphoses will be seen in later volumes. And, more broadly, the problem of the ordering of memory and emotion will receive wider and more ambitious attempts at solution. 'La Figlia Che Piange', perfect within its own terms, looks forward to further poetic development.

4

Poetic theory and poetic practice

I

We have already seen something of how Eliot's creativity as a poet is closely associated with his activity as a critic. The experiments of his poetry, his technical habits, the relation of his poetry to that of the past are all illuminated, whether directly or in passing, by his criticism. And so it is at this point, between the poetry volumes of 1917 and 1920, that many of his major critical ideas and formulations may be best examined. He published − and, it would seem, wrote − little poetic criticism before 1917; but in 1920 appeared *The Sacred Wood*, a volume which collected together various pieces already printed in periodicals, and in this volume some of his most important essays are contained. Indeed, many of the questions they raise continued to preoccupy Eliot in subsequent years, and he returns to them in later essays. So this chapter will not confine itself to the earliest criticism, but will take the opportunity to look at some of Eliot's main critical ideas about poetry across his career. Many of his ideas develop and change, and some of these developments will be examined in a later chapter, but certain of them remain constant − or at any rate remain central, with subtle shifts and adjustments and changes of emphasis occurring along the way − and a general view of them will be useful here. There are also ideas which he only formulated later, but which carry the stamp of centrality, and which fairly can be regarded as informing his poetic practice from the beginning.

We have already looked in Chapter 2 at something of Eliot's criticism of the Metaphysical poets and of Laforgue, Baudelaire, the Jacobean dramatists and Dante, since the reading of these poets was influential in some of Eliot's earliest poetry. But although Eliot was there quoted putting a high valuation on his criticism of individual poets, it would be a mistake to think that his general formulations about poetry (in essays like 'Tradition and the Individual Talent', 'The Music of Poetry', 'The Three Voices of Poetry' and 'The Social Function of Poetry') are not

71

also relevant to his own poetry and our consideration of it. One reason for this is that whether we accept or reject his ideas about the making of a poem, or the poet's relation to history or the social role of the poet, or whatever it may be, we can see in Eliot's discussions of these things pointers which may help us to understand his aims and achievements and his relative successes and failures in his own poems.

The most famous essay in *The Sacred Wood* (or the most notorious, as it has sometimes been called),[1] is the essay of 1919, 'Tradition and the Individual Talent'. It is in three parts, and the two main parts focus on two related issues which are of central importance in attempting to understand Eliot's poetic criticism and his own poetry. The first is the question of the poet's relation to history and tradition; the second is the question of how a poem is made, and involves the ideas of 'personality' and 'impersonality'. Eliot's formulation of both issues (particularly the second) is deeply problematic and has provoked all kinds of questions and disagreements.[2] But certain things in the essay caught the imagination of readers at the time, and have continued to do so. It may not be, as a whole, a 'classic' essay (in which we feel throughout an expression of certain permanent truths), but it has classic moments. And even in its most doubtful (even, we may conclude, wrong-headed) passages we feel that it engages with problems which were pressing for Eliot, and which are still alive for us.

The first part of the essay proposes a fresh idea of tradition, in particular the tradition of poetry to which the individual poet is related. Tradition is not to be confused with an inert acceptance of the past, or with simple conservatism, or 'following the ways of the immediate generation before us in a blind or timid adherence to its successes'. What it *is*, on the other hand, is formulated in one of Eliot's classic passages (*Selected Essays*, p. 14). Tradition, he says there, cannot be merely inherited, but involves 'great labour'. It involves, above all, 'the historical sense' ('nearly indispensable to anyone who would continue to be a poet beyond his twenty-fifth year'). The historical sense makes a writer aware of the order of European literature from Homer, its 'simultaneous' existence in the present; it makes a writer aware of both the timeless and the temporal, and also most conscious of his own age. Now there may be some poets who have not sought 'the historical sense', but one cannot think of many major ones. Certainly that formulation would apply to

Chaucer, to Spenser, to Shakespeare, to Milton, to Marvell, to Pope, to Keats, to Tennyson (to name a few outstanding examples). But it is particularly notable (from our point of view in a study of the poems) that it applies to no one more than to Eliot himself.

Even as early as 'Prufrock' we can see Eliot the poet beginning to acquire 'the historical sense', not always successful in detail, but certainly so in an overall effect. The epigraph from Dante may be (as has been suggested) redundant erudition; but the poem's echoes of, for instance, Marlowe (in the opening), of the King James Version of the Bible (in 'There will be time . . .'), of Marvell, and the allusions to John the Baptist and Hamlet show the beginnings of a rich technique, which was to find fuller development in *The Waste Land* and, in a changed and less ostentatious form, in *Four Quartets*. Of course, the power of borrowing and allusion — of creative erudition — which transforms what it takes into its own new substance, is not the sum total of the workings of 'the historical sense'. In a general way, as Eliot makes clear, the historical sense helps him to know what directions to take, what needs to be done; and it also provides him with a critical tool of comparison, and with a set of standards against which to judge his own and his contemporaries' work. But for Eliot the historical sense also provided a creative method within many of his own poems, a method which allowed him to explore, present, criticize and even judge both himself and his age. It enabled him to draw on what was alive for the present in poets (and other writers) of the past, to redraw the lines of tradition by giving prominence to certain poets relatively less current at the time (Donne, Marvell, the Jacobean playwrights) and dislodging, for a time, other more august names (Milton is the prime example).

The second part of 'Tradition and the Individual Talent' reflects on the processes which are at work in the composition of a poem, and the most notorious part of the discussion is the attempt at an analogy between the poet's mind and a piece of platinum which acts as a catalyst in a chemical reaction between two gases. The catalyst serves to bring about a new compound out of the two gases, but the catalyst itself is unchanged by the process. In the analogy, the poet's mind is the platinum or catalyst; 'feelings' and 'emotions' are the two chemicals. The poet's mind, then, is simply a neutral medium in the making of a poem out of 'feelings' and 'emotions', and is unchanged by the experience of the poem. The latter are distinguished, it would seem, by saying that 'emotions' belong to the general life-experience of the poet (presumably love, hate, anger, despair, etc.), and 'feelings' inhere 'in particular words or phrases or images'.

Now there are a host of problems and objections pertaining to this analogy and the account it gives of poetic creation. But the main ones would seem to be: can we imagine that the mind of the poet is so inert in the process of composition? Can we imagine that it could be so totally unchanged by the process? Can the process of composition be so completely automatic as this would seem to make it? (It is difficult to see what room there would be for the mental processes of active discrimination and choice, the critical activity in creation which elsewhere Eliot insists on.)[3] But the biggest problems arise with the concluding statements of the second paragraph of this part:

> It [the mind of the poet] may partly or exclusively operate on the experience of the man himself; but the more perfect the artist, the more completely separate in him will be the man who suffers and the mind which creates; the more perfectly will the mind digest and transmute the passions which are its material.

Firstly we may need to know what is meant by 'experience' in the first part of that sentence (in one sense of the word, the poet's mind could only operate on his own experience, but presumably Eliot means his primary experiences in 'life' as opposed to the experience of art or literature). Secondly, *can* the mind which creates be separated from the man who suffers, and would it be a desirable state of affairs if it could? This part of the statement is perhaps the nub of objections to the whole idea of 'impersonality', which is the term used in the last part of the essay to sum up the ideal state of the artist. It would seem to lead towards a state of 'dehumanization' for the artist, a term which is close to the way we usually use 'depersonalization', which Eliot uses himself (at the end of Part I of the essay) to describe the process he goes on to outline. It would seem close to the 'classiosity' which D. H. Lawrence denounced as 'bunkum' and cowardice, because of its retreat from the truth of experience.[4]

And yet, despite the fact that Eliot has been led into some doubtful formulations, it seems to me that he is still trying to get at some powerful and necessary truths — necessary both in general and in particular for himself at the time. It is clear from the essay that he wants to get away from the Romantic notion of poetry as the direct expression of personal feeling. Wordsworth's account was: 'Poetry is the spontaneous overflow of powerful feelings: it takes its origin from emotion recollected in tranquility' (Preface to *Lyrical Ballads*). The matter is subsequently qualified in Wordsworth's full discussion, and even in those famous phrases a qualification like 'takes its origin from' makes a difference which tends to be forgotten. But the popular account would have it that poetry is the direct expression of feeling, only different from the direct expression in 'life' by being in verse; the poet feels sorrow, or joy, or love, expresses it directly and autobiographically and seeks to produce the same feeling in the reader. Eliot knows as a practising poet that the matter is more complex than that; that many 'feelings' (to revert to Eliot's terms) enter into the process of creation besides direct autobiographical 'emotion'; and even more important, that the poetic medium may be far from directly autobiographical. To this extent, at least, Eliot seems to be saying something clear and salutary, and it also has large implications for his own poetic practice.

Of course, one can derive a clearer view of what Eliot is saying only by ironing out certain complexities. Eliot does not use the term 'autobiographical'; he uses the more general terms 'personal' and 'personality'. 'The progress of an artist is a continual self-sacrifice, a continual extinction of personality.' 'Poetry is not a turning loose of emotion, but an escape from emotion; it is not an expression of personality, but an escape from personality.' There may be truths or half-truths in these statements, but certain questions are bound to arise. What kind of, or how complete, an extinction of personality is the artist to aim at without becoming featureless and indeed lifeless? Is 'self-sacrifice' the same as 'extinction'?[5] How far can the artist afford to 'escape from emotion' before he becomes quite emotionless'? (We might remember 'The Dry Salvages' II and 'the emotionless / Years of living among the breakage / Of what was believed in as the most reliable'.) There are problems in these critical formulations which Eliot never completely resolved, though both his criticism and his poetry often return to them in varying ways.

Indeed, the irresolution of these problems was, one may say, a continual stimulus to the poetic and critical activity, a stimulus to the search for what has been called a 'technique for sincerity'.[6] And for our focus on the poems, the important thing would seem to be that the essay 'Tradition and the Individual Talent' reveals a pressing need to find a formula for poetry which would avoid the too importunate and direct pressure of personal experience and allow the poet to explore (through 'tradition') wider areas of human possibility. But Eliot did not abandon the 'emotional', and he returns to the problems in an essay of 1927, 'Shakespeare and the Stoicism of Seneca', where the emphasis is less problematic: 'What every poet starts from is his own emotions . . . Shakespeare, too, was occupied with the struggle — which alone constitutes life for a poet — to transmute his personal and private agonies into something rich and strange, something universal and impersonal' (*Selected Essays*, p. 137). The aim is not, this time, to escape from emotion, but to 'transmute' emotion. The change suggests that Eliot no longer felt the need to devise a formulation which kept 'the man who suffers' so sharply divided from 'the mind which creates'.

However, in the poetry up until *The Hollow Men* (1925), and indeed sometimes earlier, we feel the same kind of impulse towards a poetry that works obliquely, avoiding direct utterance and speaking through masks of *personae*, or adopting a tone of detachment, sometimes whimsical, sometimes caustic and satirical. And at this point the idea of the mask might be looked at more closely, since it is in many ways the corollary of the idea of impersonality. 'And I must borrow every changing shape / to find expression', says the narrator in 'Portrait of a Lady', and this is Eliot's own procedure, in changing ways, throughout his career. Eliot did not formulate an idea of the mask at any great length in his criticism, but there are hints here and there. There is the 'doubling' of the personality in Laforgue 'against which the subject struggles' (*The Criterion*, 12, p. 469) — and one might note that last phrase, since it suggests that the fragmentation into different personalities is not seen as a state in which to rest: some notion of wholeness beyond it is kept in view. There is the remark in Part II of the essay on Blake of 1920: 'You cannot create a very large poem without introducing a more impersonal point of view, or splitting it up into various personalities.'[7] But perhaps the best early statement of the idea of the mask comes from Ezra Pound, whose early influence on Eliot we have already briefly examined. Pound wrote in 1914:

In the 'search for oneself', in the search for 'sincere self-expression', one gropes, one finds some seeming verity. One says 'I am' this, that, or the other, and with the words scarcely uttered one ceases to be that thing.

I began the search for the real in a book called *Personae*, casting off, as it were, complete masks of the self in each poem. I continued in a long series of translations, which were but more elaborate masks.[8]

This statement stresses the idea that the use of masks is a 'search for oneself', and that is how, I think, we should see their use in Eliot – as an escape from a surface self, and a search for a deeper self, and a new way of seeing the self. Eliot did formulate some ideas about the mask in a much later essay, 'The Three Voices of Poetry' (1933), but what the formulation lacks is a clear sense of the relation between the mask and the self. The poetry of the first voice is lyric poetry (where the poet is talking to himself or to nobody); the third is that of dramatic verse (where the voice is that of a created character). The second includes the voice of the Browningesque dramatic monologue: and here we seem close to Eliot's own practice in 'Prufrock' or 'Journey of the Magi' or 'A Song for Simeon'. But the second voice is also made to include all those kinds of poetry in which the poet is speaking to an audience, including epics, satire, poetry intended to instruct, poetry with a social purpose. One feels that the 'second voice' is being made to encompass too much here: there is, after all, an immense difference between, say, the epic voice, or the didactic voice of much of Eliot's *Choruses from 'The Rock'* (1934), and the voice of Browning's Duke or Andrea Del Sarto. Eliot does not quite define, in his triple distinction, the voice of the dramatic monologue, or of that subdivision of the dramatic monologue which involves the use of mask. (I say 'subdivision' because there seems, again, to be a difference between the more external dramatic creation of the speaker in Browning's 'My Last Duchess' and the mask proper, the mask which half hides and half reveals the poet, as with Prufrock or Tiresias or Simeon.)

This brings us back again to the question of 'impersonality'. For it should be said that though the technique in 'Prufrock' or 'Portrait of a Lady' (in the latter's creation of a narrator–mask) avoids the direct autobiographical utterance, the poems feel intensely 'personal' in the indispensable sense: that is, we feel the poet's feelings, and the poet's predicament, in whatever way, and are deeply engaged in them. Thus the poems feel in many ways closer to Eliot's first 'lyric voice' (of the essay) than to that voice which is concerned with addressing an audience – a voice, as I shall later suggest, which sometimes had its dangers for Eliot – or to the voice of many of Browning's monologuists.

'The Three Voices of Poetry' does in fact contain a passage which can fittingly conclude this discussion of 'personality', 'impersonality' and *personae*, because it stresses, in a way which seems to me particularly fine and convincing, the ultimately inescapable sources of any real poem in the poet's deepest personal feelings. It also implies the irrelevance in the 'lyric' poem of any conscious 'social purpose' to the poet's first effort to come to terms with the stirrings of his creative impulse, an implication to which we shall return when considering Eliot's later poetry. At the very beginning of the creative process the poet is dealing with 'nothing so definite as an emotion in the ordinary sense', but with an 'embryo', a nameless something.

In a poem which is neither didactic nor narrative, and not animated by any other social purpose, the poet may be concerned solely with expressing in verse – using all his resources of words, with their history, their connotations, their music – this obscure impulse. He does not know what he has to say until he has said it; and in the effort to say it he is not concerned with making other people understand anything. He is not concerned, at this stage, with other people at all; only with finding the right words or, anyhow, the least wrong words. He is not concerned whether anybody else will ever listen to them or not, or whether anybody else will ever understand them if he does. He is oppressed by a burden which he must bring to birth in order to obtain relief.   (*On Poetry and Poets*, p. 98)

Eliot goes on to speak of the poet as 'haunted by a demon' of which the poem he makes is a kind of exorcism. The poem is not primarily a means of communication but a way of gaining 'relief from acute discomfort'. When the words of the poem fall into place the poet experiences 'a moment of exhaustion, of appeasement, of absolution, and of something very near annihilation, which is in itself indescribable. And then he can say to the poem: "Go away! Find a place for your self in a book – and don't expect *me* to take any further interest in you." '

That does not settle the problems of 'personality' and 'impersonality', but in its personal urgency it seems to go beneath or behind them to the very sources of lyric poetry. It also reminds us that we cannot take the full force of the ideas of a great critic if we ignore the quality of his prose, the vitality of expression

78

which, to use Wordsworth's words about poetry, is 'its own testimony'.

II

One of the ways in which Eliot saw that the dark 'embryo' or 'creative germ' could first appear was as an intimation of music, a fragment of musical rhythm, and this in turn suggests why he was often dissatisfied with the usual way of talking about a poem springing directly from an 'emotion' in the ordinary sense, emotion of the kind which everybody can be expected to feel: sometimes the impulse came in a form which was inseparable from the mode of art itself. The question of 'the music of poetry' is such a central one in Eliot's own criticism, and the music of his own verse is an element which has already been seen to be so important in the 1917 volume and which will so frequently be raised again, that it would be a good idea to look more closely at this point at Eliot's own critical discussion of the subject.

The best known of his passages on the music of poetry comes in his chapter on Matthew Arnold in *The Use of Poetry and the use of Criticism* (1933). He suggests that Arnold was perhaps not 'highly sensitive to the musical qualities of verse', and he goes on:

What I call the 'auditory imagination' is the feeling for syllable and rhythm, penetrating far below the conscious levels of thought and feeling, invigorating every word; sinking to the most primitive and forgotten, returning to the origin and bringing something back, seeking the beginning and the end. It works through meanings, certainly, or not without meanings in the ordinary sense, and fuses the old and obliterated and the trite, the current, and the new and surprising, the most ancient and the most civilised mentality.   (p. 118–19)

The manner is rather stiff ('what I call the "auditory imagination" . . .') and the ideas are in places grandiloquent rather than precise ('returning to the origin and bringing something back, seeking the beginning and the end'). There is perhaps a formal echo of Coleridge's famous passage on the balancing and reconciling powers of the imagination at the end of Chapter 14 of *Biographia Literaria*. But we still find, I think, some suggestiveness in the passage, in the sense of what is 'below the conscious levels of thought and feeling' and the idea of the fusion of the primitive and the civilized. And it is important to note the inseparability even here of 'music and meaning' ('It works through meanings, certainly, or not without meanings in the ordinary sense').

Nevertheless, we have a better, because more specific and informative (and less exalted), account of the poet's musical sense in Eliot's essay on Rudyard Kipling (in *A Choice of Kipling's Verse*, 1941, and *On Poetry and Poets*, 1947). For Kipling, says Eliot, poetry was frequently an 'instrument' – 'the poem is something which is intended to *act*' on its readers in a particular way – whereas

For other poets – at least, for some other poets – the poem may begin to shape itself in fragments of musical rhythm, and its structure will first appear in terms of something analogous to musical form; and such poets find it expedient to occupy their conscious mind with the craftsman's problems, leaving the deeper meaning to emerge from a lower level. It is a question then of what one chooses to be conscious of, and of how much of the meaning, in a poem, is conveyed direct to the intelligence and how much is conveyed indirectly by the musical impression upon the sensibility – always remembering that the use of the word 'musical' and of musical analogies, in discussing poetry, has its dangers if we do not constantly check its limitations: for the music of verse is inseparable from the meanings and associations of words.

(*On Poetry and Poets*, p. 238)

The idea that a poem should 'first of all *be*', that it may begin with fragments of musical rhythm, and that a poet may need to concentrate on 'craftsmen's problems', leaving the deeper meanings to emerge 'from a lower level', and the important proviso, again, that music is inseparable from meaning: all these are particularly important ideas, not least in relation to Eliot's own poetic practice and the question of how we should read his poetry. How many of Eliot's poems seem to establish themselves with a particular 'musical rhythm' almost before anything else – after the first three rather languorous lines of 'Prufrock', the rhyme and rhythm quickens, and we are almost snapping our fingers:

> Let us go, through certain half-deserted streets,
> The muttering retreats
> Of restless nights in one-night cheap hotels

The effect is mainly generated by that short second line, though as Eliot says it is difficult to separate the meaning of the words from the sudden effect of urgency following the effect of languor. Or take the opening of 'La Figlia Che Piange' with its distinctive lyrical lilt (unlike anything else in the 1917 volume); or, later, the tight, exact stanza of the quatrain poems of 1920, setting the tone at once for their caustic precision; or the short-winded, energyless lines of the opening of *The Hollow Men* (1925), close to a rhythmic paralysis; or the repetitive, incantatory rhythms of the opening of *Ash-Wednesday*, expanding and contracting with the thought.

In all those examples, once again, it is probably impossible to isolate rhythmic effects from the meanings of the words. But the rhythmic effects of the opening of *Ash-Wednesday*, for example (if one includes the element of repetition), certainly give the reader more than the meaning by itself: they give the insistence of a mind brooding on a question and falling into patterns of rhythm reminiscent of liturgy, which prepares us for the direction the poem is going to take. In his essay 'The Music of Poetry' (1942) Eliot wrote: 'I know that a poem, or a passage of a poem, may tend to realize itself first as a particular rhythm before it reaches expression in words, and that this rhythm may bring to birth the idea and the image' (*On Poetry and Poets*, p. 38). On the other hand he was always wary of the kind of poetry criticism which spoke of the sound of verse detached from the meaning, which spoke of musical values as being opposed to those of the intellect or of the visual imagination (see for example his essay 'Swinburne as Poet', *Selected Essays*, p. 324). He was also wary — and this is particularly germane to his own poetic practice — of any equation of music with mellifluousness or sonority: 'There are many other things to be spoken of besides the murmur of innumerable bees or the moan of doves in immemorial elms' (the phrases are lines from Tennyson); 'Dissonance, even cacophany, has its place' (*On Poetry and Poets*, p. 32). It is in fact less easy than one might think to select examples of simple dissonance of *sound* in Eliot's verse, but given the inseparable play of sense, there is '*Here we go round the prickly pear / Prickly pear prickly pear*' or 'For thine is / Life is / For thine is the' in *The Hollow Men*, or for pure cacophany the 'Hoo ha ha' and 'KNOCK KNOCK KNOCK' of *Sweeney Agonistes*.

But perhaps the most important of all Eliot's ideas related to the 'music of poetry' was that of the vital relation of poetry to common speech. 'Whether poetry is accentual or syllabic, rhymed or rhymeless, formal or free, it cannot afford to lose its contact with the changing language of common intercourse' ('The Music of Poetry', *On Poetry and Poets*, p. 29). Eliot saw that he and other poets (most notably Pound) at the beginning of the century had effected the same kind of revolution that had been effected by Donne in his time and by Wordsworth in his: they recalled poetry from straying too far in the direction of artificiality and specialized poetic diction. No word was to be thought intrinsically unpoetical; poetic language was to be made to accommodate the elements of modern life. In the late essay 'What Dante means to me' (1950), which includes several valuable reflections about Eliot's early poetic practices, Eliot wrote of how he learned from Baudelaire and Laforgue 'that the poet, in fact, was committed by his profession to turning the unpoetical into poetry' (*To Criticize the Critic*, p. 126). The language of common speech — which would often, according to Eliot, need to be based also on a *local* language, the language of a particular place — was to sound throughout his verse, whether in the tones of the poet himself, or those of his characters: the clerkly Prufrock, the effusive and precious lady of the 'Portrait', the brash American in 'Humouresque', the archly business-like Madame Sosostris, the neurotic lady and the Cockney women in 'A Game of Chess', the sad dull tones of the London girl and the sonorous intonations of Tiresias in 'The Fire Sermon'. It was a capacity for dramatic common speech which, as many have felt, seems paradoxically more alive in Eliot's poems than in his poetic dramas. And it was a quality he learned not only from his own ear for the voices around (and within) him, but from many literary sources, among them the excitingly fresh cadences (to one brought up on post-Miltonic and nineteenth-century blank verse) of the blank verse of Webster, Middleton and Tourneur; and behind them, it has been suggested, the less explicitly acknowledged but subterranean and inevitable influence (to which the essay 'Poetry and Drama' and several passing remarks nevertheless testify) of Shakespeare.

III

Before we leave Eliot's critical ideas about poetry and return to the poems themselves, two further ideas deserve some attention. The first, the idea of 'objective correlative', can be dealt with fairly briefly. It was doubtless one of those ideas which Eliot said later had had 'a truly embarrassing success in the world' (the others being the ideas of impersonality, and of 'the dissociation of sensibility' which I shall examine below); and perhaps the success of this particular idea was one of the more embarrassing cases because of the brevity and even the sketchiness of the original formulation. But it deserves some attention here because it too is related to the central problem of the poetic expression, or avoidance, of 'personality' or personal experience.

The formulation comes in the essay on *Hamlet* of 1919.

The only way of expressing emotion in the form of art is by finding an 'objective correlative'; in other words, a set of objects, a situation, a chain of events which shall be the formula of that *particular* emotion; such that when the external facts, which must terminate in sensory experience, are given, the emotion is immediately evoked. If you examine any of Shakespeare's more successful tragedies, you will find this exact equivalence; you will find that the state of mind of Lady Macbeth walking in her sleep has been communicated to you by a skilful accumulation of imagined sensory impressions; the words of Macbeth on hearing of his wife's death strike us as if, given the sequence of events, these words were automatically released by the last event in the series. The artistic 'inevitability' lies in the complete adequacy of the external to the emotion; and this is precisely what is deficient in *Hamlet*. Hamlet (the man) is dominated by an emotion which is inexpressible, because it is in *excess* of the facts as they appear. And the supposed identity of Hamlet with his author is genuine to this point: that Hamlet's bafflement at the absence of objective equivalent to his feelings is the prolongation of the bafflement of his creator in the face of his artistic problem. (*Selected Essays*, p. 145)

Now, leaving aside for a moment the application of the idea to *Hamlet*, one can see, I think, the broad principle here, though the details are often problematic. The principle is that the poet can express his emotion not by describing it directly but by finding an equivalent for it. So (for example) Keats, possessed of an emotion of fullness and ripeness stimulated by an autumn scene, though not explicable merely by that scene, evokes it, and evokes a whole sense of his experience at that point in his life, by a description of Autumn. Or Eliot himself, aware of a range of emotion in himself — of aspiration, timidity, romantic feeling, self-mockery, etc — writes a poem not about a young student of twenty-two in Harvard or Paris, but about an indeterminately 'middle-aged' character called Prufrock. The example from Eliot is a more indirect expression of feeling than the example of Keats, but the principle is not totally different. The Keats example might illustrate Eliot's 'set of objects', and the

'Prufrock' example the 'situation', both of which are 'the formula' of the 'particular emotion'.

And yet Eliot's formulation already raises problems. 'Set of objects', 'situation' and 'chain of events' are still somewhat vague terms. The objects in the Ode 'To Autumn' are not just 'objects' but objects described in a particular way, with terms which are loaded with value and significance of various kinds. The 'situation' in 'Prufrock' is not just a set of 'external facts', but a set of external facts mingled with impressions, valuations, feelings. The argument is then slightly complicated by the fact that the subsequent examples are taken from drama, and are examples not of 'correlatives' of the emotion of the *author* but of that of the *characters*. We may agree that the state of mind of Lady Macbeth is communicated partly by 'a skilful accumulation of imagined sensory impressions' – though only partly by that means: 'The Thane of Fife had a wife / Where is she now?' is not a sensory impression. But it is the emotion of the character, and only in a special sense (different from that in lyric poetry) that of the dramatist. This transition in Eliot's argument from author to dramatic character is carried on, and then reversed, in the discussion of *Hamlet*: the allegedly excessive nature of Hamlet's response to the external 'situation' in the play is used as a premise from which to argue that Shakespeare is similarly baffled 'in the face of his artistic problem'. This is certainly a possible state of affairs, but the logic of the argument is not as secure as Eliot seems to suggest.

The specific problem of *Hamlet* cannot concern us here: but the general features of the argument are significant in revealing certain things about Eliot's way of thinking. The language of the argument has a strongly scientific flavour: 'the formula of that particular emotion'; 'must terminate in sensory experience'; or, on Macbeth's speech, 'as if . . . these words were automatically released by the last event in the series'. It is as if Eliot wants to use a language which is as impersonal as possible, and which makes the process of evoking an emotion (for the reader), or expressing the emotion of a dramatic character, sound as if it were in some way 'automatic'. It is true that he writes that Macbeth's words are '*as if* . . . automatically released'; and that he puts 'inevitability' in inverted commas. The scientific terms are only metaphorical. But the language testifies to the way in which Eliot wished to characterize the artistic process in terms which avoided notions of subjectivity and direct personal expression.

And this again throws light on his own poetic practice: Eliot needed a technique for (we may still say) expressing emotion which 'objectified' that emotion as much as possible into external 'objects' or 'situations' which were far removed from direct autobiographical expression. And he needed to do this (as I shall suggest more fully in later chapters) both because of the painful pressure of actual experience of life, and (connected with this) so that his imagination might be freed from too pressing constrictions and range more widely and universally over human experience in general, including the experience of literature.

IV

The account of the 'objective correlative' suggests a need to separate artistic expression from too close an association (certainly from any identification) with the originating 'emotion'; and this brings us finally to an idea which had great influence on critical and literary–historical thought, but which also from our particular point of view throws a great deal of light on the processes and achievements of Eliot's own poems: the idea of the 'dissociation of sensibility'. There is only space to sketch the idea briefly, and the question of its historical validity (in relation to English literature and culture from the seventeenth century) will have to be left on one side. What will be important will be what it tells us about Eliot's way of seeing English literature of the past and of his own time, and about his own sensibility.

The idea is first broached in the essay 'The Metaphysical Poets' (1921). In trying to distinguish the change in 'the mind of England' between the time of Donne and that of Tennyson and Browning, Eliot suggests: 'Tennyson and Browning are poets, and they think; but they do not feel their thought as immediately as the odour of a rose. A thought to Donne was an experience; it modified his sensibility' (*Selected Essays*, p. 287). And in the next paragraph he goes on: 'In the seventeenth century a dissociation of sensibility set in from which we have never recovered; and this dissociation, as is natural, was aggravated by the influence of the two most powerful poets of the century, Milton and Dryden.' Later, in the eighteenth century, the 'sentimental' reaction followed: 'The poets revolted against the ratiocinative, the descriptive; they thought and felt by fits, unbalanced; they reflected. In one or two passages of Shelley's *Triumph of Life*, and in the second *Hyperion*, there are traces of a struggle toward unification of sensibility. But Keats and Shelley died, and Tennyson and Browning ruminated' (p. 288). Thereafter Eliot finds elements of a more 'unified sensibility' in Laforgue and Corbière, and also in Baudelaire and Racine; elements of what he calls 'the same essential quality of transmuting ideas into sensations, of transforming an observation into a state of mind' (p. 290).

Eliot revised his particular views of Donne, and of how far he achieved the ideal of a 'unified sensibility', but the idea itself, and the belief that the present age suffered from a divided sensibility, persisted. It is notably extended in the hitherto unpublished Clark lectures, which Eliot gave in Cambridge in 1926.[9] Here the idea becomes more religious in its associations, as Eliot attempts to redefine 'metaphysical' poetry. The association with the early seventeenth-century English poetry of the 'strong line' and the 'conceit', though still important in the discussion, is relegated to the secondary position, and Dante is adduced as the supreme example of the 'metaphysical' poet, or one who achieves a unity of sensibility. In the highest kind of metaphysical poetry the Word is made flesh (though it is notable that Eliot deliberately denies that there is any mysticism involved in this). Dante is more developed in this respect than Donne or Crashaw, since Dante achieves a system of thought whereas Donne only presents the process of thinking; and Dante transforms human feeling when turning to the divine, whereas Crashaw merely expresses the divine in terms of untransformed human feelings.

The importance of Dante will be returned to in a later chapter of this study. But the changing views of Donne — changing even within the course of the lectures — are particularly interesting. The first lecture stresses Donne's power to express in poetry the fusion of souls through sexual love, and cites 'The Ecstasy' as one of Donne's finest poems (though oddly, and perhaps significantly, Eliot objects to the image of the 'pregnant bank' in the first stanza). But later on he writes of the confused nature of Donne's intellectual background, and how this led him into a compromise with the physical, and judges that Donne's poetic passion is dissipated in the play of suggested ideas. Donne is entirely sincere, but though his feeling passes into thought, it does not attain belief, but simply arouses further feeling. Ultimately Eliot finds Donne a poet of chaos, his work unified only by his personality and in its final effect destructive of civilization (though Eliot rather curiously disclaims any moral intention in this criticism). Eliot has seemingly reached a judgement of Donne diametrically opposed to his view of 1921; and in the essay of 1931, in *A Garland for John Donne*,[10] he compounds this by writing of the 'manifest fissure between thought and sensibility' in Donne's poetry. But the significant thing, of course is not to convict Eliot of self-contradiction, but to show how conflicting his views were, and how much he needed to revise them even in the course of a series of lectures. And what I want to suggest is how pressingly personal these questions of 'unified sensibility' and 'dissociation of sensibility' were for him, and how much the conflict is enacted in his own poetry.

We have already seen how much the poems of the 1917 volume, *Prufrock and Other Observations*, are preoccupied with division and dissociation: with the fragmenting of perception of the self and others and of the world in general; the division of the personality between the would-be heroic and the trivial, between the public self ('I keep my countenance / I remain self possessed') and the inner turbulence in 'Portrait of a Lady', and perhaps even between Prufrock's 'you and I'. The mind may yearn after some kind of unifying Absolute behind the fragmentary appearances, as in the notion of 'Some infinitely gentle, infinitely suffering thing' in 'Preludes', but the notion is dismissed at the end of the poem to leave a final image of mere stoic or even automatic persistence. There is the division between a sense of the mind as a mere agent of animal perception and the mind as a genuine human consciousness (as in the parallel between the child – 'I could see nothing behind that child's eye – and the crab in 'Rhapsody on a Windy Night'). There are also the division between experience and language (Prufrock's 'It is impossible to say just what I mean'), between imagination and reality ('Till human voices wake us and we drown'), and between the demands of aesthetic form and the demands of moral truthfulness ('this music is successful with a dying fall, now that we talk of dying / – And should I have the right to smile'). This last division or dissociation is particularly marked as a subject in 'La Figlia Che Piange', where it combines with a sense of division between soul and body or between mind and body:

> So he would have left
> As the soul leaves the body torn and bruised,
> As the mind deserts the body it has used.

The poem, one might say, is partly about the failure to achieve that fusion and identification of souls in sexual love which Eliot spoke of as perhaps Donne's peculiar gift to humanity. And it also, as I suggested in the previous chapter, throws a critical light on the statement in 'Tradition and the Individual Talent' that 'the more perfect the artist, the more completely separate in him will be the man who suffers and the mind which creates'. This, surely, is a kind of 'dissociation of sensibility'. The idea is Eliot's diagnosis of the sickness of his time, and also, we may say, of his own sickness, out of the struggle with which he achieves the victories of his best poems. The victories are in one sense provisional, for after 1917, as we shall see, the sickness will (for a time) get worse; but in another sense they are permanent because they last beyond their time and their author's individual predicament, and record with intensity and completeness a permanent element of human experience.

5

Poems (1920)

It was characteristic of Eliot not to try to repeat his successes, and the volume of 1920 shows, accordingly, a completely new series of experiments in style, though not without significant continuities with the previous volume. Indeed, the most important poem of the volume, 'Gerontion', is in a direct line of development from 'The Love Song of J. Alfred Prufrock' to *The Waste Land*, whereas the poems in quatrain form, which constitute the majority, are in some ways a detour, an experiment which represents one side of Eliot, but not the central stream. 'Gerontion' opens the volume (Eliot had an instinct for opening with one of the best), but it was probably one of the last written, since it does not appear in any earlier published form. Eliot also, early in 1922, thought of the possibility of including it as a prelude to *The Waste Land*, but was dissuaded by Pound. For these reasons I shall discuss it at the end of this chapter.

The quatrain poems show the direct influence of Théophile Gautier (1811–72). As Eliot records: 'At a certain moment, my debt to [Pound] was for his advice to read Gautier's *Émaux et Camées*.'[1] Pound, looking back in *The Criterion* in July 1932 in an article on Harold Monro, described the process with characteristic pungency:

At a particular date in a particular room, two authors, neither engaged in picking the other's pocket, decided that the dilutation [*sic*] of *vers libre*, Amygism [the reference is to Amy Lowell, one of the original 'imagists'], Lee Masterism, general floppiness had gone too far and that some counter-current must be set going. Parallel situation centuries ago in China. Remedy prescribed 'Émaux et Camées' (or the Bay State Hymn Book). Rhyme and regular strophes.
    Results: Poems in Mr Eliot's *second* volume . . . also H. S. Mauberley. Divergence later.   (*The Criterion*, 11, p. 590).

Gautier cultivated a verse of tight forms and hard, clear images, described and exemplified in his best known, 'manifesto' poem 'L'Art', which ends:

> Sculpte, lime, cisèle;
> Que ton rêve flottant
> Se Scelle
> Dans le bloc résistant!

('Sculpt, file and chisel; let your floating dream seal itself in the obdurate block!')

But the cult of 'hardness' has its limitations, and particularly in Eliot's case. Eliot's stress on the artist's 'impersonality' is sometimes accompanied by such terms as 'hardness' and 'coldness' (Eliot admired in Hawthorne 'the firmess . . . the hard coldness of the genuine artist').[2] But an extreme of these qualities could also involve a human coldness which has to be judged in a different way, as we have already seen in the case of 'Hysteria', and many of the poems of the 1920 volume illustrate this. There is a predominant caustic tone; a stance which is close to satiric, and yet once again we feel an ambivalence, an inner preoccupation, which qualifies the 'outward-directedness' of proper satire. There are satiric targets (The *homme sensuel moyen* in Sweeney, the honeymoon tourists in 'Lune de Miel', the True Church in 'The Hippopotamus', priests and theology in 'Mr Eliot's Sunday Morning Service'), but these are rarely single and unambiguous. In 'The Hippopotamus', for instance, the 'satire' is also directed against human nature; and in 'Mr Eliot's Sunday Morning Service' the ironies are directed against both the aridities of theology and the human appetites of the modern priests. It is as though the poet is toying with conflicting views of life in a mood of disillusioned detachment, keeping them at a 'scientific' distance which is the product as much of distaste as of a genuinely objective analysis. Conflicting attitudes (which one might broadly categorize as 'spiritual' and 'sensual') are allowed to rub against one another and generate an uneasy friction. Whereas in 'Prufrock' or 'Portrait of a Lady' the conflicts within the protagonists are treated with inwardness and sympathy, the figures in the quatrain poems are held up for inspection, ridicule and sometimes contempt. At the same time the poems are often obscure, so it is not always clear why the figures are to be seen in this way, or even sometimes what the poem's final judgement on them is. This is not to say that the poems are not often 'effective' and even powerful; but their quality is such as to raise frequent doubts in the reader about *what* has been effected, about the poetic attitude and achievement as a whole.

A number of the poems are also marked by an accentuation of what one might call Eliot's 'historical method' of cultural criticism (the beginnings of which one can glimpse in 'Prufrock'), in which the qualities of past ages are held up against those of the present, sometimes in a contrast between past glory and present squalor, but just as often in a way which casts a dubious light on past as well as present. 'Burbank with a Baedeker: Bleistein with a Cigar', the second poem in the volume, is a good example. The poem begins with an epigraph which is a medley of quotations on the Venice of history and literature: there is a quotation from one of Gautier's 'Variations sur Le Carnivale de Venise', a Latin motto from a painting of St Sebastian by Mantegna ('nothing is stable except the divine'), a sentence from James's *The Aspern Papers*, a phrase from Othello followed grotesquely by one from Browning's 'A Toccata of Galuppi's', and finally a stage-direction from a masque by John Marston.[3] These are not essential for an understanding of the subsequent poem, but they briefly conjure for the informed reader a miniature kaleidoscope of Venetian 'impressions', in which carnival gaiety, Renaissance elegance and aesthetic charm mingle with darker notes (Othello's jealousy and Browning's chill of death − 'Dear dead women, with such hair, too!'). They are also fragments likely to be part of the mental furniture of Burbank, the cultured American with the Baedeker guide-book, and their main significance lies here.

Burbank meditates rather portentously on the decline of Venice in the last stanza of the poem, and throughout the poem past and present are juxtaposed. Burbank is compared implicitly with Shakespeare's Antony in the second stanza. If the reader does not recognize this allusion, the use of a 'classical' image is clear enough in its general contrast with the modern title and opening; but the comparison with Antony has two possible implications. Either Burbank is being contrasted ironically with the heroic Antony, or we are being reminded of Antony's fall and his destruction by Cleopatra (compare also 'Her shuttered barge / Burned on the water all day' with Cleopatra on the Cydnus). Is Burbank's 'fall' (several senses are possible) trite and banal in comparison with Antony's, or does it share an essential common human failing? Bleistein, on the other hand, *is* presented as debased, and the general tendency of the poem is to make a disenchanted comparison of the present with the past. We also encounter here the anti-Jewish prejudice which debases the poem. We need to remember that Eliot's perspective was not ours (he would have known of the Dreyfus case, but the horrors of the death-camps were twenty years in the future). Nevertheless we cannot avoid seeing these lines ('The rats are underneath the piles. / The Jew is underneath the lot') as a failure of moral taste and judgement.

The particular caustically analytic tone of the poem depends a great deal on the nature of the diction — a combination of demotic bluntness ('a saggy bending of the knees', 'underneath the lot', 'flea'd his rump'), a classical or archaic diction inclining to pedantry ('defunctive', 'axletree', 'protrusive'), and a technical or scientific language ('protozoic', 'phthisic'). The demotic words create an effect of vulgarity, which the elevated and scientific words mock or hold at a distance. The final effect is an uncertain one in which not only is modern capitalistic culture despised, but the past is ambiguously viewed and the status of the meditating Burbank (cultural critic or pretentious tourist?) is left in doubt. The wit is sardonic, suggesting a perpetual curl of the lip. Irony here is a means of keeping all attitudes at arm's length.

In February 1920 Eliot wrote to his brother: 'Some of the new poems, the Sweeney ones, especially *Among the Nightingales* and *Burbank*, are intensely serious, and I think these two are among the best that I have ever done. But even here I am considered by the ordinary newspaper critic as a wit or a satirist, and in America I suppose I shall be thought merely disgusting.'[4] While one does not want to share the alleged obtuseness of these newspaper critics, it is difficult to gauge the kind of seriousness constituted by these poems, or to feel that they equal the achievement of, say, 'Portrait of a Lady'. The two main 'Sweeney' poems, 'Sweeney Erect' and 'Sweeney Among the Nightingales', are on one level pungent sketches of low-life scenes; they are partly to be seen as satires against 'sensual man', but they are made complex by a play of classical allusion. 'Sweeney Erect' opens with an epigraph from *The Maid's Tragedy* by Beaumont and Fletcher which strikes an attitude of desolation, but of a rhetorical kind which gives it a particular quality of theatricality. (The heroine Aspatia, in Act II, sc. ii, who has been deserted by her lover, is posing as Ariadne, deserted by Theseus, and giving instructions to her maids, who are working on a tapestry of the subject.) The first two stanzas continue in something of the same 'classical' (or Senecan) vein, weighted with Latinate words and allusion to Greek place and myth. The command for a painting is curiously reminiscent of the opening of 'La Figlia Che Piange', but the ultimate effect is totally different. The idealized picture 'posed' there was more lyrically beautiful and less harsh, and was also the source of searching questionings and reflections. Here the classical 'picture' simply gives way to a violent contrast with the world of the modern brothel: grandeur is followed by squalor (except for the brief parenthesis from the classical world, '(Nausica and Polypheme)', which alludes to Odysseus's encounters with the young maiden and the one-eyed giant – for no very obvious reason except for the unflattering association of the latter with Sweeney. Sweeney's ape-like gestures, and the description of the prostitute's face and her epileptic fit, are done with an undeniable vividness of disgust, and the cynical reactions of Sweeney and the false prudery of the other 'ladies' are nicely observed. But the 'intense seriousness' is difficult to see, unless it lies simply in the forcefulness of the disgust. Even that, however, is qualified by a possible element of admiration of Sweeney: Emerson saw 'history' in 'the lengthened shadow of a man', but Sweeney's 'silhouette' is, one infers, priapic – an emblem of the future.

'Sweeney Among the Nightingales' continues the theme of comic disgust offset (or heightened) by a classical grandeur of allusion and diction. The epigraph is from Aeschylus's *Agamemnon*, the hero's cry at the hands of Clytemnestra, 'Alas, I am struck with a mortal blow', which connects with the ending of the poem to suggest a background of horror which, however, never becomes explicit. Again there seems to be an ambiguous combining and contrasting of classical tragedy and modern loucheness. There is an irony in juxtaposing Sweeney's bawdy pleasures with Agamemnon's passion and death, but the irony has various possible effects: the simplest one (of the grand past against the tawdry present) is the least interesting; more telling (and here perhaps we do locate the seriousness in the poem) is the way in which Sweeney is given something of the grandeur of Agamemnon, and Agamemnon is remembered as having been driven by the same sexual forces that motivate Sweeney. Both of them share in a common human fate, through there is no need to import tragedy and horror into the Sweeney narrative itself: the atmosphere is shady and slightly sinister, but Sweeney is 'Letting his arms hang down to laugh' in the second line. The common human fate is simply sexuality as Eliot saw it in 1919.

Sex and death and the relation between them indeed constitute the predominant subject of the 1920 volume; and sex and theology, a subdivision of the above, are the subject of 'The Hippopotamus' and 'Mr Eliot's Sunday Morning Service'. The caustic and sceptical note prevails, and one feels that while Eliot is obviously intensely preoccupied with questions of religious belief and dogma (even at this stage in his career), there is a detachment, a kind of 'theoretical' interest that does not suggest any tendency towards a genuine religious engagement, and which also precludes any social–satiric note. It is not so much that Eliot is satirizing the Church, but that he is holding up the ironic disparities between body and spirit, faith and dogma, asceticism and desire. 'The Hippopotamus', taking and changing an idea from Gautier's 'L'Hippopotame', develops a kind of metaphysical 'conceit', and an extended analogy between the hippopotamus and human nature. The tone is playful, and mocks both the grotesque image of humanity and the instititution of 'the True Church'. The hippopotamus is palpable 'flesh and blood', gross, weak and clumsy; the solidity of the 'True Church' is mysteriously spiritual ('based upon a rock' – the rock of the apostle Peter). The lucrativeness of the spiritual institution is slyly mocked:

> The hippo's feeble steps may err
> In compassing material ends,
> While the True Church need never stir
> To gather in its dividends.

But in the end it is the body which shall be resurrected ('I saw the 'potamus take wing')

> While the True Church remains below
> Wrapt in the old miasmal mist.

The poem is arch and sceptical. One feels Eliot is playing with theological notions ('with a puzzled and humorous shifting of the pieces', as he said of Donne in 1933) rather than, as has been suggested, denouncing 'empty idolatry of forms with the reforming zeal of his forebears'.[5] And yet there is a seriousness in the scepticism, in the ideas if not in the treatment of them: the resurrection of the body is a difficult notion, particularly for a poet who had shown (and was to show again) such a bafflement about (and even a distaste for) sexuality; and the wealth of the True Church is a perennial religious paradox.

'Mr Eliot's Sunday Morning Service' is more obscure, but the shifting ironies towards the spiritual and the physical are again at the centre of the poem. It seems most natural to take 'Mr Eliot' as the poet himself, though it has been suggested that there is a reference to a member of Eliot's family who was a minister.[6] But what is important for the reader of the poem is the *general* sardonic scepticism it displays. Marlowe's 'religious caterpillars' (priests) in the epigraph suggest the ambiguous fusion of the religious and the animal that runs through the poem. 'Polyphiloprogenitive' is Eliot's coinage, an example of the technical or mock-technical diction that often marks this volume. It suggests prolifically dispersed physical fertility ('philoprogenitive' means 'prolific' or 'loving one's offspring'), and also has theological connotations as a technical term referring to the 'begetting' of the Son by the Father (as does 'superfetation of το εν', 'the One', 'superfetation' also having a biological sense). The double reference to the word epitomizes the irony of the poem, which is about the paradoxical interpenetration of physical and spiritual, particularly in the realms of language. Priests are men of the spirit but their theological controversies are described in terms of an atavistic physicality. The 'sapient sutlers' (line 2; 'provision merchants') are mainly the bees of stanza 7, but also the 'presbyters' ('priests') of stanza 5. 'Sapient' means 'wise' (with ironical overtones) but also carries the suggestion of physical 'sap'. In a similar way the word 'mensual' in stanza 2 conveys the precise notion of time, but also has sexual overtones. At the same time the theologians are seen as characteristically physically sterile: Origen, the prolific third-century author of 'an estimated 6,000 books' castrated himself out of a desire for spiritual purity: hence the dry understatement of 'enervate Origen'. The painting described in stanzas 4 and 5 evokes a feeling of religious asceticism and purity, yet the physical is still there as a touch of the grotesque in 'the unoffending feet'. In stanza 5 the young among the penitent priests are 'pustular' with adolescent sexuality; and the souls which 'burn' in stanza 6 could be burning with lust or with religious fire. The bees of stanza 7, passing with their pollen between the male and female flowers, are like the priests spreading the Word, 'epicene' or bisexual. The poem is possibly Eliot's most obscure, and one wonders if the erudition is worth the carriage. But it conveys something of the recurring mood in this volume, toying with theological and sexual matters with a kind of dry and pedantic wit, a curious scepticism and fastidiousness, even distaste, towards soul and body. In the last stanza the appearance of Sweeney presents an alternative to the sexless fertility of the religious life as the poem has presented it: the self-satisfiedly physical balance of Sweeney's shifting 'from ham to ham' balances nicely (in sense and rhythm) with the 'controversial' (another kind of shifting from ham to ham) 'masters of the subtle schools'. Average sensual man implicitly repudiates the whole theological show (in a way comparable to the turning away from the spiritual – 'Wipe your hand across your mouth and laugh' – at the end of 'Preludes'), but the poet, of course, remains through his tone ironically sceptical towards both.

In 'Whispers of Immortality', perhaps the most successful of the quatrain poems, the irony is more clearly directed and the wit more penetrating – penetrating, like Donne in the poem, towards an apprehension of death which is at once physical and metaphysical. The quatrains in the first half (as Hugh Kenner points out) feel Jacobean and 'Metaphysical'; in the second they evoke Gautier, and the later 'fin de siècle'. 'Daffodil bulbs instead of balls / Stared from the sockets of eyes' recalls Webster's own 'A dead man's skull beneath the roots of flowers' (*The White Devil*, V.iv.137); and the opening of the second half directly echoes Gautier's 'Carmen':

> Carmen est maigre, un trait de bistre
> Cerne son œil de gitana.

It has been suggested that Eliot's poem is a criticism of the modern world's 'dissociation of sensibility',[7] but from what point of view is the criticism made? Throughout the poem 'thought' is conceived of in physical terms. Webster was 'possessed by death' (the verb is at once intellectual, pathological and sexual); 'He knew that thought *clings* round dead limbs / Tightening its lusts and luxuries' (my italics). Similarly Donne, 'expert beyond experience', possessed a knowledge beyond the physical, but nevertheless imaged in physical metaphors 'the anguish of the marrow / The ague of the skeleton'. There *is* a fusion of thought and feeling in the figurative language, but it is a fusion which images a knowledge beyond and unassuageable by the physical:

> No contact possible to flesh
> Allayed the fever of the bone.

One might contrast the embodied attitude with Donne's famous lines about Elizabeth Drury:

> her pure and eloquent blood
> Spoke in her cheeks, and so distinctly wrought
> That one might almost say, her body thought:
>> ('The Second Anniversary', line 244)

which evoke perfectly a vital union of feeling and thought, body and spirit, 'the intellect at the tips of the senses', as Eliot put it in his essay on Massinger. In 'Whispers of Immortality' there is actually a pre-emption of feeling by thought, the senses manipulated by the intellect, and the poem demonstrates 'a unified sensibility' of a different kind — the thought (of death) becoming feeling, rather than vital feeling becoming thought. The second half of the poem, with its cosy vulgar sensuality and pungency (for once with only a faint possible hint of distaste — it could equally be relish — in 'so rank a feline smell'), does not so much *contrast* with the sensibility of the first half as, in the concluding lines, corroborate it. A comparison with the ending of Gautier's 'Carmen', in which there is no alternative to, and no retreat from, the relish of Carmen's pungency, is another way of marking the quality of Eliot's poem:

> Elle a dans sa laideur piquante,
> Un grain de sel de cette mer
> D'où jaillit, nue et provocante,
> L'âcre Vénus du gouffre amer.

('She has, in her piquant ugliness / A grain of salt of that sea / From which emerged naked and provocative, / The pungent Venus from the briny gulf'). 'Grishkin is nice'; 'But our lot' (Webster, Donne and Eliot)

> crawls between dry ribs
> To keep our metaphysics warm.

From a certain point of view — from the point of view of Donne's 'The Ecstasy', for example, in which 'pure lovers' souls must descend / T'affections and to faculties, / Which sense may reach and apprehend, / Else a great prince in prison lies' — Eliot's poem might seem to be a *symptom* of dissociation of sensibility, in that there is a retreat from physical love into a contemplation of death in which the senses are merely used for an imaginative grasping of the unknown. Eliot, as we have seen, described 'The Ecstasy' in 1926 as one of Dante's finest poems, and saw it as an example of his distinctive power to convey the fusion of souls in sexual love.[8] In the vision of 'Whispers of Immortality' (and in the Donne that the poem characterizes) there can be no such fusion. Sexual love is here *only* a matter of sensuality, and the imagination, intent on grasping the reality of death retreats from sexual love to contemplate the skeleton. The whispers of immortality (which sound chilly and sinister – as opposed to Wordsworth's 'Intimations of Immortality') speak not of a life of the spirit, still less of a resurrection of the body, but, in keeping with the hardness and coldness which characterizes the quatrain poems, merely of 'the fever of the bone'.

In 'A Cooking Egg' death is treated altogether more lightly, even archly, as the speaker talks of not needing 'Pipit' in heaven since he will meet Lucretia Borgia, or Honour since he will meet Sir Philip Sidney 'And other heroes of that kidney'. The poem is slight and playful, and even (unlike the other quatrain poems) has a certain charm. The reader inevitably speculates about the identity, within the poem, of Pipit (is she, say, the speaker's wife, or mistress, an old childhood friend or nurse?) but there is little point in debating the question. The most captivating part of the poem is, I suggest, the last section, which is whimsical but also has the note of a lament for lost innocence:

> But where is the penny world I bought
> To eat with Pipit behind the screen?
> The red-eyed scavengers are creeping
> From Kentish Town and Golder's Green;

which modulates nicely to an imperial version of the 'Ubi sunt' motif:

> Where are the eagles and the trumpets?

> Buried beneath some snow-deep Alps.

The sudden change from the past of childhood (as one assumes: not 'Where is the penny bun?' but with pathetic hyperbole 'Where is the penny *world*?') to the grand historical past is effective, and highly characteristic of Eliot's play of mind. (It is slightly reminiscent of 'Prufrock', but here is a kind of reverse bathos, from private to public, domestic to imperial, 'trivial' to grand). And the last lines of the poem, with a splendid gesture of straightforward comic bathos, evoke (at any rate for the

English reader), the most familiar of London settings (A.B.C.'s were and still are a well-known cafeteria chain) with Biblical or epic grandeur:

> Over buttered scones and crumpets
> Weeping, weeping multitudes
> Droop in a hundred A.B.C.'s.

The note is comic but has genuine pathos: the humdrum sadness of great masses of people is evoked mock-heroically, in a way that renders both its banality and its grand scale. A cooking egg is below standard, not quite good enough for eating; in the poem it could refer to the speaker (in line with the epigraph from Villon: 'In the thirtieth year of my age / When I have swallowed up my shame'), perhaps to Pipit, to modern life, or perhaps to the poem itself, which overall is one of the slighter poems of the volume.

The poems in French, perhaps with the exception of 'Dans Le Restaurant', are slighter still, though amusing. 'Le Directeur' is entertaining mainly because of its form; 'Mélange Adultère de Tout' gives a glimpse of a man of many roles, 'an adulterous mixture of everything': it could be simply the mocking portrait of a type, but it could also reflect Eliot's uncertainty about his own roles ('En Amerique, professeur; / En Angleterre, journaliste' is not far from possible autobiography, though the possibility is swiftly dispelled at the end of the poem) – we might remember 'And I must borrow every changing shape to find expression'. 'Lune de Miel', too, might remind us that Eliot was married in 1915, though he spent his honeymoon in Eastbourne rather than Ravenna! But the poem is, of course, fictional, a sketch of the modern tourist which (as in 'Burbank', though with less contempt and bitterness) returns to the theme of modern banality juxtaposed with ancient splendour, second-rate hotels with a church like St Apollinaire En Classe (in Ravenna), which still preserves

> Dans ses pierres écroulantes la forme précise de Byzance.

That 'precise form', characteristic of the values admired in this volume, is still preserved, though the stone, like the civilization presented also throughout the volume, is crumbling.

'Dans le Restaurant' is more of a puzzle. Great significance has been attached to it, and yet it does not seem to be particularly successful as a poem. The narrator's encounter with the dilapidated waiter, and the waiter's anecdote, have the quality of a notation or sketch not worked up to much poetic intensity (as far as an English reader with less French than Eliot can judge). The waiter's story of his childhood encounter with the little girl seems merely a fragment of maudlin self-confession; nevertheless, a certain witty irony arises out of the poem's awareness of the narrator's snobbish condescension towards, and reluctant identification with, the waiter in 'Mais alors, tu as ton vautour!' ('So, you have your vulture!' – The narrator is perhaps like André Gide, whose 'sophistication' Eliot was later to mock,[9] who wrote 'Il faut avoir an aigle'), and in 'De quel droit payes-tu des experiences comme moi?' ('What right do you have to pay for your experiences like me?'). The poem does, in fact, show a divergence from the frame of class snobbery in which many of Eliot's ironies are set. But what is perplexing about the poem is the last stanza about 'Phlébas, le Phénicien', which reappears, translated almost word for word into English, as Part IV of *The Waste Land*, 'Death by Water'. In the present context the fragment seems to have no connection with the rest of the poem at all. The poem does not otherwise work in a fragmentary way or in a mode of collage (unlike *The Waste Land*), and this sudden transition is more difficult to make sense of than those in the later poems, since we are not prepared for it and there seem to be few connecting threads. At most one can say that it represents an escape, in the mind of the narrator (and for the poem), from the slightly disturbing encounter with the waiter; the waiter's confession of an ambiguous sexual experience at the age of seven is followed by a *memento mori*, a vision of death which has a calmness and purity.

The significance of the poem seems to be, in the end, obscure. The waiter's childhood encounter with the little girl has been compared with what Eliot has to say about Dante's formative encounter with Beatrice in *La Vita Nuova*[10]. In that poem Dante presents himself as having been struck with love for a young girl, Beatrice, at the age of nine, and the peculiar intensity of this experience became the emotional ground of his late spiritual development and of the 'idealization' (if that is the word) of Beatrice into the redemptive figure of *The Divine Comedy*. In his essay on Dante of 1929 (*Selected Essays*, p. 273), Eliot writes that it is important to grasp that the *Vita Nuova* is not a 'confession' or an 'indiscretion', and that for a reader with Dante's sense of 'intellectual and spiritual realities' it cannot be classed either as 'truth' or 'fiction'. Dante describes this sexual experience as happening to him at the age of nine: Eliot finds this neither impossible nor unique, and doubts only whether it could have taken place 'so *late* in his life' as the age of nine years, an opinion which he reports as having been endorsed by 'a distinguished psychologist'. Eliot finds that the work could 'only have been written around a personal experience', and that what 'happens to others' simply happened to Dante with greater intensity. It has been suggested, on the basis of this passage, that 'Dans le Restaurant' is related to an experience which is comparable to Dante's – comparable, but in a highly contrasting way, in that Dante's experience was an experience of goodness, and the waiter's was a cause of guilt and shame arising from cowardice and failure, but also leading, if we can see Eliot's case as parallel, to a similar spiritual development.[11] But it would seem that the difference of the shameful experience of sexuality in Eliot's poem from the quality of Dante's experience is so great that, as a founding and formative element in Eliot's experience (if it is some kind of dramatic projection of that), it would surely have led to a development different from that which we see in Eliot's poetry, where the figure of the woman which runs through the poetry (in 'La Figlia Che Piange', 'The Burial of the Dead' in *The Waste Land*, in the 'eyes' in *The Hollow Men*, and the 'blessèd face' and the Lady in *Ash-Wednesday*) has the kind of positive significance which Beatrice has in *Vita Nuova and The Divine Comedy*. Secondly, and more importantly, the quality of 'Dans le Restaurant' as a poem does not encourage us to give it great *poetic* significance. The *Vita Nuova* is, by any estimation, one of Dante's major works. It is a part of the construction of a fully realized poetic self which emerges in his works as a whole. 'Dans le Restaurant' is a minor poem written (partly, as Eliot revealed in an interview, to help him break out of a creative impasse and perhaps partly out of the need for greater 'distancing' of the subject) in a language which was not Eliot's own. It may furnish an interesting basis for biographical speculation, and may even provide certain hints and clues for a reading of other poems and an understanding of Eliot's mind. But unless we can agree that it is a better *poem* than it has usually been considered, it does not become a major part of the corpus of poems and is therefore not fully 'there' as a poem which might revise our sense of the whole *œuvre*.

In 'Dans le Restaurant' there is a use, in the narrator, of a fastidious and supercilious *persona*, and perhaps a projection of personal experience into the figure of the waiter (another kind of 'doubling' of the personality). In the quatrain poems there is technically no *persona*, but the poetic voice is deliberately dry, hard and sardonic: it is as if these poems strike a particular attitude towards the outside world in order to keep control of experience, to 'remain self-possessed' like the narrator in 'Portrait of a Lady'. The result is a certain gain in power, but a loss of inwardness and of the self-criticism which, I suggest, is a mark of Eliot's most serious and searching poems. 'Gerontion' returns to the mode of the single *persona*, and by adopting the voice of an old man speaks, with an effect which is paradoxically candid and direct, of the experience of spiritual and physical drought and impotence.

'Gerontion' is the Greek word for 'little old man', and the epigraph, from the Duke's speech to Claudio in *Measure for Measure*, III.i.32–4, suggests the dreaming of an old man. One might also recall that the Duke was in fact addressing a young man, and his 'you' is directed at humanity in general: similarly the epigraph is addressed to Gerontion, to the reader and to the poet himself. The Duke's injunction to Claudio was 'Be absolute for death': Eliot does take up such an attitude in 'Whispers of Immortality', as we have seen; he assumes an authority like the Duke's, or at least a satisfied self-commendation of 'our lot'. But in 'Gerontion' the *persona* is a figure without moral authority, a representative of fallen 'dreaming' humanity. The adoption of this *persona* is a kind of humility after the proudly superior gestures of the quatrain poems. (It may also be relevant, as I have suggested, that although the poem appears first in the volume, what little evidence there is suggests that it was written later than most of the quatrain poems.) The dryness of the poem is not the assumption of a dry wit but the consciousness of a debilitating aridity. In one sense, 'Gerontion' the old man is a logical development from Prufrock the young 'middle-aged' man: the aspirations and whimsical pathos of the latter have been replaced by the defeat and bitterness of age.

The 'free' verse of 'Gerontion' also returns to a form closer to that of 'Prufrock', though its feeling is quite different: instead of the plangent music of 'Prufrock', there is an intent, deliberative movement, sometimes clogged with the baffled energies of an old man, as in the muscular yet constricted rhythms of lines 3–6:

> I was neither at the hot gates
> Nor fought in the warm rain
> Nor knee deep in the salt marsh, heaving a cutlass,
> Bitten by flies, fought.

These are the 'memories' of a battle which was never fought ('memories' too of a classical and heroic past, 'hot gates' being a literal translation of Thermopylae, scene of the famous battle between Greeks and Persians in 480 B.C.) – the fantasies of an old man shadow-boxing. That energy is also there (again involving syntactic inversion) in

> The tiger springs in the new year. Us he devours.

The deliberative element, on the other hand, is effected by the longer lines, once or twice interrupted by shorter ones, and the hesitating effect of the line endings cutting across the syntax:

> Think at last
> We have not reached conclusion, when I
> Stiffen in a rented house,

and by the repetition of 'Think now / . . . Think now / . . . Think / Think at last / . . . Think at last' at the ends of lines. Another important element in the versification, the feel of the poem, is the use of a supple blank verse, often with one or two extra syllables to the line, of a kind that Eliot admired in Jacobean dramatists, particularly Middleton. The passage beginning

> I that was near your heart was removed therefrom
> To lose beauty in terror, terror in inquisition.

echoes closely the passage from Middleton's The *Changeling* (V. iii.150 ff.) which begins

> I that am of your blood was taken from you
> For your better health; . . .

which Eliot quoted admiringly in his essay on Middleton of 1927 (*Selected Essays*, p. 169).[12] The verse is supple, conversational, with the virtues of prose, though remaining unmistakably verse. And what must also have touched Eliot's imagination is the whole ethos of the speech, which is also the ethos of Gerontion's. Beatrice, in the play, is confessing her guilt to her father; Gerontion is confessing an obscurer guilt and failure of love to the person who was loved. Both passages have the same kind of clarity and dignity of language, the same tone of lucid and penetrating disillusion.

Like 'Prufrock', 'Gerontion' is the presentation of a consciousness. The different parts are not connected by location and narrative, but are connected in the speaker's mind. This mind is preoccupied by fragmentary thoughts of religion and of love, and the two subjects mingle and interpenetrate. 'We would see a sign!', recalls Matthew 12:38–9, where the Pharisees say to Jesus, 'Master, we would see a sign from thee', and Jesus rebukes them, saying 'an evil and adulterous generation seeketh after a sign'. Eliot's lines continue with the mystery of the infant Christ and an image of Christ's energy (possibly recalling Blake), which then degenerates into a sinister kind of communion:

> The word within a word, unable to speak a word,
> Swaddled with darkness. In the juvescence of the year
> Came Christ the tiger
>
> In depraved May, dogwood and chestnut, flowering judas,
> To be eaten, to be divided, to be drunk
> Among whispers; by Mr Silvero
> With caressing hands, . . .

The lines convey intensely a hint of baffled, then briefly flourishing, then degraded spiritual and physical power. The 'word' is both the 'Word' of St John's Gospel (the phrase is in fact a quotation from a sermon of the seventeenth-century preacher Lancelot Andrewes)[13] and the creative word of the poet. Christ is seen as beautiful and destructive. 'Depraved May' concentrates marvellously the feelings of vernal energy and corruption. The freshness of spring and power of a spiritual energy fresh from the source are contaminated, as soon as they appear, by human degradition. The 'caressing hands' suggest (in connection with later images of Madame de Tornquist 'shifting the candles' and the eroticism of the fourth and fifth verse-paragraphs) both erotic caresses and the manipulations of some sinister rite. Some primal truth about love, both religious and sexual, is seen in a brief flowering and corruption which are almost simultaneous.

'After such knowledge, what forgiveness?' The 'knowledge' is carnal knowledge in the Biblical sense, and spiritual knowledge, the 'knowledge of good and evil'. The passage on History that follows combines an analysis of 'the ways of the world' in general, of the use of History as a means to wisdom, and of History as 'the erotic'. History is figured as a woman whose 'giving' is ambiguous and deceiving, or at least which is misunderstood, received too early or too late. Neither fear nor courage, specifically human virtues, are adequate to save us. This subtle mingling of History and the erotic suggests the similar and intermingled inadequacies of the public political world and the private erotic one, the inadequacies of a merely human perspective. But the poem does not offer an alternative religious attitude. The glimpse of 'Christ the tiger' is immediately obscured and corrupted: the only energy He retains is to devour.

The 'conclusion' not reached in the next lines is the conclusion of both sex and death caught in the pun 'when I / Stiffen in a rented house'. Neither sexual consciousness nor the consciousness of death (both there in 'Whispers of Immortality' and dividing the world of consciousness between them, without a third term) are conclusive. 'This show' is presumably the show of Gerontion's consciousness, and of the poem. The presence of this implication is difficult to prove, but it is characteristic of Eliot to incorporate within a poem deprecating or ironic references to the poem itself, as with 'this music' in 'Portrait of a Lady' and, as we shall see, in 'Marina' and often in *Four Quartets*. But whether by this or other means, the line

> I would meet you upon this honestly,

comes with an especial candour and force, with an effect of sincerity which is not only Gerontion's but Eliot's. The effect is continued in the next lines about the loss of passion. It is almost impossible to keep biographical considerations completely out of our minds here, but even without them the voice of these lines seems to speak with an unusual personal directness. And it is the voice of the poem which matters, since it speaks to us also impersonally of a truth that is universal, of the mortality of merely sensual life.

The poem ends with a sudden widening of perspective to include the world of international, as if 'famous', names, and then the astrological dimension, in the processes of death:

> De Bailhache, Fresca, Mrs. Cammel, whirled
> Beyond the circuit of the shuddering Bear
> In fractured atoms.

The perspective of time is also widened by the allusion to the classical astrological tradition of the punishment of sinners by banishment to an 'eccentric, outward orbit' of space, and further, by the echo of the Elizabethan poet George Chapman's lines on the heavens and 'those that suffer / Beneath the chariot of the snowy Bear', lines which are themselves an echo of Seneca (as Eliot points out in *The Use of Poetry and The Use of Criticism*, p. 147). It is important to stress that a recognition of these associations is not necessary for an understanding of Eliot's lines: but they add layers of connotation, more or less suggestive depending on the reader's breadth and responsiveness of reading. The main thing, which is there on the 'surface', is the sudden feeling of cosmic and temporal scope, which modulates finally into the refreshing images from nature and geography, the 'Gull against the wind . . .'. The successive feelings are terror (at infinite space), release, freshness and purity (after the decadence of the adulterated senses), and finally a not unpleasant coming to rest in a 'sleepy corner'. The old man's mind drifts from impression to impression, is peopled by different thoughts, 'Tenants of the house, / Thoughts of a dry brain in a dry season'.

A degree of paraphrase can elucidate the poem, but it cannot capture the feeling. There is the satisfyingness of sound, which catches a momentary vigour in the old man's reflections, in lines such as

> Spawned in some estaminet of Antwerp,
> Blistered in Brussels, patched and peeled in London.

Or there is the dry analytic irony of the passages on the adulteration of the senses with their thin sounds and clinical and actuarial precision (and erotic pun):

> These with a thousand small deliberations
> Protract the profit of their chilled delirium,

The tone of that may seem similar to the 'superior' and sardonic tones of the quatrain poems, but its context is very different. Here, instead of a superior irony, there is a kind of weary, analytic sobriety and a sense of failure not externally observed but felt within the self. Sexuality is seen with disillusion, but is also associated with 'beauty' as well as 'vanities' or the coarseness of 'pneumatic bliss'. Religious belief is a matter of urgent but baffled glimpses, rather than of dry satiric observation and dissection. And death is seen not with the morbid relish of 'our lot crawls between dry ribs' but with the sad, serious realization of

> . . . What will the spider do,
> Suspend its operations, will the weevil
> Delay?

Through the *persona* of Gerontion Eliot gets closer to his deeper feelings than through the polished voice of the quatrain poems. And in his next work, *The Waste Land*, he will extend his use of *personae* and at the same time, not entirely paradoxically, achieve a voice at once more central and more intense.

6

The Waste Land (1922)

I

Like other of Eliot's longer works, *The Waste Land* was composed in fragments over a period of time, the earliest (which appeared in 'The Death of Saint Narcissus') dating from 1914–15. These were afterwards put together and 'edited', with the decisive help of Ezra Pound, into the final version that we know today. The process of the poem's composition can be followed in *The Waste Land: A Facsimile and Transcript*, edited by Valerie Eliot in 1971, which includes all the original drafts and Pound's annotations. The book is an invaluable insight into the way the final poem came about, and offers some interesting examples of verse which Eliot finally discarded from the poem and from his *Collected Poems*: we can see the poet's mind at work and assess his critical decisions (and Pound's critical advice) about the selection of passages, and the alteration of lines. But the final poem is what matters most in the end, and I shall not in this chapter attempt to give an account of the *ur*-version. As most critics agree, the poem is immeasurably improved in its final form, and in almost every case the material finally omitted is manifestly inferior. With Pound's help ('il miglior fabbro' – 'the better craftsman' – is Eliot's fitting tribute to him in the dedication of the poem) the poem finally 'came together'. This was Eliot's poem, and this was what he wanted the world to see; and what is most important is to read it and to make sense of it in its final version. Until we have done that, a preoccupation with the early version is out of place and may be distorting: the rescuing of the drafts is a valuable piece of scholarship, but the poem is the thing.

In approaching *The Waste Land* for the first time the reader should proceed boldly. What I have said in my Introduction about the way to approach Eliot's poetry (essentially what Johnson said of the reading of Shakespeare: 'read every play, from the first scene to the last, with utter negligence of all his commentators') applies to *The Waste Land* even more strongly than to Eliot's other poems, and in this case too, the 'commen-

tators' include Eliot himself. The supposed 'obscurity' of the
poem may be illusory, or may not matter. There will, eventually, be connections to be made, meanings to be pondered and
deepened through the exploration of allusions. But the poem, its
images and sounds, its dramatic scenes and its injunctions, is
first of all an experience − and last of all too, after we have re-
read and worked on the poem, an experience of a different kind,
though (if it is still to be a live experience) containing the earlier.
Eliot's words in a later poem, 'The Dry Salvages' (1941), can be
taken as a statement of the ideal of one aspect of criticism:

> We had the experience but missed the meaning,
> And approach to the meaning restores the experience
> In a different form,

In discussing *The Waste Land* (as with other poems) I shall begin
with the experience, with the surface which is 'intimate with the
depths', and then in the second part of this chapter go on to examine the role of myth in the poem, the question of allusion
(and the problem of Eliot's own Notes), and other matters which
will, I hope, help towards a nearer 'approach to the meaning'.

'The Burial of the Dead'

The opening lines of 'The Burial of the Dead' contrast with the
title in a way that alerts us at once to paradoxes of death and
life which are to recur throughout the poem. The note is harsh
but vital, the deployment of line and syntax accentuating the
feeling of painfully stirring life: not 'April is the cruellest month,
/ Breeding lilacs out of the dead land, / Mixing memory and
desire', but

> April is the cruellest month, breeding
> Lilacs out of the dead land, mixing
> Memory and desire, stirring . . .

'Winter kept us warm': the 'us' is general, all of us, and the next
lines make it sound as if 'we' are vegetable life as much as
human. But

> Summer surprised us, coming over the Starnbergersee
> With a shower of rain;

− the 'us' is here suddenly human and particular (a particular
group of people in Munich), suddenly and 'surprisingly': the
reader is reorientated with a sudden enlivening shift. And the
description that follows gives us European social life and a

snatch of talk from a nostalgic aristocrat talking about her childhood and her nervous adult life (the nervousness there in the tone as well as in 'I read, much of the night'). It has been said that reading *The Waste Land* is like turning the tuning-knob on a powerful radio receiver and catching a succession of different voices (English, French, German, Italian, and later even Hindu) – voices out of Europe and the world; and though that exaggerates the fragmentariness it suggests something of the effect. But it also soon becomes clear that the voices all speak with variations of the same accent of despair.

Marie's voice is succeeded in the next verse-paragraph by a harsher note, from another place and another time:

> What are the roots that clutch, what branches grow
> Out of this stony rubbish? Son of man,
> You cannot say, or guess, . . .

– a note we recognize as prophetic and biblical, as is the subsequent landscape. One might wonder if the transition is entirely successful here: is the note too heavily prophetic, too solemnly condemnatory for the glimpse of life we have just seen? (William Empson said that Eliot here was doing down the glimpse of childhood happiness which we get in Marie's memories.)[1] 'Stony rubbish' also belies the 'stirring / Dull roots with spring rain' of the opening, and is perhaps curiously difficult to read aloud with conviction. It may be too soon for the prophetic note – the prophetic urge was sometimes a snare for Eliot, as Prufrock saw. Later the poem is to justify it more fully, but we might ask in general terms: does the prophetic note, the note of social condemnation, represent the deepest element in the poem, or is that to be found elsewhere? At any rate, the tone soon modulates: '(Come in under the shadow of this red rock)' has a note of 'wit', of ironic politeness, and the transition allows a movement to an accent which is less 'biblical' and more personal, culminating in the powerful and original image:

> I will show you fear in a handful of dust.

Then, another sudden transition to the snatch of German lyric (in English: 'Fresh blows the wind / Towards the homeland / My Irish Child / Where dost thou dwell?'). The lines are romantic, song-like (whether or not we recognize them as the sailor's song from Wagner's *Tristan und Isolde*), and allow the shift from the admonitory voice to this:

'You gave me hyacinths first a year ago;
'They called me the hyacinth girl.'
− Yet when we came back, late, from the Hyacinth garden,
Your arms full, and your hair wet, I could not
Speak, and my eyes failed, I was neither
Living nor dead, and I knew nothing,
Looking into the heart of light, the silence.
Oed' und leer das Meer.

One needs the whole context to get the full force of this − the
way in which it comes after the previous snatch of song, as a
sudden feeling of release from the prophetic heaviness, the sudden 'lifting of a burden' with a consequent deepening, and inten-
sifying of feeling. It is a moment of remembered passion, and
of passion present in the speaking, a passion which is a mystery
poised between emptiness and fullness, between failure and
fulfilment. 'My eyes failed . . .', and yet, 'Looking into the heart
of light'. It is a moment of insight into a profound yet visionary
emptiness; and as if this intensity cannot be sustained for long,
the passage concludes by falling back into the more romantic
pathos and melancholy of the Wagnerian song: 'Wide and
empty the sea'. The passage is one of the most inward and intense in the poem (and indeed in Eliot's work as a whole). And
one might note in passing its echoes of earlier poems of 'Elle
était toute mouillée, je lui ai donnée des primevères' ('She was
all wet, I gave her primulas') from 'Dans Le Restaurant' and
'Her hair over her arms full of flowers' from 'La Figlia'. But
here the 'memory' is more powerful and the insight more intense. It is the momentary glimpse of something central and
formative.

Madame Sosostris introduces quite another, and spurious,
kind of mystery; although like all fortune-tellers she may speak
more wisely than she knows. The tone ('Had a bad cold, nevertheless / Is known . . .') places her, and yet she may have her
surprises. 'The drowned Phoenician sailor', 'Belladonna', 'the
one-eyed merchant' − as yet we know nothing of these (though
the first will stir a memory for the reader of 'Dans Le
Restaurant'). 'I do not find the Hanged Man.' A good thing too,
one might think; or is it? The atmosphere is one of charlatanry;
but the Tarot pack is an ancient device, and we cannot be sure
what these perhaps traditional images may, by chance, relate to
in the listener's (and our) life. But Madame Sosostris is more
concerned with her money ('Thank you') and her reputation

than with any truth: she brings the horoscope herself presumably because it is carefully 'prepared' – or perhaps because she is afraid of what other horoscopes might reveal. A horoscope is an astrological diagram of planets which is said to reveal one's pattern of fate at birth, and 'hora' is Greek for time. Madame Sosostris is anxious to tamper with evidence of fate and to doctor the records of time, unlike the poet (one might say), who tries to discover his fate and open himself to the voices of the past in all their multiplicity and confusion.

'Unreal City' – Madame Sosostris's unreality colours the vision of London 'Under the brown fog of a winter dawn'. The crowd flowing over London Bridge is a crowd of living dead, but the tone avoids melodrama by its formality: 'I had not thought death had undone so many'. The echoes of Dante can be considered later; primarily we are on London Bridge, which with King William Street and St Mary Woolnoth roots the poem in an actual London setting, an important source of the sense of immediacy of actuality in the poem as a whole. But with ' "Stetson! / You who were with me in the ships at Mylae" ' we are thrown into a wider world and a longer perspective of time: the comrade is not from the Somme, but from the seas of Greece. The effect is again one of surprise and reorientation, and the surprise is compounded by the sinister questions. Our immediate sense is of the shades of Crippen and crime stories in tabloid newspapers, and of a macabre parody of one commuter talking to another about gardening. But the corpse 'planted' and perhaps about to 'sprout' and 'bloom' touches other remote chords: John Barleycorn? Forgotten rituals? The remoteness is an important part of our experience of this passage and should not be destroyed by dragging too much to light (as the Dog does). But something is there: a guilty secret? A hidden obsession? We do not know. And whose secret? Who is Stetson? The answer is unequivocally directed at us: ' "You! hypocrite lecteur – mon semblable – mon frère!" '[2] It is we who are touched and disturbed by this passage of macabre levity, this sinister chaffing.

That is all we know, at the moment at any rate – and, one might almost say, all we need to know at this stage. April mixes 'memory and desire': memories of past passion and of remoter history; desire for present feeling and for some revelation of hidden truth, and the fear of these things too. But the 'idea' is almost nothing, nothing at any rate than can be grasped. The evocation is everything. We are walking over London Bridge, and we are at the same time members of a human race with an unfathomable depth of passions and guilts. We only half grasp 'meaning' but we are troubled, quickened and stirred.

'A Game of Chess'

This part of the poem is a triptych, in which the first 'panel' merges into the second. Each section — the picture of the grand lady in the lavish classical or renaissance setting (possibly anticipated by 'Belladonna' at line 49), the modern upper-middle-class couple of lines 111–39, and the dialogue between the two working-class ladies in the pub (lines 139–72) — has, in varying forms, a common theme of despair and the failure of sexual love, and an atmosphere of varying kinds of claustrophobia. Between them the three parts offer a wide view of human suffering across social classes and historical periods.

Beyond this clear structure, however, each section varies considerably in terms of style, and, I would suggest, in terms of poetic success. The first section (lines 77–100) gives us a rich picture of decadent grandeur. The verse recalls the late renaissance, a kind of loose blank verse which is closer to Jacobean than Elizabethan (but without the cool clarity of the Middletonian blank verse of 'Gerontion', or indeed any very specific verse echoes, except of Shakespeare in the first two lines). And the furnishings of the room are given a classical or even baroque tone, with the 'Cupidon', 'candelabra', 'laquearia', the 'carved dolphin' and the classical picture of Philomel. The confused and 'synthetic' quality of the scene is caught partly (as William Empson has pointed out)[3] in the ambiguous syntax, as in the end of second line here which hovers between looking back and forward:

> Unstoppered, lurked her strange synthetic perfumes,
> Unguent, powdered, or liquid — troubled, confused
> And drowned the sense in odours;

The splendour quickly becomes ambiguous or excessive.

Phrases like '*fattening* the prolonged candle flames' and 'huge sea-wood *fed* with copper' suggest a kind of excess. And the 'trompe-l'œil' picture above the mantel takes us back into a myth of violent and debased passion, 'The change of Philomel, by the barbarous king / So rudely forced'. The verse gives us the essentials, and we scarcely need to recognize the precise story from Ovid.[4] Philomel's metamorphosis *into* the nightingale may be more obscure, but even there we have '*yet* there the nightingale . . .' and 'And still she cried, and still the world pursues, / Jug jug to dirty ears' — the pursuit of the nightingale is the pursuit of Philomel, and it still goes on in the present. The scene then darkens again into the sinister and vaguely surreal 'withered stumps of time', 'staring forms'.

The transition to the next section and the words of the modern woman is effected through a surreal and timeless (either renaissance or modern) image:

> Under the firelight, under the brush, her hair
> Spread out in fiery points
> Glowed into words, then would be savagely still.
>
> 'My nerves are bad tonight. Yes, bad. Stay with me.
> Speak to me. Why do you never speak. Speak.'

And we are suddenly in a world of new emotional intensity. The urgent, anxious tones of the neurotic woman are exactly caught, and the dull pondering undercurrent of the man's unspoken replies. The woman urges the man to reveal his thoughts, or even just to think; suggesting his silence and his evasiveness, even from himself:

> 'What are you thinking of? What thinking? What?
> I never know what you are thinking. Think.'

— which may recall for us Gerontion's deliberate insistence on thought ('Think now / . . . Think now / . . . Think / . . . Think at last', etc.) as if thought had to work against invisible pressing barriers. The man's unspoken replies are gnomic; but 'I think we are in rat's alley / Where the dead men lost their bones' suggests squalor and skeletal dismemberment or pillaged graves, and recalls 'Or with his nails he'll dig it up again' in 'The Burial of the Dead'. More distinctly, 'I remember / Those are pearls that were his eyes' recalls Madame Sosostris (or her listener's thought) at line 48; and 'Are you alive, or not? Is there nothing in your head?' perhaps recalls the hyacinth garden and 'I was neither / Living nor dead, and I knew nothing'. By these echoes in the mind of an unspeaking interlocutor the poem begins to create the sense of a central consciousness in the poem, an awareness which runs beneath the surface of the various semi-dramatic scenes, speaking in riddles, making obscure connections, and giving the impression of a deeper knowledge. The intensity of this scene comes from the counterpoint between the anguished volubility of the woman and the weary knowledge of the man, touched with vivid moments of horror. The woman can think only of the blank future (' ''What shall we do tomorrow? / What shall we ever do?'' '); the man looks back either to fragments of distant memory or to the routine life, seen as both dull and horrifying:

> Pressing lidless eyes and waiting for a knock upon the door.

It is a contrast between what Freud called 'hysterical misery' and a deeper and more conscious despair. Because of the presence of the 'unspeaking' voice and because of the intensity, we seem to come close here to something very central to the poem. One might call it more 'personal; but in spite of the fact that it is perhaps impossible, given biographical knowledge, not to think of the unhappiness of Eliot's first marriage, one does not feel that the passage in any way depends on this recognition. If it is personal, it is personal with the force of a completely realized art, independent of its sources.

By contrast, the scene with the working-class women in the pub feels relatively external and unintense (though one might remember Eliot's later observation that a long poem cannot remain always at the same level of intensity). This scene is a matter of sharp social observation and an ear for Cockney speech. It completes the picture, in Part II as a whole, of loveless relationships and sterile sexuality, with one or two touches that link it with the other sections (the aristocratic lady had her 'strange synthetic perfumes'; Albert gave Lil some money to get herself some teeth). But it has something of the quality of expert pastiche: we feel that the details of language are being enjoyed, condescendingly, for their own sake, rather than being there entirely for the sake of the experience they evoke. To put it another way, there is little sympathy or insight in the passage. Neither of the women is allowed any equivalent of the middle-class woman's *cri de cœur*, 'What shall we ever do?' One might contrast their treatment with that of Conrad's insight into Winnie Verloc in *The Secret Agent*. The barman's refrain is a nice 'find' (though its irony is perhaps a shade too obvious) and serves something of the same function, though with less force, as the undercurrent of the man's asides in the previous section. But it is not until the end, with the modulation from the pub goodbyes to Ophelia's lines in *Hamlet* (well known enough, perhaps, to be allowed to be part of the 'surface'), that the passage reaches a

deeper note. It is not just a matter of an 'ironic' contrast between the tough pub ladies and the tragic innocence of Ophelia,
still less of a shift to the comment of a detached and superior
onlooker (though it can have both these effects). The deeper
note is the recognition of an identity of suffering between
Ophelia and the modern London women. Ophelia's madness
and tragedy is caused by a failure of love as well as by the
murder of her father; her mad songs reflect a sexual passion
thwarted and turned tragically awry. Her suffering is raised to
a greater level of intensity and pathos by her youth and innocence. The London women are inured to suffering and survive
through toughness (like the 'ancient women / Gathering fuel in
vacant lots' in 'Preludes'), but they too suffer an unconscious
despair at lovelessness and callousness. Their social circumstances, sensitivity, moral awareness are all different; but
their malaise, as the poem sees it, is the same, and the women
gain a momentary dignity from the association.

'The Fire Sermon'

The Waste Land is a poem about drought and sterility, but it is
filled with images of water, and this is not, perhaps, paradoxical. For there is an intensity of imagination in the poem which
yearns after what is absent, and which grasps at any fleeting
image of what it lacks. So 'The Fire Sermon' opens with an image of the Thames, its modern squalor not forgotten but held in
balance by the lyrical note of 'Sweet Thames run softly till I end
my song' and the 'nymphs', whose effect is not wholly ironic.
The squalor of the modern river is 'there' in the words of the
passage, and yet not there; 'The river bears *no* empty bottles
...' etc. (my italics). The tone of the opening is elegiac: summer
has gone, 'the nymphs are departed'. But the total effect is complex because of the presence of the note of modern disenchantment ('Departed, have left no addresses').

The lines on the 'dull canal' (187–95) perhaps strike one firstly
with their urban imagery: it is remarkable how vividly we get the
feel of *place* in various parts of the poem, not just for its own
sake but as part of a larger experience (which indeed is what helps
to make the places vivid: we might remember Eliot's remark
about Henry James making a place real by something happening there).[5] The rat is vivid in itself, but also recalls 'I think
we are in rats' alley' in 'A Game of Chess' (line 115). 'The king

my brother's wreck' takes us into another world, but it is striking how easily it consorts with the modern one, the reason being
(to make the point again) that we are not so much in a place as
in a mind. Some of the relevant literary associations here will be
looked at later; it is important firstly to register the linear movement from one moment to the next, the modulation from
'death' to 'spring' whereby the vivid image of 'White bodies
naked on the low damp ground' has associations of both death
(from the lines before and after) and sex (the latter taken up by
Sweeney and Mrs Porter, and the echo of Philomel in 'A Game
of Chess': 'Jug jug jug jug jug jug / So rudely forced. / Tereu').
In this context, too, it is difficult not to see the proposal by Mr
Eugenides, the Smyrna merchant, as a sexual one. We are in a
world of back-street liaisons.

The episode of the typist and the house agent's clerk (lines
215–56) follows from this. The verse begins as 'free' (lines
215–25) but quickly adopts a more regular metre, and its rhyming pattern, which is first of all irregular but with a hint of
the quatrain, becomes firmer as the passage continues, until
from the beginning of the 'love-making' passage (lines 235ff.) it
takes on a regular iambic quatrain pattern. The versification is
important to note because it contributes a great deal to the effect
of fastidious observation and holding at a distance – the effect
of distaste – which dominates the episode. The return to a
tighter quatrain form as in the 'Sweeney' poems, though this
time decasyllabic and with a more 'Augustan' feeling, might be
noted: the feeling of cold detachment is very similar. It is a
modulation in feeling as well as form from the beginning of the
passage, where the 'violet hour' is felt to be a time of relaxation
and possibility ('when the human engine waits / Like a taxi
throbbing waiting'), and may recall those earlier 'violet hours'
in Eliot's poetry, like the opening of 'The Love Song of J.
Alfred Prufrock' or the evening of 'The Boston Evening
Transcript'. And one might suggest that the passage here is
highly symptomatic of what has happened to Eliot's sensibility
since those poems. The possibilities and energies of 'the violet
hour' – never indeed realized in the earlier poems – here
become subject to a far more negative and disillusioned treatment
as the possibilities of sexuality are contemptuously dismissed.
The snobbery and thin disdain of the passage make it unpleasant
in a way which is not that of the unpleasantness that Eliot admired in Blake (*Selected Essays*, p. 317), the unpleasantness that

comes from a penetrating vision, for the effect is as of a shrinking from experience.

But the passage is only a part of *The Waste Land* and part of a very different total effect; and the feeling I have described is, indeed, only part of the passage. The introduction of Tiresias, the blind, androgynous prophet of Thebes, gives the episode at least some degree of prophetic impersonality and also a certain identification of the poetic voice with the couple: '(And I Tiresias have foresuffered all . . .)'. Tiresias is, at this point in the poem, a very useful figure in that he combines the role of prophet with the role of sufferer. But it is doubtful whether the combination succeeds, and whether Tiresias attains within the poem as a whole the importance that Eliot attributes to him in his Note on this passage (which will be discussed below). Tiresias might have given this episode a tone of sad dignity comparable to that achieved in the 'Gerontion' passage beginning 'I would meet you upon this honestly'. But his presence is scarcely felt, in the tone, beyond the passages in which he talks of himself. The solemn four-line parenthesis

> (And I Tiresias have foresuffered all
> Enacted on this same divan or bed;
> I who have sat by Thebes below the wall
> And walked among the lowest of the dead.)

(except perhaps in the redundant, or fastidious, 'or bed') sounds like Tiresias. But the description of the typist's flat, the 'young man carbuncular', 'one of the low . . .', is the disdainful snobbery of one side of Eliot. The *persona* of Tiresias fails to control the tone of the whole passage and the result is a failure of proper impersonality.

However, it is one of the virtues of Eliot's technique of fragmentation and swift, sometimes concealed, transition, that it can allow marvellous recoveries and fresh beginnings. The phrase 'When lovely woman stoops to folly' has already introduced a note of lyricism which is not entirely negated by the ironic effect of its placing; and the 'gramophone' allows the transition to this:

> 'This music crept by me upon the waters'
> And along the Strand, up Queen Victoria Street.
> O City city, I can sometimes hear
> Beside a public bar in Lower Thames Street,
> The pleasant whining of a mandoline

> And a clatter and a chatter from within
> Where fishmen lounge at noon: where the walls
> Of Magnus Martyr hold
> Inexplicable splendour of Ionian white and gold.

The poetic voice, the 'I' (I think we can call it the central voice in the poem — and it is obviously not still Tiresias) escapes from the previous arid scene and is moved to a powerful expression of positive feeling for London, for the ordinary human community, and a feeling of wonder at the 'inexplicable splendour' of Wren's church. The drafts of the poem show that Eliot looked a long time for that perfect adjective: the beauty is inexplicable in itself, but so also is its relation to the belief it celebrates; and there is also the fine 'glitter' in the sound of the word.

The river that follows is still predominantly lyrical in movement and visually picturesque rather than sordid, despite the 'oil and tar'.[6] Elizabeth and Leicester are primarily splendid in their 'gilded shell', and the snatches of wordless song ('Weialala leia') have an effect of music which predominates over any negative element in the association with Wagner's Rhine-daughters.[7] So the three utterances which follow regain some of the feelings of the preceding lyricism and their moral bleakness is rendered sad and wistful rather than bitterly resentful or scathing. The formality of syntax which combines with an effect of laconic notation also helps to achieve this effect:[8]

> 'Trams and dusty trees.
> Highbury bore me. Richmond and Kew
> Undid me. By Richmond I raised my knees
> Supine on the floor of a narrow canoe.'

We are back to the world of seduction and betrayal, but the effect is very different from the contemptuous vision of the typist and the clerk. The three women here speak in their own voices and are allowed their own kind of sadness and even dignity. But the voice to which we finally return in this part is the voice of the poetic 'I', for whom a harsher note of self-condemnation is reserved. 'The Fire Sermon' here earns its title. After the various moods of despair (and the fleeting moment of warmth and splendour) through which 'The Fire Sermon' has passed, it concludes (although 'we have not reached conclusion', and there is no final full stop) with the fires of suffering and the prayers of supplication:

Burning burning burning burning
O Lord Thou pluckest me out
O Lord Thou pluckest

burning

The broken syntax is part of the point. The three women's monologues, the snatch of song, the fragment of some past journey, are followed by yet another more broken fragment; and although it ends this Part, we feel that its status is provisional, and that the burning and the hope may both only be glimpsed for a moment, though 'burning', in its typographic isolation, has the last word.

'Death by Water'

The coolness of water comes as a relief after the burning of 'The Fire Sermon'. This Part is a complete poem, a brief *memento mori*, classical in its simplicity; but although it speaks of death, the effect at this stage is as much of respite and calm after the varieties of sadness, anguish and horror which we have encountered in previous Parts. Phlebas the Phoenician fulfils the veiled half-prophecies of Madam Sosostris ('Here . . . / Is your card, the drowned Phoenician Sailor' and 'Fear death by water') but in a way that feels as much beneficient as malign. This might also be the place to recall the epigraph to the whole work, from Petronius's *Satyricon*, which translated reads: 'For once I myself with my own eyes saw the Sibyl of Cumae hanging in a jar, and when the boys said to her: "Sybil, what do you want?" she replied, "I want to die." ' Much of the poem implies a longing for death, and Part IV answers that longing. Death is felt as a release from worldly concerns, 'The profit and loss' (which also recalls Mr Eugenides, the Smyrna merchant). But there is no suggestion of resurrection (as some critics have tried to find). The tone of the ending is classically philosophical and admonitory: *Respice finem*, 'Consider Phlebas, who was once handsome and tall as you.'

'What the Thunder Said'

Eliot wrote of Part V of *The Waste Land* that it 'in my opinion is not only the best part, but the only part that justifies the whole at all' (letter to Bertrand Russell, 15 October 1923). He wrote the

Part in Lausanne where he was being treated for his nervous illness, and it is notable that, unlike the other parts of the poem which were heavily revised with Pound's suggestions, it scarcely needed any revision at all. The point is relevant to a critical consideration since it confirms an impression of the completeness and power of this Part; and it also relates to a comment Eliot made about Pascal in his essay of 1931, where he said that some forms of illness are favourable to religious illumination and to artistic and literary composition, and that a piece of writing, thought about for a long period, may suddenly under these conditions take shape in passages which need little revision (*Selected Essays*, p. 405). It is in this Part of the poem that we reach a kind of crisis, and the sickness of the Waste Land is diagnosed and pronounced upon, though not finally cured.

The opening verse-paragraph conjures a vivid scene of some historical tumult, strongly recalling (an impression confirmed later) Christ's agony in the garden, and crucifixion; but only, as yet, recalling it rather than signalling it clearly, for it is important that we come upon the scene, at first, as strangers, and with a sense of uncertainty and discovery. The verse is urgent, with the repeated 'After . . .', the accumulation of nouns, and the thrilling effect of the drawing out of the 'reverberation / Of thunder of spring' over the line ending, in

> The shouting and the crying
> Prison and palace and reverberation
> Of thunder of spring over distant mountains

The passage that follows is insistent and mesmeric with its repetitions, like the beating of the sun or the throbbing of the mind in the desert; and vivid in the striking metaphor which relates the external landscape to an internal condition (a metaphor which recurs in other forms in later poems): 'Dead mountain mouth of carious teeth that cannot spit'. The 'water' that is not 'there' is repeated continually in the verse, and then the scene of hostile desert gives way to a lyric dream, the 'water-dripping song' as Eliot called it. Of the whole passage he wrote: 'There are *I* think about 30 good lines in *The Waste Land*. Can you find them? The rest is ephemeral.' And later: 'As for the lines I mention, you need not scratch your head over them. They are the 29 lines of the water dripping song in the last part' (letters to Ford Madox Ford, 14 August and 4 October 1923). The passage, particularly the most song-like part (lines 346–58),

effects an extraordinary example of the power of imagination
and desire to create in the poem the illusion, almost the
substance, of that which is desired; it is a representative example
of the creative achievement of the poem as a whole, in making
vividly present a sense of life which counters the human and
natural aridity which is the poem's subject.

> If there were water
> And no rock
> If there were rock
> And also water
> And water
> A spring
> A pool among the rock
> If there were the sound of water only
> Not the cicada
> And dry grass singing
> But sound of water over a rock
> Where the hermit-thrush sings in the pine trees
> Drip drop drip drop drop drop drop
> But there is no water

The figure in the next section is not identified: the lines begin
and end with a question. The 'white road' and the 'brown man-
tle' coming after the desert scene and 'the agony in stony places'
have their associations, but we cannot be sure. The 'murmur of
maternal lamentation' also takes its place among these associations, and the city which 'cracks and reforms and bursts in the
violet air'. But these too are the objects of questioning ('What
is that sound . . .', 'What is the city . . .'). The accumulation
of these elements to suggest that this may be Christ on the road
to Emmaus, the lamentation that of Mary and Anne, the earth-
quake that which followed the Crucifixion (Matthew 27:51), is
unobtrusively, mysteriously done, and the vision is unfixed, the
episode dissolving into a vision of the collapse of successive
civilizations into dream-like unreality:

> Falling towers
> Jerusalem Athens Alexandria
> Vienna London
> Unreal

Eliot's first Note to Part V (to anticipate briefly) signals that the
journey to Emmaus was one of the things in his mind
throughout the Part. But it is important, in the experience of the

poem, not to lose the sense of uncertainty and indeterminacy. These are still merely the fragments of a consciousness, and fragments, too, often only in the shape of questions.

The next section ('A woman drew her long black hair out tight') compounds the shift into dream ('Unreal') with a surrealistic nightmare like a Hieronymous Bosch painting (a source that Eliot confirmed),[9] a nightmare which ends with 'empty cisterns and exhausted wells' and prepares the transition to the 'decayed hole among the mountains' in the next section, and the 'empty chapel'. After the hints of the Crucifixion and Resurrection this comes as if with a sense of failure and loss. And yet the empty feeling is without horror this time ('Dry bones can harm no-one'), and 'the grass is singing'. Once again, we do not *need* to identify this as the 'Chapel Perilous' of the Grail legends, as we are bound to do if we follow up Eliot's Notes; and the ready identification of it by critics, and the confident reference to it in discussions of the passage, seem misleading. For its identity is not made clear in the poem, and the elusive play of suggestion and connection, the sense of *lost* significances, as also in 'Only a cock stood on the rooftree' (the cock that crowed three times to Peter? The emblem of resurrection? Of the banishing of evil spirits?) is an essential part of the effect.

At line 393 there is 'a damp gust / Bringing rain', but in the next lines

> Ganga was sunken, and the limp leaves
> Waited for rain, . . .

The sense of refreshment comes and then goes swiftly, as it does at other points in the poem. In a few touches the ominous oppressiveness before a storm is palpably evoked, building up, heavy with coiled power and unspoken voice, to the first thunder-clap and utterance.

DA
Datta: . . .

And then comes the response and the further admonitions of the thunder. First of all these are enigmatic sounds for us, clarified only partially by what follows. It has been said that whereas the English have an expression 'It's Greek to me', Americans sometimes say 'It's Hindu to me'; and whatever meaning we may later discover for the sounds *Datta*, *Dayadhvam*, *Damyata*, that is an element in the primary effect and should remain a part of the final effect. When we know that the words mean 'Give', 'Sympathize' and 'Control' we can begin to interpret the moral meaning of these injunctions. But although the injunctions are intelligible and powerful in any ethical system they are here also part of a tradition quite alien to Western readers. Their force comes with a sense of freshness, of discovery, but also of obscurity, accentuating the difficulty of understanding and obeying the injunctions.

But the atmosphere of tense expectation in the opening lines means also that they come with a feeling of gathered force:

> *Datta*: what have we given?

And the answer is a controlled and passionate statement, 'blood shaking my heart' referring both, such is the ambiguous syntax, to the original experience and to the present telling of it:

> My friend, blood shaking my heart
> The awful daring of a moment's surrender
> Which an age of prudence can never retract
> By this, and this only, we have existed

The 'surrender' is unspecified, but in the context of the following injunction and of the whole poem, and in the feeling, it impresses us mainly as a statement about a personal relationship. The other replies to the thunder confirm this. That to *'Dayadhvam'* ('Sympathize') suggests a consciousness locked within itself, its confinement confirmed by the thinking about it. And the reply to *'Damyata'* ('Control') has a delicacy of movement which conveys a moment of exceptional tenderness and insight:

> The boat responded
> Gaily, to the hand expert with sail and oar
> The sea was calm, your heart would have responded
> Gaily, when invited, beating obedient
> To controlling hands

'Would have responded': the sense of missed opportunity, of something lost, is nowhere more poignant in the poem.

This whole passage of the thunder's injunctions is the climax of *The Waste Land*, and together with the hyacinth garden, the invocation of 'O City city . . .', and the 'water-dripping song', one of the focal creative moments in the poem — those moments in which 'the burden of the mystery' is lightened and we feel that passionate feeling of possibility (even if it is lost possibility) which makes the poem a dramatic and creative encounter with the Waste Land, and not a merely passive and defeated description of it. But we feel this only if we refuse to take the glimpses of life and significance for the secure possession of these things, and refuse to see a firm structure where we should only see 'A heap of broken images'. The central consciousness, the central 'I' (whose presence has been accumulating, as I have suggested, throughout the poem), reaches its strongest voice in the replies to the thunder.

Finally, in the last section:

> I sat upon the shore
> Fishing, with the arid plain behind me

At the beginning of 'The Fire Sermon' he was 'fishing in the dull canal'. Little has changed except the place, though the arid plain is now 'behind'. Setting 'my lands' in order has still to be begun (and 'Shall I . . .?'), and thereafter the poem breaks down into a babel of past voices and echoes.'These fragments I have shored against my ruins' is the most that can be affirmed by the poem as a whole, and the process of 'fitting' them together brings in Hieronymo and the possibility of madness.[10] The ending is a heap of images and a medley of motifs which have occurred in the poem (London Bridge, fire, birds, 'falling towers', the words of the thunder).[11] It is a masterly coda, a brilliant close to the 'musical organization'. But like the 'music' at the end of 'Portrait of a Lady' or the compositional art of the opening vision of 'La Figlia Che Piange', the completeness of the art, the finality of the aesthetic effect is poignantly at odds with the sense of unanswered questions and of significances just out of reach. The closing line 'Shantih shantih shantih' completes the musical effect; but even for Christian believers it cannot mean 'The Peace which passeth all understanding' (which Eliot gives as 'our equivalent' in his Note), since it comes from what is for Western readers an alien tradition, and in these matter there can be no 'equivalents'. The poem (like Eliot elsewhere) knows this, even if the Note momentarily forgets it. For the fact that such elements can be deployed (with complete sincerity) for artistic effect, and yet not be grasped as matters of firm belief, is what generates the drama of consciousness – the life – of the poem.

II

One of the recurring critical questions about *The Waste Land* is whether its technique of fragmentation (Eliot himself, in an interview, called it 'structureless')[12] leads to a debilitating incoherence, a lack of *any* kind of the unity which we feel is, in some form, necessary for a successful work of art. I shall later look more fully at the nature of these objections, but for the time being I hope that the preceding commentary has shown that even on the 'surface', the work is held together by a network of echoes and parallels and by the strong presence of certain preoccupations. The poem is a vision of sterility in human and natural life, and above all in the former. The recurrence of the theme of failed sexual love is alone enough to show the pressure of a unifying concern through many varying instances: the couple in the hyacinth garden, the woman in the palace, the chess-playing middle-class couple, the conversation of Lil and her friend, the 'nymphs' and their friends ('the loitering heirs of city directors'), Sweeney and Mrs Porter, the typist and the clerk, the three women of London (and Margate), the isolated consciousness who speaks to 'my friend' of 'a moment's surrender' and to an unnamed companion of how 'your heart would have responded' – all these are facets of the same despair and sustain the burden (psychological and musical) of the poem. Secondly, this is reinforced by a common and recurring landscape, the 'dead land' of April and the desert of 'stony rubbish' in 'The Burial of the Dead'; the 'stony places', rock, sand and mountains, 'exhausted wells' and 'arid plain' of successive moments in 'What the Thunder Said'; and the urban equivalents in 'the brown fog of a winter dawn', 'rat's alley', the 'brown land' of the Thames's winter banks, the dull canal and the gas-house, the typist's flat, Margate sands. Whatever the structure or structurelessness of the poem, these elements of theme and imagery contribute powerfully to the sense of an artistic whole.

But as well as the kind of unity which these elements establish there is a kind of partial structure suggested in the play of reference and allusion in the poem, in particular in the use of myth. This cannot be denied, though I would suggest it is less important, in the experience of the poem, than some critics have suggested.[13] The question also brings us to the problem of Eliot's Notes, for it is a moot point whether, without the Notes, critics would have been so ready to lay such a primary stress on the mythic structure of the poem. It is the Notes that direct us so clearly towards the fertility rituals (*via* Sir James Frazer's *The Golden Bough*) and the connection with these of the legend of the Holy Grail proposed by Jessie Weston in *From Ritual to Romance*. The fertility gods are nowhere mentioned directly in the poem, and the Fisher King is not named. Nor does the chapel in Part V necessarily suggest, in any of its details, the Chapel Perilous of the Grail story. It would be foolish to deny that once these connections have been pointed out, they open up new avenues of possible suggestion; and the Notes are now an inescapable part of the poem. However, particularly in our first approaches to the poem, they should be kept in proportion and not allowed to usurp the experience and meaning of the poem, or we are in danger of seeing it as nothing but a repository of erudition.

Eliot's own attitude to the Notes was ambiguous. They did not form a part of the first publication of the poem in *The Criterion* (London, October 1922) or *The Dial* (New York, November 1922). Eliot later wrote in his essay 'The Frontiers of Criticism' (1956) that the Notes were added to the text of the first publication in book form (Boni and Liveright, New York, December 1922) because the poem was 'inconveniently short', and the result was 'the remarkable exposition of bogus scholarship that we see today' (*On Poetry and Poets*, p. 109). Eliot was inclined later in life to make disparaging remarks about his early works, not all of which need be taken as gospel. Arnold Bennett recorded that he asked Eliot whether the Notes were 'a lark or serious' and Eliot replied that 'they were serious, and not more of a skit than some things in the poem itself'.[14] Nevertheless it would seem that readers of the poem would do well to bear in mind Eliot's confession that he was 'penitent' about the Notes, because they aroused 'the wrong kind of interest'. He did not regret his just tribute to Jessie Weston, but added: 'I regret having sent so many enquirers on a wild goose chase after Tarot cards and the Holy Grail' (*On Poetry and Poets*, p. 110). What then should a proper attitude to the Notes be? Firstly, one should clearly distinguish between those Notes which merely give supplementary information (like the one that tells us about the hermit thrush) and those which are pointers of general significance (like the references to the myths of the Waste Land in Frazer and Weston), and also between those that simply give us a source reference and those which point us to sources which may modify our sense of a passage. This is partly a matter of trial and error (as well as time and interest), but the poem itself and our response to it is the final test. Any further exploration *via* the Notes (or any other route) must be guided by a sense of the poem as a whole and the life of individual passages. The Notes, compounded by later source-commentaries, can give the depressing and stultifying impression that the enjoyment and understanding of the poem depends entirely on a mass of previously acquired erudition, and this is quite false. For all its hidden suggestions and sources and its deliberately disorienting procedures, the poem − since it *is* a poem − is still 'a man speaking to men', however enigmatically. And it is better to ignore the Notes and the source-hunters entirely than to lose sight of the poem beneath a mass of supposed scholarship.

What, then, of the role of myth within the poem? Eliot himself wrote of what he called 'the mythical method' in an essay of 1923, '*Ulysses*, Order, and Myth':[15] Joyce, he wrote, was pursuing a method which drew parallels between the ancient and modern worlds, and other writers would follow him. He calls Yeats the first contemporary to be conscious of the method, and points to the influence on writers of psychology and Frazer's work of comparative anthropology, *The Golden Bough*. The way Eliot describes this method perhaps suggests his own poem *The Waste Land* as much as or even more than *Ulysses*: 'It is simply a way of controlling, of ordering, of giving shape and a significance to the immense panorama of futility and anarchy which is contemporary history . . . It is . . . a step towards making the modern world possible for art . . .' (*Selected Prose of T. S. Eliot*, ed. Kermode, pp. 177–8). Clearly this implies that he took the mythic element in *The Waste Land* very seriously. But the question remains, what kind of role does it have, and how central is it in the poem?

The short answer is, I think, not as central as Eliot's comments above and many critical accounts would have us believe. The myth of the Dying God and the story of the Holy Grail seem to be not so much a way of 'controlling and ordering' or of 'giving significance to' events, as a way of providing a shadowy background of half-remembered significances which play their part in the drama of consciousness in the poem. There is not a 'structure' of myth but a dimly perceived pattern of allusions and echoes which remain elusive, and the elusiveness is what gives a sense of mystery and a haunted atmosphere to the poem.

But the actual explicit elements of myth are really very few. Madame Sosotris's cards, the drowned Phoenician sailor, the man with three staves, the one-eyed merchant and the Hanged Man may carry some initial associations for some readers, and some of them begin to accumulate significance when echoed later by Phlebas the Phoenician, Mr Eugenides the Smyrna merchant (perhaps), the corpse in Stetson's garden (perhaps) and the crucified Christ. But the association of the man with the three staves with the Fisher King of the Grail legend is, as Eliot says in his Note, 'quite arbitrary', and without the Note we would not have made the connection. The corpse planted in the garden ('Will it bloom this year?') may recall, once we have got the gist of Frazer, the buried fertility god (perhaps Osiris), and connect with the spring and rebirth at the beginning of 'The Burial of the Dead' ('breeding lilacs out of the dead land'). It may also anticipate the resurrected God of Part V, Christ on the road to Emmaus.

Nevertheless, these things do not amount to a structure. It is no bad idea to get hold of at least the rudiments of what is in Frazer and Weston (and 'purist' critics of the text and nothing but the text sometimes forget that the subject may also be interesting for other reasons!). Frazer records, in the two volumes which Eliot mentions, the various beliefs and rituals surrounding the fertility gods Adonis, Attis and Osiris (Greek/Phoenician, Phrygian and Egyptian respectively), involving such things as the burial of effigies of the god, filled with seeds, to encourage the crops and perhaps to symbolize immortality, or the ceremony of committing an effigy of the god to the sea, from which it is later retrieved. These things may add resonances to the corpse in the garden or the drowned Phoenician sailor, but they are enigmatic and often contradictory ones. (As we saw, there is little hint that the sprouting of the corpse is to be welcomed — rather the opposite — and no suggestion of rebirth in 'Death by Water'.) Again, Jessie Weston's basic notion was that the Arthurian stories of the quest for the Holy Grail showed patterns of derivation (through symbols, narrative elements and thematic content) from the fertility myths, and that the legend of the Grail was not primarily to be associated with either folklore or Christianity (though it carried overlays of association with these) but with far older beliefs. The main features of the Grail legend itself are the Waste Land ruled over by a sick or impotent King (whose sickness is often the cause of the wasting of the land), and a quest by a knight–hero for the Grail which will heal the King and restore the land, or a quest involving ritual tests which, successfully performed, will lead to the same result. Jessie Weston also discusses the Tarot pack in connection with the Grail legend, since its four suits (Cup, Lance, Sword and Dish) correspond to the sacred objects associated with the Holy Grail. But only a few of the basic details find any echo in *The Waste Land*. Eliot's association of 'the man with three staves' with the Fisher King is 'arbitrary' as we have seen, and only made in the Notes. The speaker in the second section of 'The Fire Sermon' 'fishing in the dull canal' and 'musing upon the king my brother's wreck / And on the King my father's death before him', and the speaker at the end of the poem 'Fishing, with the arid plain behind me' do, in the light of Eliot's Notes, stir more audible echoes. And line 202 in 'The Fire Sermon', 'Et O ces voix d'enfants, chantant dans la coupole!', is from Act III of Wagner's *Parsifal*, just before the healing of Amfortas, the Fisher King; in Eliot's poem it gives a sudden glimpse of ascetic purity immediately after Mrs Porter and her daughter. But, as I have already pointed out, the chapel in 'What the Thunder Said', though associated with the Chapel Perilous in the Notes, echoes no actual details of the chapels in the legends.

The most we can say, then, is that even for the reader with the 'relevant' knowledge, the associations work as significances barely glimpsed, faint intimations. What seems to have attracted Eliot to these 'sources' is the suggestion they offered of a set of lost connections, of beliefs and rituals which related pre-Christian myth to Christian beliefs, the idea of the sterility of the land and the body to that of the disease of the spirit. As in 'Gerontion' the failure of physical potency is closely connected with the failure of belief (for instance in the sexual and theological connotations of 'I that was near your heart was removed therefrom / To lose beauty in terror, terror in inquisition'), but the echoes are deliberately faint. The poem is about a consciousness full of fragments of past significance which haunt it like ghosts, perplexing, confusing, perhaps holding out the hope of something to pursue (there is a very faint feeling of a quest in 'What the Thunder Said'), but mainly coming and going in the mind with a tantalizing clarity of image and indistinctness of meaning. The poem is not a diagnosis of modern ills in the light of myth, so much as a dramatization of the elusive play of those myths in the consciousness, an elusiveness which is an integral part of the disease.

The other allusions in the poem generally work in the same way. Once again, one must distinguish mere sources from allusions. It is irrelevant to an understanding of the poem to learn that Marie in 'The Burial of the Dead' is based on a Countess Marie Larisch whose autobiography Eliot may have known,[16] and whom he certainly met;[17] or that the description of the lady's palace in 'A Game of Chess' has echoes of a story by Poe[18] (though these things may have their biographical or other interest). But the allusions to (or quotations from) Dante or Shakespeare or the Bible have a more significant effect. In a general way the feeling of a literary patchwork, or palimpsest, is an important part of the poem, since it is about (among other things) the confused elements of history and past culture in a consciousness and the mind's attempts to make sense of this confusion. Lines from *The Tempest*, quoted or half-changed ('Those are pearls that were his eyes', 'Musing upon the king my brother's wreck') add an enigmatic connotation of death by drowning, and of possible transfiguration, to those parts of the poem where they appear (linking with other deaths by drowning, and other kings). Lines from *The Divine Comedy* add other suggestions: 'So many I had not thought death had undone so many'[19] (line 62) brings the solemnity of the *Inferno* to the crowds flowing over London Bridge, but again the effect is equivocal: it partly suggests (like Shelley) 'Hell is a city / Much like London', or more precisely the condition of the 'lukewarm' in Canto III of the *Inferno*; partly, too, the distance, of the consciousness that perceives the Waste Land, from the firm clarities of judgement and belief which inform Dante's vision. So, too, the line from *Purgatorio*, XXVI, 'Poi s'ascose nel foco che gli affina', in the closing section of the poem conjures the 'refining fire' which cleanses the Provençal poet Arnaut Daniel of his sins of lust and replaces the fire of the end of 'The Fire Sermon' with another kind — but conjures it only for a moment along with a babel of other voices (between an English nursery rhyme and a Latin hymn). Historical allusions have a similar duality: Elizabeth and Leicester in 'The Fire Sermon' bring primarily, as we saw, a vision of beauty and freshness; but (as Eliot's Note reinforces) the history of their relationship[20] suggests another example of the pervasive failure of love which stretches across the Waste Land and back in time.

Those quotations and allusions, and others like them, like the myths in the poem, provide glimpses of meanings rather than a structure of meaning. They may be immediately apparent to the reader (as, say, the quotation from Ophelia and the allusion to Cleopatra in 'The Chair she sat in, like a burnished throne . . .' will be to most readers) or they may be the discovery of repeated explorations of the poem and explorations of the other literature (since needless to say a mere source-reference carries no association at all). But though they may provide elements which the critic is made to feel useful by revealing, they are not the main source of the poem's meaning, still less the poem itself, and they should not be the main focus of criticism. That can only be the poem itself, the poet's unique creation with its play of sound, rhythm, the individual word with its denotation and connotations, created figures and landscapes, dramatic dialogue and central voice — 'the whole consort dancing together'.

The mythical and allusive method did, however, serve an important purpose. It enabled Eliot to stand back from his experience and to generalize it into a view of life; and in another way it also helped him to get closer to his experience, that is, to deal with matters which would have been too painful to approach in any more direct way. This seeming paradox perhaps accounts for the various remarks which Eliot later made about the poem. In his essay of 1931, 'Thoughts after Lambeth', Eliot wrote that he disliked the word 'generation', and that to praise *The Waste Land* for expressing 'the disillusionment of a generation' was nonsense. 'I may have expressed for them their own illusion of being disillusioned, but that did not form part of my intention' (*Selected Essays*, p. 368). Part of Eliot's irritation here was clearly aroused by the critics' self-approving identification of their own feelings with his. In a lecture of 1947 he said that he had written the poem 'simply to relieve his own feelings' ('On Poetry', an address at Concord Academy, p. 10),[21] a remark which must also have been prompted by critical discussion of the poem which dealt with it primarily as an impersonal myth or a description of the state of civilization. The remark quoted as an epigraph to the *Waste Land Facsimile*, that 'To me it was only the relief of a personal and wholly insignificant grouse against life; it is just a piece of rhythmical grumbling' (the only source for which is a quotation in a lecture by Professor Spencer as reported by Henry Eliot, the poet's brother), was presumably a joke prompted by irritation at portentous criticism. But in an interview in *The Paris Review* in 1959 Eliot put the matter more positively. Asked whether it was part of his intention to make *The Waste Land* a Christian poem (as some critics had found) rather than express 'the disillusionment of a generation', Eliot replied that it was not, and that in 'Thoughts after Lambeth' he had been trying rather to say what his intentions had not been. His tone in the interview implies a general unease with the whole idea of 'intention': 'I wonder what intention means! One wants to get something off one's chest. One doesn't know quite what it is until one has got it off. But I couldn't apply the word intention positively to any of my poems. Or to any poem.'[22]

All these comments point towards the initially personal nature of the poem, to its roots in personal experience. And they help to confirm what is surely the feeling in the poem of a central consciousness burdened, except at brief thrilling moments of relief and insight, with an intolerable despair. This central consciousness may be thought of as Tiresias, as Eliot's Note suggests:

Tiresias, although a mere spectator and not indeed a 'character', is yet the most important personage in the poem uniting all the rest. Just as the one-eyed merchant, seller of currants, melts into the Phoenician sailor, and the latter is not wholly distinct from Ferdinand Prince of Naples, so all the women are one woman, and the two sexes meet in Tiresias. What Tiresias *sees*, in fact, is the substance of the poem.

But this seems an added idea rather than one fully realized within the poem; and although it is suggestive, it is not necessary to think of the central consciousness in this way. Indeed, to do so may obscure some important and more personally intense elements at the centre of the poem. For Tiresias is a prophet, and a prophetic solemnity characterizes his utterances about himself, even though this tone does not, as I suggested above, entirely dominate the whole passage. The prophetic tone is in fact too solemn and impersonal to be the tone which we hear at the very centre of the poem. This latter tone is not, however, the limited personal contempt which intrudes in the passage with the typist and the clerk (it may be indeed that this is allowed to intrude *because* of the not entirely central pose of Tiresias which is interspersed with it). The voice at the centre is rather the voice of:

> I was neither
> Living nor dead, and I knew nothing,
> Looking into the heart of light, the silence.

> I remember
> Those are pearls that were his eyes.

> O City city, . . .

> My friend, blood shaking my heart

> . . . your heart would have responded
> Gaily, when invited, beating obedient
> To controlling hands.

This voice, of course, sometimes merges with others. The 'I' in 'While I was fishing in the dull canal / . . . Musing upon the king my brother's wreck / And on the king my father's death before him' is partly the central voice, partly that of Prospero and of Ferdinand Prince of Naples in *The Tempest*. But it remains distinct, like an undertone, a voice in the mind (as it is in the unspoken replies to the woman in 'A Game of Chess'). It is this voice, of which the other voices in the poem provide variations and echoes, which lies at the heart of the poem, and rather than being essentially the voice of the prophet, it is the voice of personal suffering.

But personal suffering felt at such a profound level, and reflected on in relation to so wide a consciousness of general human experience, becomes a vision for which we can use that difficult word 'impersonal'. And to those remarks of Eliot's on the nature of *The Waste Land*, already referred to, we may finally add a remark from a talk of 1951, 'Virgil and the Christian World', where the general reflection applies precisely to Eliot's own poem. He wrote that a poet may believe that he is only expressing his private experience, and that his poem may be simply 'a means of talking about himself without giving anything away', but for his readers it may express their own feelings and the 'exultation and despair of a generation'. However, the poet does not need to be aware of this meaning for others, just as 'a prophet need not understand the meaning of his prophetic utterance' (*On Poetry and Poets*, pp. 122–3). In *The Waste Land* Eliot did not set out (despite Tiresias) to be a prophet, a man who sees profoundly the ills of his own age, but by exploring his own malaise at a profound level he did finally create a poem which spoke to his time.

How far, finally, can we say that the poem is also an expression 'for all time' – that is, an expression of a permanently applicable view of life? Eliot's vision did not cease to develop with *The Waste Land*, and indeed, some of his irritation at others' use of the phrase 'the disillusionment of a generation' (even though he later used a similar phrase himself) may also have come from the feeling that the poem represented a phase that he had made a great creative effort to move beyond. With all its broad reflection on experience, we may finally feel that whatever the poem achieves, it does not 'see life steadily and see it whole', and indeed that its virtues, particularly its intensity, are bound up with its partiality. Its inability to see anything *but* sterility in human relationships suggests not a central point of view but a very particular one. But to have realized the vision in an entirely new form, at such a level of intensity and with such a consciousness of the pervasiveness of this condition through time and across society, is an extraordinary achievement. Eliot's remarks about *The Revenger's Tragedy* in his essay on Tourneur of 1930 are applicable to the poem:

the play is a document on humanity chiefly because it is a document on one human being, Tourneur; its motive is truly the death motive, for it is the loathing and horror of life itself. To have realized this motive so well is a triumph; for the hatred of life is an important phase − even, if you like, a mystical experience − in life itself.

(Selected Essays, p. 190)

It is from this point of view that one might best begin to answer one of the major adverse criticisms of *The Waste Land*, the view that rather than diagnosing and putting into perspective a confused and negative sense of life, it succumbs to the malaise and the confusion. This criticism is perhaps put most powerfully by Yvor Winters in his study *On Modern Poets* (1943), where he compared Eliot unfavourably with Baudelaire. 'Eliot,' he wrote, 'has surrendered to the acedia that Baudelaire was able to judge; Eliot suffers from the delusion that he is judging it when he is merely exhibiting it'; and a little earlier in the same essay:

Eliot, in dealing with debased and stupid material, felt himself obliged to seek his form in his matter: the result is confusion and journalistic reproduction of detail. Baudelaire, in dealing with similar matter, sought to evaluate it in terms of eternal verity: he sought his form and his point of view in tradition, and from that point of view and in that form he judged his material, and the result is a profound evaluation of evil. The difference is the difference between triviality and greatness.[23]

Now it may be that Baudelaire *had* a sure grasp of 'eternal verity' and a sure grasp of the form and of the point of view, if indeed there is a single point of view, of tradition. And we may agree that in *The Waste Land*, for all his constant preoccupation with 'tradition' in his poems and in his prose, Eliot did not. But form has to be worked out afresh in each generation; and it may be that 'eternal verity' is for many poets, even great poets, as for the rest of us, elusive. We may say that while *The Waste Land* shows little firmness of belief, it is precisely the honesty and intensity with which it dramatizes both its confusion and its moments of insight and conviction that make it a great poem.

7

From *The Hollow Men* (1925) to 'Marina' (1930)

The Hollow Men, published in 1925, can be seen both as a continuation, in some ways a culmination, of the creative mood that produced *The Waste Land*, and, to a lesser extent, an attempt at a new beginning. Indeed, the conflict between these two tendencies, in which the former finally dominates, is what creates the tension in the poem. There are glimpses of a new imagery (the 'perpetual star / Multifoliate rose'), and there is a new element of abstraction in Part V ('the idea' and 'the reality', 'the conception' and 'the creation', etc.), but the general mood of the poem is that of a kind of tense enervation which culminates in a shrill and desperate frivolity. But by 1930, with the publication of *Ash-Wednesday*, Eliot had reached a point of new religious orientation, and in 'Marina' a new and achieved sense of hope and expectation. This chapter will attempt to trace that progression through the poems.

Eliot said of *Ash-Wednesday* that like *The Hollow Men* it grew out of separate poems and that he gradually came to see it as a sequence. He felt that this was the way his poetry had often evolved.[1] Part I of *The Hollow Men* ('We are the hollow men') was published separately in the winter of 1924–5. Part III ('This is the dead land') was published as the third of 'Doris's Dream Songs' in November 1924. Parts I, II and IV were published together in March 1925.[2] The whole poem, with Part V, appeared in *Poems 1909–1925* later in the same year. As with *The Waste Land*, the fragmentary composition partly accounts for the poem's lack of narrative sequence or argument (its separate meditations circling round a single mood) and its changes in tone, though there is a deliberate monotony about the whole which is quite different from *The Waste Land*.

The first two of 'Doris's Dream Songs' ('Eyes that last I saw in tears' and 'The wind sprang up at four o'clock'), republished as the first two poems in *Minor Poems* in *The Complete Poems and Plays*, are closely related to the material of *The Hollow Men* and throw a certain light on it, so it will be useful to consider them here. 'Eyes that last I saw in tears' is a poem about a remembered relationship, and may recall 'La Figlia Che Piange'. The 'division' and 'Eyes I shall not see again' suggests a memory of parting, as in the earlier poem. The phrase 'golden vision' would be apt for the vision of the first stanza of 'La Figlia' with its 'Weave, weave the sunlight in your hair'; and the 'eyes of decision' and which 'outlast a little while / A little while outlast the tears' are not so distant from the implied action and 'fugitive' resentment in

> Fling them to the ground and turn
> With a fugitive resentment in your eyes:

But, of course, all the lyricism of the earlier poem has gone, to be replaced by short (as if short-winded) lines which move with a broken effect (accentuated by the almost complete absence of punctuation). With their repetitions, the lines also have a partial effect of incantation, and this is a significantly new note in Eliot's verse. It is not the lyrical, refrain-like repetition of 'Weave, weave the sunlight . . .' in 'La Figlia', but it has the beginnings of an effect of liturgy, particularly in the second stanza:

> This is my affliction
> Eyes I shall not see again
> Eyes of decision
> Eyes I shall not see unless . . .

The grief of remembered sorrow is subdued here to a calmer meditativeness and a quieter affliction (though still touched with fear of the future), as if calmed by the semi-hypnotic effect of the incantation.

The other new element is the imagery of 'death's dream kingdom' and 'death's other kingdom'. Parts of *The Waste Land* were *like* dreams, but this is the first point at which the dream is seen consciously as a separate realm or 'kingdom'. This suggests a new kind of reflection on experience – rather than just a dramatic presentation of it – which becomes increasingly marked in the poems from *The Hollow Men* onwards. And together with 'death's other kingdom' the phrase also suggests a new kind of symbolic (or perhaps even allegorical) landscape, which is mysterious as yet, but points the way (as we shall see) towards a drawing on Dante. The same 'death's dream kingdom' in the 'The wind sprang up at four o'clock', together with 'the surface of the blackened river', also point towards that landscape, which is explored more fully in *The Hollow Men* as a whole. Otherwise this second poem is more baffling, though still haunting: it seems to consist of a mingling of more importunate and turbulent experience ('a face that sweats with tears') with an imagery derived from some literary or historical source which relates that experience to a wider and more general context. But this imagery, the 'camp fire' and the 'Tartar horsemen', unlike that in the previous poem, must have been felt by Eliot to be more arbitrary since it did not survive into the final poem, *The Hollow Men*.

In looking at *The Hollow Men* itself, my procedure will follow roughly the same pattern as with *The Waste Land*: that is, it will begin with the 'surface' of the poem and try and establish the impression it makes and the meanings it suggests, without digging too deeply into 'sources'. I would suggest that many commentators have greatly exaggerated the importance, both for responding to and understanding the poem, of the Gunpowder Plot, Conrad's *Heart of Darkness* and Dante's *Divine Comedy* (and still more of a lesser source like *Julius Caesar*). The epigraphs do point us in the direction of the first two, and there are one or two other echoes in the text. A knowledge of *The Divine Comedy* does enrich and illuminate the poem rather more than the other 'sources'. But unless the poem can be seen to stand by itself and to impress us *with* itself an exploration of these sources will do it little good.

The epigraphs at first give us fleeting impressions: 'Mistah Kurtz he dead' will recall briefly, for those who know Conrad's story, that moment when the death of the colonial leader Kurtz is announced with laconic brevity, and will recall Conrad's hollow man, the idealist with no substance within. And 'Penny for the Old Guy' will more surely recall the straw man of 5 November (an association to be echoed later in 'our dry cellar'). But these are fleeting impressions, transitory images: they awake vague associations but not precise meetings; they alert us towards certain possibilities and whet the imagination. We move on to the poem.

> We are the hollow men
> We are the stuffed men
> Leaning together
> Headpiece filled with straw. Alas!

Our dried voices, when
We whisper together
Are quiet and meaningless
As wind in dry grass
Or rats' feet over broken glass
In our dry cellar

The short, breathless lines create a sense of absolute enervation, and the repetitions of syntax and vocabulary ('dried . . . dry . . . dry') at the same time an effect of muttered incantation. And the sounds are both suggestively described in the similes ('rats' feet over broken glass' suggesting a kind of painful vulnerability as well as the faint tinkle of sound) and echoed in the sibilant consonants. 'Headpiece', in the singular, is a touch which suggests the hollow men's uniformity, an effect as of 'clones'. The passage, which sets the metrical pattern for the poem as a whole, gives the rhythmic equivalent of the 'Paralysed force, gesture without motion' described in the next lines. In fact that phrase (together with 'Shape without form, gesture without motion') describes the paradoxical effect of the whole poem, which consists both of a sense of exhaustion and of a last concentration of baffled energy, the short lines conserving a remnant of energy into a concentrated statement.

The next lines, and Part II, bring us to death's kingdoms. 'Death's other Kingdom' would seem to be that kingdom of actual death to which the living death of the hollow men is parallel, but to which they have not yet 'crossed'. 'Death's twilight kingdom' at the end of Part II (and the end of Part IV) may be some further and transcendent state (as the phrase 'that final meeting' might suggest); or it may be synonymous with the 'dream kingdom' (as the syntax would allow), a state between light and darkness, touched as if with intimations of purgatory and paradise. This latter reading gains force from the recurrence of similar imagery in *Ash-Wednesday* VI, 'The dreamcrossed twilight between birth and dying' and 'The place of solitude where three dreams cross'. And twilight in Eliot's poetry is generally evocative of states of transition between worlds, shiftings of consciousness. The distinctions are not fully clear (even with the help of recourse to Dante, as we shall see), and surely deliberately so. Rather than trying to pin down the 'kingdoms' too definitely it is probably more in keeping with the spirit of the poem to allow these various suggestions their mysterious ambiguity. But at least there is here a dream of death, which holds out the possibility of either some feared meeting with the 'eyes I dare not meet in dreams' or some transfiguration of them.

For although some kind of quasi-allegorical landscape seems to be at work behind the 'kingdoms', the poetic suggestiveness seems to derive from the thought of the 'eyes'. In his poetry Eliot has always been particularly conscious of eyes, of the power of others' looks: the 'eyes that fix you in a formulated phrase' ('Prufrock'); the eye of the woman in 'Rhapsody on a Windy Night', which 'twists like a crooked pin', and the 'child's eyes', behind which the speaker could 'see nothing'; the 'patient curious eye' of the parrot in the early poem 'On a Portrait', whose disconcerting look disrupts the dreamy atmosphere of the woman's portrait; and above all those of 'La Figlia Che Piange' whom the speaker bids 'turn / With a fugitive resentment in your eyes'. There are also the failures of the poet's own sight, as in the hyacinth garden in *The Waste Land*: 'I could not / Speak, and my eyes failed, I was neither / Living nor dead'; the memory of which gives an added point as a contrast to 'Those who have crossed / With direct eyes, to death's other Kingdom'. But in Part II of *The Hollow Men*, these disturbing or resentful or admonishing or derisive eyes, which the hollow man cannot face 'with direct eyes', become beautifully transformed and removed to a distance. There is a feeling of dispersal, the voice is drawn out by the rhyme words, and there is a mingling of sense impressions in the comparison of the 'voices' and the 'star':

> There, the eyes are
> Sunlight on a broken column
> There, is a tree swinging
> And voices are
> In the wind's singing
> More distant and more solemn
> Than a fading star.

This distance makes evasion possible, as do the 'deliberate disguises of the next verse paragraph, the 'rat's coat' and the rest of the scarecrow (or Guy) — disguises which makes us think of the various *personae* or masks of Eliot's poetry, which have enabled him to express himself obliquely, to write without direct confrontation with painful experience.

Part III has a double movement, of construction and collapse. We are back in a desert landscape like those of *The Waste Land*, but as opposed to a 'heap of broken images' there ('The Burial

of the Dead', line 22), here 'the stone images / Are raised'.
There are the beginnings of a new constructiveness, reflected too
in the curiously 'composed', pictorial quality of

> here they receive
> The supplication of a dead man's hand
> Under the twinkle of a fading star

− like some surrealist painting. But the next stanza puts a question, without a question mark, so that by the end it feels as much
like a statement.

> Is it like this
> In death's other kingdom
> Waking alone
> At the hour when we are
> Trembling with tenderness
> Lips that would kiss
> Form prayers to broken stone.

The stone images which were 'raised' are now 'broken'. It is an
intense image − personal and yet made impersonal by the context and the generalizing 'we' − of baffled passion turning to
a religious expression, but one which as yet has only the ruins
of a past tradition to appeal to.

A feeling of 'Wandering between two worlds, one dead / The
other powerless to be born' (Arnold's words are surprisingly
appropriate) continues in Part IV. This is a valley of 'dying
stars', unless a 'perpetual star' reappears. 'This broken jaw of
our lost kingdoms' is a vivid image both of arid landscape and
of the subjective feeling of impotence in the perceiver. 'We
grope together / And avoid speech' suggests either a desperate
attempt at physical intimacy (like the typist's and the clerk's in
The Waste Land) or refugees huddling together for solace.
'Sightless, unless / The eyes reappear': here in a concentrated
phrase is the idea that the hollow men's ability to see depends
on the eyes of another − they are sightless without those eyes
to see by, and sightless unless they see those eyes. 'As the
perpetual star / Multifoliate rose': the eyes reappear as
something else. The introduction of this completely new imagery
is sudden and unexpected, and, I think we must say, baffling:
we cannot simply invoke Dante to make sense of it. Or rather
we can in order to explain its provenance (discussed below), but
not to gauge its effect in the poem. As yet it seems an imagery
plucked out of the air, beautiful but mystifying. And the poem

recognizes this in 'The hope only / Of empty men' — either it is *only* hope, or it is only the hope of men who are empty, and therefore not much hope at all.

Part V (which appears to have been written last) falls away from the intense concentration of the previous parts into the parody of nursery rhyme. It is a bitter moment of desperate frivolity, preceding a passage of philosophic statement new in Eliot's verse, as if the frivolity dispels the semi-mystical atmosphere of the preceding Part, leaving the mind empty of images and ready only for pure abstractions. The 'Shadow' which falls between 'the idea / And the reality' and the rest is surely primarily (and sufficiently) the shadow of death (which is also the shadow of doubt) — whatever other literary shadows it may recall from Conrad or Dowson.[3] We have seen in the poem the 'Shadow' falling between the idea and the reality ('The eyes reappear' and 'the hope only'), the desire and the spasm ('Lips that would kiss / Form prayers to broken stone'), the motion and the act ('gesture without motion') the potency and the existence ('paralysed force') the essence and the descent ('the eyes are / Sunlight' and 'Let me be no nearer'). Now these images are concentrated into a distilled knowledge of intense but 'bloodless' categories, in counterpoint with phrases of prayer (*'For Thine is the Kingdom'*) and despair (*'Life is very long'*) which struggle against them, and which peter out in stammered fragments. The concluding lines fall back into the thin mocking jingle which opened this part. It is a conclusion of deliberate, painful bathos and banality, suggesting only the collapse of creative effort.

In a graph of Eliot's spiritual progress, *The Hollow Men* would be at the lowest point. There is as yet no new beginning after *The Waste Land* (except perhaps in the fact of its having been written at all): the new symbols of hope are fleeting and feel arbitrary and hollow. It is like a last concentration of exhausted energy. And yet this arid condition is still made into a poem; the energy is there, desperately gathered for the hollow men's chorus which at least bears witness to their condition. All this is in the poem. The allusions are secondary and do not change the picture. The 'old guy' epigraph simply reminds us of another rather different group of 'hollow men', political desperadoes, who *were* 'lost / Violent souls', and gives an added resonance to the 'dry cellar', and perhaps (though this seems to me strained) to 'Not with a bang but a whimper' (the gunpowder did not explode and Guy Fawkes was tortured). Conrad's 'Mistah Kurtz' is an exemplary hollow man and commentators have found other echoes of Heart of Darkness in the poem, but they are not necessary for either our response or our understanding.

The connection with Dante is more important, but again a knowledge of Dante does not change our primary understanding of the poem (though it can add to and deepen it). For the images of *The Divine Comedy* are echoed pervasively throughout the poem. The hollow men recall the crowd of the 'trimmers' or the 'uncommitted' on the banks of the Acheron in Canto III of the *Inferno*, who have not yet 'crossed / . . . to death's other Kingdom' (hell itself, in the *Inferno*) and who are 'gathered on the beach of this tumid river' (*The Hollow Men*, lines 13–14 and 60). The 'Multifoliate rose' of Part IV directly recalls Dante's vision of the court of heaven in the form of a Rose in the *Paradiso*, 'multifoliate' (though Dante does not use the precisely equivalent word) because of the tiers of 'petals' of the ranks of the redeemed (Canto XXX, lines 112ff. and Canto XXXI, lines 1ff.). Further, the 'eyes' of Eliot's poem recall the marked awareness of eyes and sight throughout those Cantos of the *Purgatorio* in which Dante encounters Beatrice (XXX, particularly lines 66–78, and XXXI, particularly lines 118–22). The parallels intensify the feeling that *The Hollow Men* is reaching after some experience in which a love which has failed is transformed into a spiritual awareness ('unless / The eyes reappear / As the perpetual star / Multifoliate rose'). But the critical problem is to decide *how far* Eliot has been able to incorporate – which would mean to recreate – elements of Dante's vision in his poem, and how far he is still struggling towards them. At any rate we cannot, of course, import Dante's scheme into Eliot's poem. Eliot's 'kingdoms' seems to bear some resemblance to Dante's traditional Catholic division of the afterlife into Hell, Purgatory and Heaven, but any attempt to find exact equivalents breaks down. The hollow men gathered on the bank seem to be like those on the near side of the Acheron in *Inferno* III: the 'other kingdom' to which some have 'crossed' may recall Hell itself (where prayers are futile, 'prayers to broken stone'). But the 'twilight kingdom' has elements of both the *Purgatorio* (where Dante has his 'final meeting' with Beatrice) and the *Paradiso* (where the multifoliate rose appears); and the features of the 'dream kingdom' in Part II ('the wind's singing', the 'fading star'), which have been thought to echo the imagery of *Purgatorio* XXVIII–XXIX,[4] seem to me more tenuously connected.

What we have, then, in *The Hollow Men* is not a clear allegorical scheme but the echoes and fragments of such a scheme which cannot be grasped in its fullness (the men's hollowness precludes this possibility). The elements are as much tantalizing as reassuring, and as in the final Part of the poem, the 'Shadow' falls between the 'idea' of them and the 'reality', the 'conception' of them and the 'creation'. There is a kind of progress from the condition of *The Waste Land*, in that the creative imagination, though more constricted, concentrates itself on the possibilities of a single scheme, a single source of order (rather than drawing almost randomly on wide-ranging and dispersed sources, from St Augustine to the Buddha or the *Bhagavad Gita*). But the effort to make sense of traditional wisdom and spirituality is still a struggling and, at the very end of the poem, a despairing one. In his dealings with tradition the poet's task is to give an honest rendering of his relation to it and not to impose an order from the past on personal experience which cannot authenticate that order. *The Hollow Men*, in both its aspirations and its stammered conclusion ('For thine is the . . .'), with its mocking commentary, is notable above all (like *The Waste Land*, but at a different point of the spiritual journey) for the sincerity of its effort to achieve that end.

II

The three *Ariel Poems*, 'Journey of the Magi' (1927), 'A Song for Simeon' (1928) and 'Animula' (1929), written and published between *The Hollow Men* and *Ash-Wednesday*, show a marked change of poetic style and mood. They are more discursive in manner, less 'Symbolist' and closer in their rhythms to prose than either *The Hollow Men* or *The Waste Land*. They also strike one as being written at a lower level of poetic intensity, as experiments in a deliberately flatter style. They are also the first poems written and published after Eliot's baptism and confirmation in the Anglican Church in June 1927, and show an attempt to come to poetic terms with his conversion. There is an interesting passage at the end of Eliot's essay of 1929, 'Second Thoughts About Humanism', which relates primarily to T. E. Hulme but which also seems to describe the process of Eliot's own conversion. He writes of the way in which it is often supposed that some Christians are prepared to put up with dogma because they enjoy 'the luxury of Christian sentiments and the excitement of Christian ritual'. But for some the process is the opposite of this, and rational assent and intellectual conviction, though they may come late and slowly, often precede the appropriate feelings. 'To put the sentiments in order is a later, and an immensely difficult task: intellectual freedom is earlier and easier than complete spiritual freedom' (*Selected Essays*, p. 491). One might say that these three *Ariel Poems* were part of the process for Eliot of putting 'the sentiments in order'. They are in a sense exercises, experiments in expressing a new religious state of mind by means of *personae* in the first two poems, and meditative reflection in the third. They do not strike one, I suggest, as being among Eliot's most outstanding poems (unlike the fourth Ariel poem, 'Marina'), mainly because of this lower intensity, this style of discursive low-key reflection. It was a mode which Eliot was to use again in *Four Quartets*, but there it is part of the dynamics of a long poem, where intensity (as Eliot pointed out) needs to be varied.[5]

'Journey of the Magi' adopts the *persona* of one of the magi themselves, and, beginning with a quotation from a Christmas sermon of Lancelot Andrewes (about whom Eliot had written in an essay of 1926, reprinted in *For Lancelot Andrewes*, 1928), develops an imaginary monologue about the journey to Bethlehem and the magus's reactions afterwards to the birth of Christ. The narrative is flat in tone and deliberately anticlimactic: the only comment on the discovery of Christ's birthplace is the dry understatement of 'it was (you may say) satisfactory'. The details of the journey are not espcially vivid, and the 'prophetic' elements (the 'three trees on the low sky', the hands 'dicing for pieces of silver') seem rather obvious. Eliot clearly chose the magus as a *persona* because he represented the experience of being caught 'between two worlds', of having had an intimation of faith but now being left 'No longer at ease here, in the old dispensation' – the experience of conversion without the full benefit of assured faith. The ending of the poem rises to a certain intentness of reflection with the deliberateness of

> but set down
> This set down
> This:

146

But although the poem seems to reflect (or stand as a 'correlative' for) Eliot's state of mind, as a poem it perhaps suffers from a certain lack of imaginative life. As a piece of historical evocation, one might compare it unfavourably with Browning's 'Karshish'; and Browning's poem is also more effective in its use of a historical *persona* to convey the experience of a particular attitude to Christianity.

'A Song for Simeon' (1928) also uses a figure from the Gospels as a 'correlative' of the poet's state of mind and faith. The story of Simeon is told in Luke 2: 25–35. A 'just and devout' Jew living in Jerusalem, he was told by the Holy Ghost that 'he should not see death, before he had seen the Lord's Christ'. He encounters the infant Christ in the temple to which the child has been brought for circumcision. He prophesies to Mary: 'Behold, this child is set for the fall and rising again of many in Israel; and for a sign which shall be spoken against; (Yea, a sword shall pierce through thy own soul also,) that the thoughts of many shall be revealed.' Eliot makes Simeon an old man: many of his words echo those of Gerontion, and the poem is like a recasting of Gerontion's experience in the light of faith and revelation. Gerontion's

> White feathers in the snow, the Gulf claims,
> And an old man driven by the Trades
> To a sleepy corner.

becomes

> My life is light, waiting for the death wind,
> Like a feather on the back of my hand.
> Dust in sunlight and memory in corners
> Wait for the wind that chills towards the dead land.

The image of the feather is perhaps the most delicate and finely imagined in the poem, together with the Roman hyacinths and the winter sun of the first two lines, which convey a sense of wonder and fragile new life. Otherwise the poem is characterized by a deliberately Biblical language, interwoven with actual phrases from the Gospels. Like 'Journey of the Magi', the 'Song' presents a figure to whom revelation has been granted but to whom it has come too late for this life. The magus says 'I should be glad of another death'; Simeon's life is waiting for the death wind, and his monologue closes with the words of St Luke's Gospel and the 'Nunc Dimittis': 'Let thy servant depart,

/ Having seen thy salvation'. It is striking how often Eliot's imagination projects itself into the *personae* of older men (first Prufrock, then Gerontion, and now the Magus and Simeon): it is as if the life of youth or of young middle age (Eliot was forty in 1928) was missing, or lost almost before it was there, and the poetic imagination has above all to come to terms with that loss. But 'Prufrock' and 'Gerontion' are both also acutely aware of what has been lost, and the sense of tension is partly what makes them such memorable poems. The problem with 'Journey of the Magi' and 'A Song for Simeon' is that they are poems about a state of weariness as well as self-sacrifice to faith, and it is difficult for that weariness not to be felt in the verse in a way that qualifies the sense of creative activity. Their reliance on Biblical figures (unlike the invented figures of Prufrock and Gerontion) and, particularly in the case of the Song, the actual phrases of the Bible, is also problematic. Is Eliot simply falling back on a traditional language in the absence of fresher and more original poetic inspiration? Is the dialogue between 'tradition' and 'the individual talent' (or 'making it new', in Pound's phrase) too much weighted towards the former? But these questions are also involved with the 'problem of belief' in Eliot's religious verse (briefly, how far does the reader's appreciation of these poems depend on his or her own beliefs?), and we shall return to them in discussing *Ash-Wednesday* and in the next chapter.

'Animula' (1929), the third Ariel poem, is Latin for 'little soul', and Eliot perhaps took it from the first line of a poem by the Roman Emperor Hadrian, 'Animula vagula blandula' ('Little soul − fleeting away and charming'). It is itself a charming title for a poem much of which is about childhood, and also one which carries, as it turns out, a moral judgement which is revealed in the last part of the poem (beginning 'Issues from the hand of time . . .'). The details of childhood are pleasantly observed but with no great imaginative life or vividness of language. (One wonders about the appropriateness of 'a *flat* world'; and 'the pain of living and the drug of dreams' is hackneyed, though improved by the line that follows. In particular one wonders why 'dreams' should be so glibly disparaged, since Eliot elsewhere so often finds a positive value in them.) The rhythm is ponderously meditative, a semi-regular iambic pentameter, and a little bit like the prose of an old-fashioned *Times* leader. There are touches of ironic juxtaposition

('Content with playing cards and kings and queens'), and, for the reader today, of 'period' charm in 'What the fairies do and what the servants say'. On the whole, though, it is a somewhat distant picture described in the tones of a patronizing middle age. But it is something to have caught at least a hint of the quality of childhood in a poem whose real point and moral comes at the end. After childhood (lines 1–15) and adolescence (lines 16–23) comes adulthood. 'Issues from the hand of God the simple soul' – of the child. (The line is a quotation from Dante, *Purgatorio* XVI, 85–8, in which with a briefer and perhaps less laboured charm Dante imagines the soul 'a guisa di fanciulla / Che piangendo e ridendo pargoleggia': 'like a little girl who plays crying and laughing'). But 'Issues from the hand of *time* the simple soul',

> Irresolute and selfish, misshapen, lame,
> Unable to fare forward or retreat,
> Fearing the warm reality, the offered good,
> Denying the importunity of the blood,

(contrasting with the child's 'Advancing boldly . . . / Retreating . . .'). And the last line of the verse-paragraph comes with a sobering force:

> Living first in the silence after the viaticum.

The viaticum is the last sacrament of communion given to the dying: as in the first two Ariel poems, real life for Eliot, at this time, seems to have consisted only in the consciousness at a point just before death. The last verse-paragraph, a brief prayer, recalls 'Gerontion' again with its fictitious names; and Boudin 'blown to pieces' recalls in particular the 'fractured atoms' of 'De Bailhache, Fresca, Mrs. Cammel'. The world of power, violence and success is briefly conjured, and then (rather quaintly, perhaps, and according to Eliot without any specific allusion)[6] a legendary world, medieval or classical (Adonis or Actaeon), is suggested in 'Floret, by the boarhound slain between the yew trees'. The last line, 'Pray for us now and at the hour of our birth' clinches, with a nice effect of surprise, the moral meaning of the poem with the double suggestion that we need prayer at our birth because life is more dangerous to us than death, and that we need prayer to assist at our rebirth (or real birth) into religious consciousness.

III

The three Ariel poems discussed above are experimenting in new stylistic modes, and expressing obliquely a religious faith newly acquired and yet uneasily held, experienced with something of a sense of anti-climax. And yet their obliqueness and their predominant feeling of weariness leads to a rather dulled poetic effect. *Ash-Wednesday* is altogether more striking as a development. It is still a poem of obliquities and of exploration – indeed more explicitly so. There may in fact have been something as yet slightly evasive and 'hypothetical' about the first two Ariel poems, with their assumption of traditional Biblical figures as *personae*. How close, finally, was Eliot's experience to that of the Magus or Simeon, who had been granted unique and miraculous revelations? *Ash-Wednesday* speaks instead in the first person, and this may be the most important element in the development it represents. In the earlier poems the 'I' of the poet only appears in one or two notable instances like 'La Figlia Che Piange', and in certain central moments in *The Waste Land* (where it is also, however, at times amalgamated with Tiresias or Ferdinand Prince of Naples). But here at the opening of *Ash-Wednesday* is Eliot speaking, or meditating, in his own person:

> Because I do not hope to turn again
> Because I do not hope
> Because I do not hope to turn
> Desiring this man's gift and that man's scope
> I no longer strive to strive towards such things
> (Why should the agèd eagle stretch its wings?)
> Why should I mourn
> The vanished power of the usual reign?

There is still a touch of the old 'self-masking' habit in the parenthesis – the pose of being an old man (Eliot was only forty when Part I was published, separately, in 1928). But one should probably see the line partly as a self-mocking joke, which the imperial connotation of the eagle intensifies; and generally the note struck is that of straightforward, intimate self-communion.

The other major new element is the style, part meditative, part incantatory. The style may have been influenced by the prose of Lancelot Andrewes, whom Eliot praised for his 'ordonnance, or arrangement and structure, precision in the use of words, and relevant intensity'. 'Ordonnance' one finds in Eliot's finely controlled long second sentence which runs from line 9 to line 23, withholding the first of the main verbs for emphatic effect until line 20, and 'precision in the use of words' in 'veritable', which means both 'real' and 'rightly so called' — earthly love is the one 'power' rightly so called ('transitory' coming as a sad, necessary, opposite term after 'veritable'). Eliot also quotes Canon Brightman on Andrewes: 'Every line tells and adds something. He does not expatiate but moves forward: if he repeats it is because the repetition has a real force of expression; if he accumulates, each new word or phrase represents a new development, a substantive addition to what he is saying.'[7] So in the first three lines of *Ash-Wednesday* the repetition with variation is not only incantatory (inducing a liturgical feeling) but also functional for meaning: 'Turn again' means turn back; the second line suggests a more fundamental, inclusive 'hopelessness'; the third perhaps the thought that the speaker does not hope even to turn *to* anything new, including, at this stage, faith, which has, as we discover, to be 'constructed' (line 24) and not just 'turned to'. The repetition in 'strive to strive' is also precision: the condition of real striving had never even been reached.

The effect of the whole is of a deliberative meditation which is also incantation — which employs the resources of rhythm and rhyme to create a musical movement, allowing an emotional accommodation to the moral renunciation which is being made. The shorter lines often embody a thought checked by its finality, or by the need to revise it, the longer lines and more expansive rhythms and rhymes a more elegiac feeling of regret for the beauty that has been lost — as in this passage, where the first two lines both affirm a cessation of thought and revise 'think' to 'know', and the penultimate line has a bluntness which is softened to elegy by the unexpected flow into the next line:

Because I do not think
Because I know I shall not know
The one veritable transitory power
Because I cannot drink
There, where trees flower, and springs flow, for there is nothing again

The syntax, rhythm and rhyme look constantly forward, the repeated 'Because' leading one on to the main clause, and the rhymes often coming in mid line ('power' / 'flower'; 'voice /

rejoice') so that we linger on them less. The 'having to construct something' is thus embodied in the verse.

What is renounced is earthly love and happiness. 'The infirm glory of the positive hour' has echoes of Wordsworth's 'hour / Of splendour in the grass / And glory in the flower' and Shakespeare's 'O how this spring of love resembleth / The uncertain glory of an April day'. And the imagery of 'drink / There where trees flower, and springs flow' has associations with human as well as natural fertility, not least from their constant association in Eliot's previous poetry. 'Time' and 'place' and the 'actual' concentrate in abstractions those preoccupations with particularities in Eliot's earlier poetry ('Under the brown fog of a winter noon / A crowd flowed over London Bridge'), and make those particularities bearable by finding them 'actual only for one time / And only for one place' instead of generally representative. And 'the blessèd face' is surely the face of the 'Eyes I dare not meet in dreams' in *The Hollow Men* (which were the eyes of 'fugitive resentment' in 'La Figlia Che Piange'), and the 'voice' one of those which in 'death's dream kingdom' was 'in the wind's singing'. But these associations are not indispensable for understanding, and may be pressed too far. The 'blessèd face' carries its own significance, and criticism needs to take warning from the subsequent lines about 'These matters that with myself I too much discuss / Too much explain' (and indeed from 'Teach us to sit still') and to give due weight to the self-clarifying movement of the whole. Nevertheless it is worth stressing that the argument is important in the poem — though it is not directed at persuading the *reader* — and that the poem could not be further from the 'beautiful gibberish' which was all that one early critic found in it.[8]

The poem is partly an argument directed at the speaker himself (a meditation), but even more than that it is a prayer, or at least repeatedly cast in the form of a prayer. It is a 'performative utterance' (to use Austin's suggestive term), an utterance which is more an action than a statement: 'And I pray that I may forget . . .'. In Part II of the poem the description of the leopards and the bones is not *merely* a description — it is a description addressed or offered to the Lady: 'Lady, three white leopards . . .' And the song of the bones is of course a kind of liturgical chant, like the Roman Catholic Litany to the Virgin Mary. Part III ends with the words of the Centurion to Christ in Matthew 8:8: 'Lord I am not worthy / but speak the word only', and Part IV with the ambiguous line 'And after this our exile', which suggests as it stands 'And after this will come our exile' but which also quotes from the Catholic prayer to Mary, 'And after this our exile show us the fruit of thy womb Jesus'. It is one of those points in the poem when we must be equally alert to surface meaning and to possible quotation or association, for it exemplifies the tension in the poem between what can be said sincerely by the poet and the implications of quotation from traditional sources of scripture and liturgy. The completed quotation is a prayer to the Virgin; the half-quotation has an ambiguous status between prayer and a promise of further suffering. The poet is concerned above all to show how traditional belief and traditional forms of language can be 'lived' (in Eliot's phrase in his essay 'Poetry and Propaganda')[9] — how they can be 'made our own'; and sometimes he has to demonstrate only a half-success, or an ambiguous fusion of the personal and the traditional.

A recurring instance of this ambiguity, which is central to the undertaking of the whole poem, is the double relation between 'the word' and 'the Word', between the poet's creativity and the Word of God. We have partially encountered this already in 'Gerontion', 'The word within a word, unable to speak a word, / Swaddled with darkness', which is mainly the *Verbum Infans*, the 'Infant Word' of Andrewes's Christmas sermon of 1618 (which the other phrases echo) but also the 'word' of the poet's unrealized speech. So at the end of Part III of *Ash-Wednesday*, the centurion's words to Christ in Matthew 8:8 are used by the poet to pray for God to 'speak the word only', to reassure him in his faith, but also more specifically to 'speak the word' in his poetry. At the end of Part IV the bird 'sang down':

> Redeem the time, redeem the dream
> The token of the word, unheard, unspoken

— which is again the Word of St John's Gospel ('In the beginning was the Word') but also on another level the unspoken word of the poet's inspiration. In Part V the mesmerizing verbal play of the opening is not just an exercise in sound effects but relates the 'lost' or 'spent' or 'unspoken' word of the poet to 'the Word unheard' and 'The Word without a word' of God. Later in Part V (line 22) the poet is 'torn on the horn' between 'word and word', both in the ordinary struggle of composition and the more particular struggle of material word against spiritual Word. The poet's 'devoted, concentrated . . . purpose' is to let God's Word speak through his word. But at the same time this is possible only if a more humble, primary aim is realized – to compose his own mind and feelings in the light of God's will. So the poet must listen as much as speak, listen to the other voices in the poem, to the song of the bones in Part II, to the figures 'going in white and blue, in Mary's colour' in Part IV, the veiled sister in Part V (whom we do not hear but whose prayers are prayed for), to the voice of Christ in the refrain of Part V ('O my people, what have I done unto thee' – from Micah 6:3, and given to Christ in the 'Reproaches', a part of the Roman Catholic Mass for Good Friday), and to the 'whispers' and 'voices' from the yew trees in Parts IV and VI. (In the case of Christ's words, however, there is again, perhaps, an ambiguity: undifferentiated as it is from the poet's words except by linear separation, it might be read at first as spoken by the poet. Would it be too strained a reading to see this as also the poet speaking to his audience and repenting his former influence? As another instance of a tension between poetic surface and allusion, between personal utterance and traditional meaning?)

To turn to another aspect of the poem: the yew trees mentioned above are one instance of a further new element in Eliot's art in this poem, the use of allegory or seeming allegory. It might indeed be better to call this symbolism, if one accepts the distinction between allegory, in which precise concrete equivalents are given for abstract ideas or qualities, and symbolism, where there is less precise denotation and more suggestiveness, and where the symbol seems to partake of or to contain the quality it represents, as opposed to just 'standing for' it. One of the most notable instances is the striking vision of the 'three white Leopards' in Part II. They seem like beasts from some moral bestiary, and have Dantesque echoes, but there is no allegorical meaning to pin down. Their role in the poem is self-explanatory: they represent – and indeed are – a power, both dangerous and beautiful (one might remember 'Christ the tiger' in 'Gerontion'), which destroys the physical body. The whole passage, with the curious, almost quaint, 'chirping' of the bones, is an extraordinary vision, like some Indian or oriental pictorial allegory, of physical death made peaceful and beautiful. The bones have a kind of innocence and bird-like (or insect-like) charm which is both grotesque and convincing (bolder even than

Yeats's striking 'unless / Soul clap its hands and sing'). The desert imagery of *The Waste Land* and *The Hollow Men* is not abandoned for images of fertility and rebirth, but transformed into a positive symbol. Aridity is perceived as something spiritually and indeed physically satisfying. It is a masterly stroke to be able to imagine (recalling Genesis) 'the cool of the day' in the desert, the 'blessing of sand' and 'the quiet of the desert'. There is a varied wit in this Part too, which is there in the very light irony of '(which were already dry)' and 'chirping' (irony because it seems to recognize and allow for the element of quaintness and absurdity), and which helps to produce this fusion of opposing qualities – the dry cool beauty and the un-compromising listing of 'My guts the strings of my eyes and the indigestible portions / leopards reject'. For the first time in Eliot's poetry death is seen in a positive way, and not only as mere release (as in 'Death by Water').

A full consideration of this passage takes us well beyond con-siderations only of allegory and symbolism, but the *air* of allegory and the broader symbolic suggestions play their part. The Rose of the central passage of Part II also has allegorical overtones (the Virgin Mary is a Rose in the Litany, the Rose is a symbol of Christ's passion) but its meaning is primarily ex-plained in the poem: 'Rose of memory / Rose of Forgetfulness' is cryptic, but clearly relates to the preoccupation with the right and wrong uses of memory and forgetfulness in the poem as a whole and in other poems. (Compare 'Let the whiteness of bones atone to forgetfulness' in Part II, and the destructive memories that have to be left behind and the ambiguously distracting yet strengthening memory of the pasture scene in Part III, and also Part III of 'Little Gidding', 'This is the use of memory . . .') The Rose also becomes 'the Garden / Where all loves end' (cease, *and* find their culmination) – recalling Eden, but also there in the poem in Part IV. But allegorical precision is not part of the effect: there is no final way of saying, for instance, whether the Lady of Silences (who is the Rose) is the Virgin Mary herself, or still the Lady who is addressed in the first section (who 'honours the Virgin').

Part III of the poem has an even fuller semblance of allegory, but again it is semblance rather than the fully schematized thing itself. The turnings and the stairs recall Dante's *Purgatorio*, but the image of spiritual ascent is self-explanatory enough. Eliot indeed removed the more explicit pointer to *Purgatorio* XXVI (the Canto in which Dante meets the poet Arnaut Daniel who is suffering for the sin of lust) by removing the original title to this Part, 'Al som de l'escalina', in the final published version of the complete poem. It is the 'surface' that is vivid; 'the same shape twisted on the banister', the stair 'Damp, jagged, like an old man's mouth drivelling, beyond repair / Or the toothed gullet of an aged shark' (Eliot was drawn to this particular image of decay – we may recall the 'Dead mountain mouth of carious teeth that cannot spit' in 'What the Thunder Said', and 'This broken jaw of our lost kingdoms' in *The Hollow Men*, IV). The whole of this Part is a striking imaging of spiritual ascent and a struggle with the past and memory (in 'A Game of Chess', 'Footsteps shuffled on the stair'), and with hope (compare Part I, 'Although I do not hope', and 'East Coker' III: 'Wait without hope / For hope would be hope for the wrong thing').

The most beautiful and enigmatic passage in this struggle with memory comes in the third verse-paragraph of Part III. The 'slotted window bellied like the fig's fruit' is satisfyingly physical (there is no recoil from the senses) and the 'pasture scene' has a picturesque and fairy-tale quality, the 'antique flute' also recalling Pan and his pagan energies. There is a surprising parallel here with the painting in 'A Game of Chess', 'As though a window gave upon the sylvan scene' (line 98), as if the image of violence and unhappiness which that picture involved were here recast and transformed into an image of sweetness and enchantment. And the evocation of

> Blown hair is sweet, brown hair over the mouth blown,
> Lilac and brown hair;

also recalls those earlier images of love in 'La Figlia Che Piange' ('Her hair over her arms and her arms full of flowers'), the lilacs of 'Portrait of a Lady' and the opening of *The Waste Land* and the hyacinth garden later in 'The Burial of the Dead' ('Yet when we come back, late, from the hyacinth garden, / Your arms full, and your hair wet, I could not / Speak . . .'). These memories prompt a lyrical rhythmic flow, an accession of positive feeling, which is at the same time 'distraction'. The memories of beauty both distract and aid the spiritual ascent, with a fine ambiguity caught in the delicate hesitating movement and the ambivalence of 'stops and steps' – where the stops are both hindrances and the stops on a flute, sounding a music which both hesitates and

carries forward on the upward progress, a music both fading
and yet providing a kind of strength:

Distraction, music of the flute, stops and steps of the mind over the
    third stair,
Fading, fading; strength beyond hope and despair
Climbing the third stair.

It is a fine example of the whole movement of Eliot's mind in
the poetry of his middle and later periods — a movement which
continually looks to the past, yet not so much with nostalgia or
with regret as with a regathering and reassessment of past experience and imagery and a recasting of it into a new pattern. An
observation by Eliot on the poems of Yeats's later period comes
to mind: 'The interesting feelings of age are not just different
feelings; they are the feelings into which the feelings of youth are
integrated' (*On Poetry and Poets*, p. 259).

    The life of *Ash-Wednesday* lies in the tension generated by
this attempt to integrate the memories of past feeling with the
movement towards a kind of asceticism and spiritual purification. In Part IV we have the picture of the nun-like 'silent sister
veiled in white and blue', perhaps the same figure as (and certainly recalling) the Lady of Part II. The sensuous imagery is
refined and delicate, with cool colours associated with religious
paintings of the Virgin — violet, green, 'blue of Mary's colour'
— and with touches of a Dantesque imagery of light ('White
light folded, sheathed about her, folded'). But there are also still
echoes of earlier experience, for example in:

      The new years walk, restoring
      Through a bright cloud of tears, the years, restoring
      With a new verse the ancient rhyme. Redeem
      The time.

The 'bright cloud of tears' recalls again 'La Figlia Che Piange'
— the 'Eyes that last I saw in tears' — as well as suggesting the
poet's tears (a double reference which was also present in *The
Hollow Men*, who were 'Sightless, unless / The eyes reappear');
and it suggests again the progress of an originating image, from
La Figlia to the Lady or sister of *Ash-Wednesday*. The 'ancient
rhyme' here is therefore both the language of Christian tradition
and the former rhyme of the poet's own work. And 'Redeem /
the time' suggests both the Pauline sense of 'make good use of
the time' (see e.g. Colossians 4:5) and the more personal sense

of 'recall and save past time, past experience'. If *Ash-Wednesday* is about renunciation, it is a renunciation that salvages and transfigures nature rather than abandons it. The 'flute' of the 'garden god' (with its suggestion of Pan) is 'breathless'; and yet at the sign from the veiled sister 'the fountain sprang up and the bird sang down'.

But in the poem as a whole there is no easy resolution or conclusion, and it is the tension of a continuing struggle that should be stressed – the prayer sought for 'Those who are torn on the horn between season and season, time and time, between / Hour and hour, word and word, power and power'. The incantatory rhyme and rhythm registers the tension and yet also effects a therapeutic easing of the mind, leading it beyond the over-insistent demands of 'explanation' and false knowledge ('spitting from the mouth the withered apple seed' at the end of V, recalling the apple of the Tree of Knowledge). And the concluding Part VI registers this tension more sharply still. The 'Because I do not hope . . .' of Part I, which was a prelude to an act of rejoicing and renunciation, is replaced by 'Although I do not hope . . .', a prelude to an evocation of how the past still wells up in the mind and imagination. This welling up is ostensibly – in the light of certain admonitory words – a negative force, disconcerting the spiritual powers, pulling back. 'The lost heart stiffens', suggesting stubbornness as well as vitality (in the Old Testament the Jews are a 'stiff-necked' people); and the heart is 'lost' in more than one sense; the 'weak spirit' rebels; the 'blind eye' creates 'empty' forms between 'the ivory gates' (which were the gates in the underworld, in Homer and Virgil, through which *false* dreams passed). And yet in the passage as a whole the feeling of vitality cannot be gainsaid and has a positive force which gives especial intensity to the verse:

>   though I do not wish to wish these things
> From the wide window towards the granite shore
> The white sails still fly seaward, seaward flying
> Unbroken wings
>
> And the lost heart stiffens and rejoices
> In the lost lilac and the lost sea voices
> And the weak spirit quickens to rebel
> For the bent golden-rod and the lost sea smell
> Quickens to recover

The cry of quail and the whirling plover
And the blind eye creates
The empty forms between the ivory gates
And smell renews the salt savour of the sandy earth

Despite the fact that these things are distractions and are not 'wished', they cannot be felt, in the verse as a whole, to be entirely negative. Despite the ascetic aim of the spiritual man, the poet cannot help living in the world and responding to its beauty. As the beginning of the next verse-paragraph confirms: 'This is the time of tension . . .' And the final prayer to the 'Blessèd sister' is a prayer to be taught 'to care and not to care' for these things. 'Suffer me not to be separated' — from the sister and mother, from God but also surely from the self (in one sense), and from the past (pulled apart by the 'tension'), from the experience which makes the integrity of the whole man. Once again the sense of this line as a quotation from (we are told)[10] the Roman Catholic hymn 'Anima Christi' ('The Soul of Christ') needs to be balanced against the possible sense of the line in its immediate context. And indeed the two senses may not be finally separable; the image of lady, sister and mother in the poem is as much the transformation of earlier images of women (as we have seen in various echoes in the poem) as it is of a new discovery. Without a living sense of the human experience the religious experience will lack body, the word will not be made flesh.

Ash-Wednesday is remarkable in its new departures and its transfigurations of the earlier verse, in its new rhythms, both incantatory and discursive, and in its attempt to rediscover and revitalize the traditional language of the Bible and the liturgy. But a critical question remains, as to whether the work does not rely too heavily on traditional quotation and whether all the allegorical (or quasi-allegorical) and mystical elements are entirely integrated with the rest. The line which ends the fourth verse-paragraph of Part IV, 'While jewelled unicorns draw by the gilded hearse', is beautiful, but arbitrary and fanciful, signifying nothing beyond itself. (It will not do simply to invoke Beatrice's chariot drawn by the griffin in *Purgatorio* XXIX: Eliot may have been influenced by the memory of this, but Dante's image has a clear allegorical meaning, unlike Eliot's, and griffins and unicorns, chariots and hearses are not interchangeable unless one wants only vague effect of the mysterious!) Similarly the two yew trees in Parts IV and VI seem to have a symbolic meaning: one of them is easily and traditionally associated with death; but the other can be only associated with resurrection by the hopeful inference of the reader (perhaps with very distant help — but not much — from the two apple trees in *Purgatorio* XXII and XXIV, the first of which is identified, doubtfully, by the commentators as the Tree of Life in Eden and the second, with more assurance, as the forbidden Tree of Knowledge). It seems that Eliot is experimenting with a mystical imagery some of which remains mysterious and private and gives the air of meaning rather than meaning itself.[11] In some ways he is still in the position of the poet in *The Waste Land*, who moves among images whose significance may be lost and irrecoverable. And yet the air of purpose and 'having to construct something' makes one feel that the images here are being used differently, and sometimes to give substance to a conviction and a structure of meaning which they are not in fact fully able to support.

But it might be wise to adduce at this point the *caveat* which Eliot offered in the first lecture in *The Use of Poetry and the Use of Criticism* (1933). He said that if *Ash-Wednesday* ever ran to a second edition he had thought of prefixing to it Byron's lines from *Don Juan*:

> Some have accused me of a strange design
>   Against the creed and morals of this land
> And trace it in this poem, every line.
>   I don't pretend that I quite understand
> My own meaning when I would be *very* fine;
>   But the fact is I have nothing planned
> Except perhaps to be a moment merry . . .

I have not been able to discover any reviews of the poem which did accuse Eliot of a 'strange design' (these accusations seem to have come rather in reviews of *For Lancelot Andrews*, 1928), and 'a moment merry' is a good joke (if *Ash-Wednesday* was the result of a plan to be merry one wonders what would have been the result of a plan to be sad and serious) — but the confession about meaning is worth noting. Like other of Eliot's poems, *Ash-Wednesday* is not well served by over-interpretation.

Finally, what of the status of the poem in relation to Eliot's other major work after his 'conversion', *Four Quartets*? No one, I think, would dispute the superiority of the latter poems, but it might be worth reflecting on the reasons. One would seem to be that in *Ash-Wednesday* Eliot is to some extent a 'religious' or 'devotional' poet, in the sense that Eliot defines in his essay 'Religion and Literature' (1935):

> For the great majority of people who love poetry, '*religious* poetry' is a variety of *minor* poetry: the religious poet is not a poet who is treating the whole subject matter of poetry in a religious spirit, but a poet who is dealing with a confined part of this subject matter: who is leaving out what men consider their major passions, and thereby confessing his ignorance of them. (*Selected Essays*, p. 390)

In a letter to W. F. Stead of 9 August 1930 Eliot argued on the other hand that in *Ash-Wednesday* he was trying to explore a field 'between the usual subjects of poetry and "devotional" verse – the experience of a man in search of God, and trying to explain to himself his intenser human feelings in terms of the divine goal'. This is a good description of *Ash-Wednesday*; as we have seen, Eliot does not entirely leave out his 'major' (or other) passions but tries in the poem to show the tension between them and the religious aspiration. But such a description would also be true of a 'devotional' poet like Herbert, in a poem like 'Affliction'. And when so much of the poem is cast in the form of prayer, when so much of it relies on quotations of traditional religious sources and echoes of Dante, we feel that it can be justly described as 'devotional'. At any rate, each of the *Four Quartets* succeeds in relating wider areas of experience to perceptions which could in a fundamental sense of the word be called religious. And these perceptions are themselves imagined with a more radical originality – involving what D. W. Harding has called 'the creation of concepts'[12] – and without such a reliance on traditional forms.

IV

The last of the *Ariel Poems*, 'Marina' (1930), is a genuine culmination of Eliot's poetic progress since *The Hollow Men*, and perhaps the finest poem of Eliot's middle period. And its success seems to come from its closeness to the springs of Eliot's personal feelings. In it we see a resurgence of the imagery of the poet's childhood, and above all a reconciliation with human relationship which is also the condition of an awareness of 'a world of time beyond me'. Unlike 'Journey of the Magi', 'A Song for Simeon' or *Ash-Wednesday* it does not rely on any traditional religious language or allusion, and this (I suggest) is a mark of its radical creativity. It does, of course, contain allusion – above all to Shakespeare's *Pericles*, which provides its title and part of the inspiration for its sea imagery and its subject, recognition and reconciliation, and also in its epigraph to Seneca's *Hercules Furens* ('What is this place, what region, what shore of the world?'). But an understanding response to the poem does not depend on a recognition of these 'sources', and the language of the poem (unlike *Ash-Wednesday*'s reliance on Bible and liturgy) does not draw directly on Shakespeare or Seneca, but effects a completely new expression which echoes mainly the imagery of Eliot's own earlier poems.

The opening lines are rapt and expansive – the feeling is as much one of wonder as of questioning (there is no question-mark as there is in the Senecan epigraph):

> What seas what shores what grey rocks and what islands
> What water lapping the bow
> And scent of pine and the woodthrush singing through the fog
> What images return
> O my daughter

The images that 'return' live independently in the poem in the tone of wonder and rediscovery with which they are uttered. But they gain an added association if we recall the 'water-dripping song' from Part V of *The Waste Land* and the intensity of the imagined 'sound of water over a rock / Where the hermit thrush sings in the pine trees'. The refreshment which could only be imagined there ('But there is no water') here becomes real. Once again, Eliot gathers up an image or memory from the past (ultimately from the New England coast of his childhood) and transforms it, in a new symbolic and dramatic context. The context is dramatic because this is a monologue addressed to 'my daughter'. But although the daughter is 'Marina' it seems misleading to refer to the speaker as Pericles: the details of the poem do not otherwise recall Pericles; the speaker is 'the poet', whose identity is not quite that of Pericles or T. S. Eliot but is unique to the poem. The poem (to use a worn but indispensable phrase) 'creates its own world', which is self-contained and self-explanatory; and only secondarily echoes or points to the larger worlds of Eliot's poetry as a whole, the literary tradition and the world of personal experience (Eliot's and ours).

The insistent and admonitory passage that follows characterizes the sins of anger (or cynicism), pride, sloth and lust in vivid concrete images. But the sermon-like or prophetic tone is not there primarily for its own sake (for the sake of denunciation) but as a part of the emotional drama of the poem: all these things, in the extended syntax of the sentence

> Are become unsubstantial, reduced by a wind,
> A breath of pine, and the woodsong fog
> By this grace dissolved in place

Sin and death 'become unsubstantial', but so does the tone of the moralist's anger: *its* bitterness is also dissolved in the poem. And what dissolves it and the other things are, significantly, sensations of sound and smell, rather than of sight, just as the images of the opening lines were those of 'water lapping', 'scent of pine' and 'woodthrush singing'. The imagery of Eliot's early poems is predominantly, even insistently, visual ('in the lamplight downed with light brown hair', 'Stand on the highest pavement of the stair', 'Slowly twisting the lilac stalks', 'Those are pearls that were his eyes, Look!' 'White bodies naked on the low damp ground'). The visual surface is importunate and usually disturbing. Now the other senses are called in (or more accurately, rise to consciousness) to counter this importunacy and evoke a more intimate awareness. (In a similar way Wordsworth spoke of the 'despotism of the eye' and how the poetic imagination conjures up different senses 'to counteract each other').[13]

This deeper and more intimate awareness is continued in the next lines:

> What is this face, less clear and clearer
> The pulse in the arm, less strong and stronger −
> Given or lent? more distant than the stars and nearer than the eye
>
> Whispers and small laughter between leaves and hurrying feet
> Under sleep, where all the waters meet.

The face, I think one can say, of 'fugitive resentment', of the 'eyes I dare not meet in dreams', here becomes less clear in a visual sense but clearer in other ways (emotionally and spiritually); and 'the pulse in the arm' does not have the pulsing insistence of feeling of earlier experiences, of the rhythm of 'Compelled my imagination many days, many days and many hours / Her hair over her arms and her arms full of flowers' or the passion of 'My friend, blood shaking my heart', but a quieter more telling pulse, 'less strong and stronger'. Possession of this face is beside the point ('Given or lent?'), and the image of 'stars' and 'eye' recalls *The Hollow Men* Part II, where in dreams 'the eyes are / Sunlight on a fallen column' and 'voices are / . . . More distant and more solemn / Than a fading star'. The line here, 'more distant than stars and nearer than the eye', captures just the mysterious combination of intimacy and distance (or, one might say, personality and impersonality) which is the condition of the new sense of relationship. The 'whispers and small laughter between leaves and hurrying feet' also evoke sounds, this time of childhood, rising from a buried dream-world or unconscious ('under sleep'), an echo of innocent relationship which looks forward to 'Burnt Norton' ('for the leaves were full of children, / Hidden excitedly, containing laughter'). The passage evokes a miraculous sense of the return of a profound yet mysterious human relationship.

The passage that follows seems to involve a symbol of the poet's 'craft', the double sense of which is implicit. It is as if the poet turns to this clear, concrete, objective image almost with relief after the half-tangible and half-impalpable qualities he has been evoking. 'Bowsprit cracked with ice and paint cracked with heat': we are not, of course, aware first of all of the analogy, but of the object, and this is a necessary part of the effect (just as, one can imagine, the practicalities of boating were a necessary part of Eliot's experience as a boy on the New England coast, as well as the awareness of the 'breath of pine' and the 'woodsong fog'). The passage alternates between the suggestive intimation of meanings on the edge of consciousness and the solid sense of practicalities. The spiritual state is impalpable but still a firm possession; the craft is all too fallible:

> Made this unknowing, half conscious, unknown, my own.
> The garboard strake leaks, the seams need caulking.

It is as if, in this strangely effective use of technical language, the poet turns almost gruffly from the indeterminate nature of the experience to the hard, satisfying technicalities of this craft. The boat becomes a symbol of the whole process of 'making' ('I have made this'), of the ambition expressed in *Ash-Wednesday*, 'having to construct something / Upon which to rejoice'. The concluding lines of this penultimate section seem to have a double reference, both to the girl of the title and to 'this unknowing, half conscious, unknown' of two lines before:

> This form, this face, this life
> Living to live in a world of time beyond me;

The visual memory of 'this face' is put into perspective by being placed between the less visual 'this form' and 'this life'. And in its syntactic relation to 'this . . . unknown', 'this form' would seem to be also the 'form' of the poem, so that it is to the poem as well as to Marina that the poet wishes to 'Resign my life' (and in a sense they are both the same thing, since Marina does not exist outside the poem), his 'speech' to the 'unspoken' speech of the poem, and also the unspoken speech of poems to come (his own and others),

> The awakened, lips parted, the hope, the new ships.

But one does not want to complicate the general sense of wonder and anticipation in these lines with too specific a set of associations. All these significances (together no doubt with others) are, I suggest, playing within the lines; but the feeling of awakening, of the breath caught in wonder or drawn for speech ('lips parted'), is there in the exultant accumulation of phrases, in the rhythm, music and surface meaning. The concluding lines repeat the opening with slight changes. The woodthrush is 'calling' through the fog (with a new sense of urgency – and perhaps calling 'My daughter'), and the new 'granite' islands towards 'my timbers' we have a note which, it has been suggested, is slightly ominous, a hint of shipwreck. But the hint seems slight, and it is surely going too far to suggest that 'We are not yet, apparently, out of the world of 'Journey of the Magi', where birth feels more than a little like death'.[14] The note of hope and anticipation at the end of the previous verse-paragraph has been so marked, and the 'dissolution' of the deadly sins so finely effected earlier in the poem, that we surely feel this poem represents a new state of mind, and a new achievement beyond that of the other Ariel Poems and *Ash-Wednesday*. It is true that there is one other dark note in the poem which is difficult to explain. The epigraph from *Hercules Furens* is the outburst of Hercules in that play when he recovers from his attack of madness to discover that he has killed his wife and children, and Eliot said in a letter: 'I intended a criss-cross between Pericles finding alive and Hercules finding dead – the two extremes of the recognition scene.'[15] But it is not easy to see what this 'criss-cross' adds, beyond an ironic allusion (for one or two very erudite readers of Seneca's Latin) which simply comments on the poem by way of contrast — the horrifying and tragic recognition being simply that which has been escaped or avoided. There is no other note of tragedy in the poem, and one cannot help feeling that the Senecan epigraph is an intrusion (though its questions seem to provide the pattern for Eliot's opening and suggest some mysterious alchemy of poetic imagination whereby these tragic accents are turned to the account of hope and new life).[16]

What is most notable is that the poem achieves a sense of renewed life without the help of specifically religious language (except in the 'sermon' passage and the word 'grace'). And the importance of the virtual absence of religious language lies in the fact that the strongest elements in the future development of Eliot's poetry were not, I suggest, his use of traditional religious language and the expression of orthodox Christian belief, but those which continued his effort to come to terms with his past and the problems of human life and history. This is not to deny, of course, that the attempt to create a new awareness of the transcendent is a central element in *Four Quartets*; but it is to suggest that what is most successful in that work is its creation of a new language for experience 'out of time', a language which draws its strength from Eliot's experience as a whole.

8

Poetry, pattern and belief

I

Between the publication of *The Hollow Men* (1925) and that of 'Burnt Norton' (1936) Eliot's thinking about poetry, as well as his own poetic style, underwent some radical changes and developments; and the changes in the style are so closely linked to the critical thinking that it is illuminating to consider these changes and developments in the criticism in relation to the poems. We can identify three main areas of critical thinking which are particularly relevant to the poetry after 1925: the consideration of the qualities of good verse, with a particular consideration of the virtues of prose qualities in verse on one hand, and on the other those qualities of music and symbolism which take verse to an opposite extreme from prose; the interest in the pattern made by a poet's work as a whole (where the main examples are Shakespeare and Dante); and finally the question of the relation of poetry to philosophy and belief.

Of Eliot's poetry and poetic criticism up until 1922 and the publication of *The Waste Land*, it is fair to say that there is a widespread emphasis on values derived from Donne and the Metaphysical poets, together with those of certain French poets, in particular Laforgue. What these groups had in common (for all their differences) was a striking heterogeneity of imagery, and a tendency to 'difficulty', a need 'to force' — in Eliot's words, 'to dislocate if necessary' — language to their meaning.[1] Their emphasis was on a poetry of intense passages and images, on effects of surprise, on a frequently 'imagistic' clarity, and although Eliot denied any direct involvement with the Imagist movement itself,[2] something of their practice too emerges in his verse (particularly in the 1920 poems, as we have seen, *via* the hard clarity of Gautier). This kind of poetry lends itself particularly to effects of dissonance and fragmentation, of the kind that we see in 'Prufrock', 'Gerontion' and *The Waste Land* and *The Hollow Men*. Even though these poems are not without qualities of organization, they tend to depend on vivid glimpses, sharp juxtapositions, sudden changes of tone, and movements from sublimity to bathos, from tragedy to farce. There is little discursive argument or extended statement (although one begins to see such statement in Part V of *The Hollow Men*). Images are predominantly visual (rather than aural, tactile or olfactory) and 'literal' (that is, with their meaning contained on the 'surface' of the image itself, as in 'Her hair over her arms and her arms full of flowers' or 'White bodies naked on the low damp ground') rather than symbolic (where they also point or seem to point to a hidden significance, as in the 'Multifoliate rose' or 'the first turning of the second stair').

With *The Hollow Men*, *Ariel Poems* and *Ash-Wednesday* one sees a movement, in varying degrees, towards techniques of discursive statement on the one hand and symbolism on the other. And this corresponds to a more deliberate procedure in the poetry, a fuller attempt to order and discipline experience – in the words of *Ash-Wednesday*, 'to construct something / Upon which to rejoice' and also, through symbolism, to reach 'beyond the limits of the normal world' and to discover 'objects suitable to arouse new emotions' ('Note Sur Mallarmé et Poe', 1926).[3] Both the style of discursive statement and the Symbolist technique are extended further still in *Four Quartets* (with varying degrees of success), and so the present discussion looks back to the last chapter and forward to the next. Hugh Kenner has written that to combine in *Four Quartets* 'a Symboliste heritage with an Augustan may have been Eliot's most original act';[4] and a concern with both these modes is reflected in much of the criticism written in this period (and occasionally outside it).

Eliot's sense of the discursive possibilities of poetry appears first in his essay on Dryden of 1921, where he praises Dryden for his ability to write a poetry of 'statement': 'Swinburne was also a master of words, but Swinburne's words are all suggestions and no denotation; if they suggest nothing, it is because they suggest too much. Dryden's words, on the other hand, are precise, they state immensely, but their suggestiveness is often nothing.' After quoting the whole of Dryden's elegy upon Oldham he comments: 'From the perfection of such an elegy we cannot detract; the lack of suggestiveness is compensated by the satisfying completeness of statement' (*Selected Essays*, pp. 314–16). In his little book on Dryden of 1932, *John Dryden: The Poet, the Dramatist, the Critic*, Eliot takes the matter further, noting how Dryden 'restored English verse to the condition of speech' and how he showed 'that if verse should not stray too far from the customs of speech, so also it should not abandon too much the uses of prose' (pp. 13, 15). The effort to restore the element of speech into poetry is of course a recurring preoccupation with Eliot in his own verse and in his criticism, where he finds the quality variously in Donne, in certain Jacobean dramatists (most notably Middleton and Tourneur), in Laforgue and (more conventionally but with equal justice) in Wordsworth (in *The Use of Poetry and the Use of Criticism*, pp. 71–4). But in the discussion of Dryden it is associated particularly with the discursive qualities of prose — with Dryden's ability, for instance, to elevate political and religious controversy to the level of poetry (*John Dryden*, p. 16). And in an essay on 'Poetry in the Eighteenth Century' (1930)[5] Eliot sums up what he is getting at in discussing the 'prosaic' element in much good verse. He writes that there are essential qualities which are common to good verse and good prose, that the originality of some poets has consisted in their ability to say in verse what had previously only been said in prose, and that 'to have the virtues of good prose is the first and minimum requirement of good poetry' (pp. 272–3). We may feel that some of his discussion here overstates the case, particularly the last remark, which would surely rule out much of Eliot's own practice in a poem like *The Waste Land* (the ending of 'The Fire Sermon', to cite just one example). Nevertheless, this kind of consideration is highly pertinent when we consider the 'prosaic' qualities in poems like 'Journey of the Magi' or, mingled with other qualities, in Part I of *Ash-Wednesday*, as we have already seen; and even more so in the varying kinds of discursive poetry in *Four Quartets*, which we shall examine in the next chapter.

As regards his interest in 'Symbolist' technique, Eliot had read and studied the French Symbolist poets from as early as 1908, when he read Arthur Symons's *The Symbolist Movement in Literature*. But it would seem that he was at first more interested in Laforgue and Corbière (mentioned in the 'Metaphysical Poets' essay) and Verlaine and de Nerval (who make brief appearances in *The Waste Land*) than in the most extreme of the Symbolists, Mallarmé. He later said that it was in 1925 that he began to re-read Mallarmé seriously. Mallarmé represents the extreme movement of Symbolism away from the use of language to refer to objects in the world, and towards a poetry in which words exist as far as possible independently of their referents, with a significance which is to a corresponding degree defined by their relation to other words in the poem. This procedure obviously lends itself to the intimation of a world beyond ordinary experience. As Eliot said in the 'Note Sur Mallarmé et Poe', the work of Donne, Poe and Mallarmé was an expansion of their sensibility *'beyond the limits of the normal world*, a discovery of new objects suitable to arouse new emotions' (my translation; italics in the original). Mallarmé transmutes 'the accidental' into 'the real' by means of 'incantation . . . which insists on the primitive power of the Word'. But this does not involve Mallarmé and Poe in 'the merely sonorous or melodious', which they could have exploited: in fact it makes them set it aside in favour of a syntax which 'prevents the reader from *swallowing at a gulp*' their sentence or line.[6] Mallarméan Symbolism is not for Eliot a departure from meaning; nor is it, as it is sometimes seen, an avoidance of 'life' or experience; as another remark in relation to Mallarmé makes clear, where Eliot says that 'verse is always struggling . . . to take up to itself more and more of what is prose, to take something more from life and turn it into "play" . . . The real failure of the mass of contemporary verse is its failure to draw anything new from life into art.'[7] The statement about drawing something new from life has an obvious pertinence to *The Waste Land*, which Eliot was writing at the time, just as his description of Mallarmé's and Poe's 'firmness of tread when they pass from the tangible world to the world of phantoms' illuminates for us the quality of those moments when Eliot sees the leopards in *Ash-Wednesday*, enters the rose garden in 'Burnt Norton' or treads the pavement 'in a dead patrol' in 'Little Gidding'.

We have already seen how the emphasis on 'new objects' and on 'incantation' bears fruit in *The Hollow Men* and even more in *Ash-Wednesday*. The meaninglessness, on a literal level, of 'the eyes are / Sunlight on a fallen column' or 'The eyes reappear / As the perpetual star / Multifoliate rose' does not preclude a Symbolist logic of the emotions and a poetic significance. The same is true of 'The single Rose / Is now the Garden / Where all loves end'. And the vision of the 'three white leopards' in *Ash-Wednesday* is both literal and something more. As for 'incantation', the repetitions, rhymes and assonances of *Ash-Wednesday* create a music, as in the opening of Part V ('Against the Word the unstilled world still whirled / About the centre of the silent Word'), which involves meaning, but which also alleviates the sense of present loss ('the lost word is lost')

170

and avokes a feeling of harmony. Finally, to look forward to 'Burnt Norton', we can see the Mallarméan Symbolist mode at work in the opening of Part II, where the first two lines,

> Garlic and sapphires and the mud
> Clot the bedded axle-tree.

echo Mallarmé's line from his sonnet 'M'introduire dans ton histoire' − 'Tonnerre et rubis aux moyeux' ('Thunder and rubies up to the axles') − and follow the same procedures of non-referential and 'illogical' combinations of images. In a lecture of 1933 Eliot had some interesting reflections to make on Mallarmé's line. Citing the whole poem, he said that it is a mistake to suppose that a simile or a metaphor is always something intended to be visual; and he went on to quote the sestet of Mallarmé's sonnet, containing the line quoted above, which he described as one that cannot be visualized at all. He went on to say that the elements of rationality, precision and vagueness are all proper to poetry, and that in poetry as distinct from prose each word has absolute value in itself. Poetry is incantation as well as imagery; and Mallarmé's 'thunder and rubies' cannot be visualized or heard or thought together, but their being set side by side brings out the connotation of each.[8] The 'Burnt Norton' passage will be discussed more fully in the next chapter (since there are, I suggest, fundamental differences as well as similarities between the modes of Eliot's passage and Mallarmé's poem); and Eliot's use of Symbolist procedures in *Four Quartets* can be over-stressed. But something of the Symbolist procedure is at work in Eliot's poetry after 1925, not only in its extreme form (as in 'While jewelled unicorns draw by the gilded hearse' in *Ash-Wednesday*) but also in a modified form in a poem like 'Marina', where although the images have a narrative and dramatic status, which is clearer than it often is in Mallarmé, they also combine images which do not 'fit' into any narrative or dramatic logic or syntax, as in 'hurrying feet / Under sleep, where all the waters meet' or the sequence of 'I made this . . . / The rigging weak . . . / . . . Made this unknowing, half conscious unknown, my own', where the boat is associated with something quite intangible.

II

Eliot had always been interested not only in the music of sound and incantation, but in the practice (as one can see in *The Waste*

Land), and increasingly also the theory, of the idea of pattern or 'musical design' in poetry. In 'The Music of Poetry' (1942) he wrote of the 'musical design' in particular scenes and in whole plays of Shakespeare, and referred to G. Wilson Knight's studies of 'recurrent and dominant' imagery in the plays (*On Poetry and Poets*, p. 36). He also later wrote in his Introduction to Valéry's *The Art of Poetry* (1958) that the Symbolists understood music essentially as aiming for 'an unattainable timelessness . . . a yearning for the stillness of painting or sculpture', where again the idea of a musical pattern is implicit. We have already seen the elements of a musical pattern in single longer poems like *The Waste Land* and *Ash-Wednesday*, and we have also begun to discern a kind of pattern, which is partly musical, emerging in Eliot's *œuvre* as a whole: the pattern of recurring words, images, motifs and situations which grows out of a continual re-examination of experience and a casting of it into different forms. And this recasting of experience and forming of it into a new pattern achieves its fullest and most varied realization in *Four Quartets*, where, in Part V of 'Burnt Norton', we find an earlier discursive formulation of the idea that Eliot later applied to Valéry and the Symbolists:

> Only by the form, the pattern,
> Can words or music reach
> The stillness, as a Chinese jar still
> Moves perpetually in its stillness.

After 1925 Eliot became more and more concerned with the question of the ordering of experience and the creation of pattern or design. I have already touched on Eliot's praise of Dante's *Divine Comedy* in 1920 ('the most comprehensive and the most ordered presentation of emotions that has ever been made'). Of that work he also wrote that Dante does not contemplate emotion for its own sake. The emotions of the people in Dante's Hell, Purgatory or Paradise, or the emotion invested in them by our attitude, 'is never lost or diminished, is always preserved entire, but is modified by the position assigned to the person in the eternal scheme, is coloured by the atmosphere of that person's residence in one of the three worlds' (*The Sacred Wood*, p. 167). In relation to Eliot's own work, one might reflect here that in 1920 Eliot was undergoing the upheaval of personal experiences which were to find expression in *The Waste Land* and *The Hollow Men*, and that the order and perspective seen here in Dante is at a far remove from any which Eliot could command or endorse himself. There was as yet no commitment to any faith in an 'eternal scheme', let alone the ability to make his own any kind of system which allotted 'residence' (the slight quaintness of the word in this context itself suggests an awkward distance form the idea) to 'one of the three worlds'. An order for experience could not be simply taken up from outside, but had to be struggled for; and the struggle goes on, in all the later work, to see that order in the achievements of former literature and to realize it in his own poetry. It was an order that he perceived in the work of certain Elizabethan and Jacobean dramatists, particularly Shakespeare, in whom he found 'a continuous development' throughout the plays; 'the whole man' was revealed not by his greatest single work but by the pattern as a whole (*Selected Essays*, p. 193). And later in the same essay he wrote that in all the Elizabethan and Jacobean dramatists whom he admired 'there is the essential, as well as the superficies of poetry; they give the pattern, we may say the undertone, of the personal emotion, the personal drama and struggle, which no biography, however intimate, could give us; which nothing can give us but our experience of the plays themselves' (p. 203). It is a statement which one can apply with complete justice to Eliot's own poetical works, and particularly so because in his case the poems themselves explore the ideas of order and pattern which they also exemplify.

It should be added that there is also an awareness in *Four Quartets* of the danger of *imposing* a pattern which will distort the true nature of experience (for instance, by over-valuing one side of life at the expense of another) and precluding a proper and vital response to further experience. In the words of 'East Coker' Part II:

> There is, it seems to us,
> At best, only a limited value
> In the knowledge derived from experience.
> The knowledge imposes a pattern, and falsifies,
> For the pattern is new in every moment
> And every moment is a new and shocking
> Valuation of all we have been.

The danger of concern with 'pattern' and 'order' is that the pattern and order will solidify and distort the perception of fluid reality. The kind of pattern that Eliot admired was one which showed a continual development like that of Yeats, within whose work Eliot felt could be discerned what he called, using Henry James's phrase, 'The Figure in the Carpet' (in 'Rudyard Kipling', *On Poetry and Poets*, p. 235). But the figure was not a static one, for 'maturing as a poet means maturing as the whole man, experiencing new emotions appropriate to one's age, and with the same intensity as the emotions of youth' (p. 254). And the evolution of the pattern also involves the re-examination and recreation of earlier feelings within a new perspective. Of Yeats's poems 'The Winding Stair' and 'Coole Park' Eliot wrote: 'In such poems one feels that the most lively and desirable emotions of youth have been preserved to receive their full and due expression in retrospect. For the interesting feelings of age are not just different feelings; they are feelings into which the feelings of youth are integrated' (pp. 258–9). I have quoted this last sentence already in relation to Part III of *Ash-Wednesday*, and it is worth quoting again, for this sense of the continual development and revision of experience and the gradual establishment of a more clearly defined pattern is even more relevant, as we shall see, to *Four Quartets*.

III

The reviewing of experience and the gradual establishment of a pattern are assisted to an important degree, particularly from the time of *The Hollow Men* onwards, by an element of philosophical thinking which becomes incorporated into the poetry, and even more by the growing influence of Eliot's beliefs (particularly religious beliefs) as these become more firmly established. And it would be appropriate at this point to look more closely at these factors as they relate to the poetry. Eliot, a poet who had studied philosophy at Harvard and Oxford, was always clear about the fact that the activities of the poet and the philosopher were quite different and distinct, but the poet could, he felt, show the relation of a philosophy to the rest of experience. As he wrote in 'Poetry and Propaganda' (1930), 'What poetry proves about any philosophy is merely its possibility for being lived . . . It is the making of the Word Flesh.'[9] But Eliot also came to feel that an abstract philosophic language could at times be incorporated into verse itself. It has been suggested that he learned this to a great extent from Valéry, to a translation of whose poem 'Le Serpent' he wrote an introduction in 1924.[10] He admired the way in which Valéry gave a firm structure to Symbolist verse. But much later, in a lecture in France in 1952, he expressed himself more fully on the philosophic element in Valéry's poetry, while talking of the poem 'Le Cimetière Marin':

'Valéry's poem has what I call the philosophic structure, an organization not only of successive reactions to a given situation but of reactions to his first reactions.' And later in the same lecture he said that in Valéry's poems 'the abstract mode and the poetic mode are united better than in the work of any other poet'[11] (my translation).

One element of the 'abstract mode' can be seen already in Part V of *The Hollow Men*, in the abstractions of 'the idea', 'the reality', 'the motion', 'the act', and so on, and Eliot's successive balancings ('Between the conception / And the creation' etc.) even echo directly, as Ronald Bush has pointed out, Valéry's line from 'Le Cimetière Marin', 'Entre le vide et l'événement pur' ('Between the void and the pure event'). And an abstract and discursive language also plays its part in *Ash-Wednesday*, in Part I in particular and the passage that begins 'Because I know that time is always time'. And in *Four Quartets*, as we shall see, the mode is more fully developed throughout the four poems, either in the more strictly philosophical meditations like that which opens 'Burnt Norton' ('Time present and time past / Are both perhaps present in time future') and the use of abstract nouns in Part II ('*Erhebung* without motion, concentration / Without elimination'), or the more discursive meditations like Part III of 'Little Gidding' ('There are three conditions which often look alike') and frequent other examples in the poems. These are, as it were, 'reactions to reactions', an attempt to formulate in general reflective and abstract terms the nature of experience (rather than simply to present it or to reflect only its particularities). But it should be stressed that these abstract reflections are also woven into the musical pattern of the poems as a whole, so that they do not provide definitive, encapsulating statements as much as reflections which are themselves just one mode of experience, and which play their part in a larger movement of consciousness.

Some observations by Eliot in an essay of 1926 on the Elizabethan poet Sir John Davies also suggest his growing concern with the question of the role of ideas and beliefs in poetry. They also show his increasing sense of the limitations of the method and sensibility of Donne (an attitude we also see in the Clark lectures of 1926 and the essay in *A Garland for John Donne*, 1933). Eliot suggests that Davies not only is more restrained in his use of figurative language, but has a more serious attitude towards ideas. Donne merely entertains ideas and explores the ways in which they affect his sensibility, whereas Davies has a greater 'capacity for belief' and pursues a single idea with complete seriousness (*On Poetry and Poets*, p. 136).

This idea, the 'capacity for belief' and pursuit of 'thought', together with my previous discussion of the 'poetic' status of statements of ideas or beliefs within *Four Quartets*, brings us to the general issue of the relation between poetry and beliefs, a question which preoccupied Eliot repeatedly throughout his career, both explicitly in his criticism and implicitly in the poems themselves. It will be useful to divide this issue into two parts: firstly there is the question of how Eliot's developing religious (and other) beliefs after 1925 affected his own poetry (not the fact that they did, which is obvious enough, but the *way* that they did); and secondly there is the question of how far, if at all, the reader of Eliot's poetry (and indeed of poetry in general) has to share the beliefs of the poet in order to be able fully to appreciate the poetry.

Eliot's growing religious beliefs after 1925 became, it is clear, the major element in his experience and provided the central subject for his poetry – not as a matter for the exposition of dogmatic truths, but as a matter for exploration, and integration with the rest of experience. In the Clark lectures of 1926 (pp. 53–4) Eliot spoke of two ways in which poetry can add to human experience: firstly by recording accurately the world of sense and feeling (as in the poetry of Homer or Chaucer or Catullus), and secondly by extending the frontiers of the world (as in the poetry of Dante or Baudelaire). We might say, I think, that up to *The Hollow Men* Eliot's poetry is mainly of the first kind, and afterwards it is of the second, as he began to explore a world of experience beyond the senses. Religious belief also helped to provide a structure through which to order other experience, just as Eliot saw in Dante's *Vita Nuova* a way of ordering the experience of adolescence (pp. 72–3). Eliot's poetic effort became similar to that which he saw in Dante, a way of extending human love until it led towards the divine (pp. 123–4). But it should also be remembered that Eliot had reached this stage after a radical experience of failure and despair, recorded in his earlier poems. There was no easy assumption of a traditional religious framework. We can say of him, to a great extent, what he said of Baudelaire: that he was 'discovering Christianity for himself', rather than taking it up for social or political reasons. 'He is beginning, in a way, at the beginning; and, being a discoverer, is not altogether certain what he is exploring and to what it leads'

(*Selected Essays*, p. 422). The idea of exploration and discovery is particularly relevant to *Ash-Wednesday*, 'Marina' and parts of *Four Quartets*.

The effect of Eliot's newly confirmed religious belief on *Ash-Wednesday* will, I hope, have been clear enough from the discussion of that poem. It is, in one sense of the word at any rate, a 'personal' poem in which the 'I' is the poet, and the poet (we have no reason not to believe) is T. S. Eliot the man. Thus, when he writes 'Consequently I . . . / . . . pray to God to have mercy upon us' we believe that he believes in a God and that he means what he says. The poem does, of course, avoid particular biographical detail of a circumstantial kind, so that the 'I' does have a certain impersonality; we are led to respond to a man, who may be representative of men in general, rather than to the individual T. S. Eliot. But there is not the dramatic projection into a *persona* that we find, say, in 'Prufrock', and we feel that Eliot the man is in his deepest convictions (and doubts) at one with the speaker of the poem. Eliot's religious belief is, then, the very subject of the poem – belief in all its fluctuations and feelings of strength and weakness, certainty and uncertainty. The poem is both a record of a spiritual ordering of the mind and feelings, and the act of ordering itself. But there is no sense in which the poem aims, like a piece of argument or a sermon, to persuade the reader to certain beliefs. Eliot does not, in his poems, become a propagandist or apologist for Christian belief (whatever he may be in some of his critical and polemical writings, and, perhaps, in some of his plays). *Ash-Wednesday*, and I would argue also *Four Quartets* (for all its element of statement and exhortation, its passages of 'We must . . .'), are essentially the poetry of personal experience, the poetry of what Eliot called 'the first voice', poetry in which the poet is first of all 'talking to himself – or to nobody' and concerned only with 'finding the right words'. *Ash-Wednesday* is variously cast in the forms of personal record, vision, song and prayer, but never of persuasive argument or sermon. Again, in *Four Quartets*, although there is argument it is generally an argument with the self, 'the language and tone of solitary meditation', to use the phrase Eliot applied to Sir John Davies's poetry; and where there is (rarely) exhortation, it is, I shall try to show, exhortation directed more at the self (and perhaps the single private listener) that at a congregation. Eliot's religious beliefs are a matter for record, examination, questioning and presentation (making us feel what they feel like) in his poetry, not a matter for propaganda and persuasion (still less proselytizing). Nor is there any complete break in respect of belief with the poetry before 1927. In reply to a comment from I. A. Richards that Eliot in *The Waste Land* had effected 'a complete separation between his poetry and *all* beliefs', Eliot replied that (although he could not claim to pronounce authoritatively on his own poem) he could not see such a separation, and that the 'sense of desolation, uncertainty, and futility' which Richards found was far from proving such a separation: 'for doubt and uncertainty are merely a variety of belief'.[12]

The mention of the reader or audience in the previous paragraph, and the reaction of I. A. Richards, brings us to the second half of the issue of poetry and belief: the question of how far the reader's attitude to the poet's beliefs should affect his judgement of the poetry — or to put in another way, how far the reader needs to be able to share the poet's beliefs in order fully to appreciate the poetry. It was to this part of the question that Eliot himself gave most thought in his critical writing. In all his discussions he is pulled between two opposing positions: between wanting to say that the reader can detach himself from the beliefs of the poet by 'suspending' the question of belief and disbelief (to use a term originally used by Coleridge about the experience of watching a play, and revived by I. A. Richards in his discussions of poetry and belief), and wanting to say that any full engagement with a poem must engage also with any belief the poet may be trying to express. The question is one which is clearly relevant to our reading of Eliot's own poetry, particularly the poetry after 1925. To put the question rather summarily, do we have to share Eliot's Christian beliefs in order to enjoy and benefit from his later poetry?

Eliot's main discussion of the question of poetry and belief comes in the essay on Dante of 1929, and here he makes certain distinctions which are useful. While saying the reader cannot afford to ignore Dante's philosophical and theological beliefs, he makes the distinction between 'philosophical *belief*' and 'poetic *assent*': he says that the reader can give poetic assent to the beliefs while he is reading the poem even if he does not share the beliefs (which seems to be the same idea as 'the suspension of disbelief' while reading). This 'poetic assent' obviously involves at least an 'understanding' of the beliefs: 'You are not called upon to believe what Dante believed, for your belief will not give you a groat's worth more of understanding and appreciation; but you are called upon more and more to understand it' (*Selected Essays*, pp. 257–8). The middle part of that statement, the idea that sharing the belief will add nothing to understanding and appreciation, is surely questionable; and Eliot himself modified his position on that in a footnote to the same essay, when he admitted that Dante's statement 'la sua voluntade e nostra pace' ('His will is our peace') had a greater beauty for him because his own experience had deepened its meaning for him (so that, in effect, he 'shared' the belief). But the distinction between poetic assent and philosophic belief still holds: we can say perhaps that we can suspend philosophic belief while we read, and that we need only to 'understand' the poet's beliefs, but that there is a deeper state of appreciation (other things being equal) that can come from the experience of sharing the poet's beliefs.

A further distinction which Eliot makes is between 'what Dante believes as a poet and what he believed as a man'. (One might note here the distinction between the tenses: what Dante 'believed' as a man is a matter of history, 'one time and one place'; but Dante 'believes' as a poet, because the beliefs are living in the poem, *The Divine Comedy*). Dante's poem may rely profoundly on a theological system which found its supreme expression in the *Summa* of Thomas Aquinas, but

We are not to take Dante for Aquinas or Aquinas for Dante. It would be a grievous error in psychology. The *belief attitude* of a man reading the *Summa* must be different from that of a man reading Dante, even when it is the same man, and that man a Catholic.　　　　(p. 259)

And we can apply this, *mutatis mutandis*, to Eliot himself. We are not to take Eliot's writings after 1927 for an expression of Anglican doctrine, not only because the beliefs may have their own individual peculiarities, but also because we should not be reading the poems as if they were doctrine. Elsewhere he describes this as a distinction between 'beliefs as *held*' and 'beliefs as *felt*', the latter being the material of the artist (*The Use of Poetry and the Use of Criticism*, p. 136). Described in this way the distinction may seem difficult to discern, but it would seem to be one between the deliberate willed adherence to a belief, and the unwilled feeling about a belief. We may recall in this connection Eliot's remarks about poetry and philosophy, already quoted: 'What poetry proves about a philosophy is merely its possibility for being lived' – that is to say, its possibility for both prompting and regulating the feelings and for providing principles which are acted upon (both in life and art, for poetry is also a kind of action). Poetry can embody the way in which a belief is integrated with the rest of experience.

The question of how far we can enjoy (which means also benefit from) poetry which treats of or is imbued by beliefs we cannot share still, of course, remains after the above distinctions have been made. And although in the essay on Dante of 1929 Eliot states categorically, 'I deny, in short, that the reader must share the beliefs of the poet in order to enjoy the poetry fully' (p. 269), in particular cases we find him very much affected in his appreciation of a poet by his attitude to the poet's beliefs. In the case of Shelley, for example, he describes how Shelley's ideas are for him a major obstacle in the appreciation of the poetry: 'I find his ideas repellent; and the difficulty of separating Shelley from his ideas and beliefs is still greater than with Wordsworth' (*The Use of Poetry and the Use of Criticism*, p. 89). And his discussion of the problem here takes it a stage further than in his essay on Dante, for he is led to distinguish between beliefs in poetry which the reader simply does not share, and those which he finds positively antipathetic. Although not a Buddhist, he is still profoundly affected by some of the early Buddhist scriptures, and he enjoys Fitzgerald's *Omar* though he finds his view of life 'smart and shallow'. But his dislike of Shelley's views impedes his enjoyment of certain poems, and in others the views seem so 'puerile' that he cannot enjoy the poems at all (p. 91). And this leads him eventually to a general position which, while it leaves several problems, has the virtues of breadth and common sense:

When the doctrine, theory, belief, or 'view of life' presented in a poem is one which the mind of a reader can accept as coherent, mature, and founded on the facts of experience, it interposes no obstacle to the reader's enjoyment, whether it be one that he accept or deny, approve or deprecate. When it is one which the reader rejects as childish or feeble, it may, for the reader of well-developed mind, set up an almost complete check. (p.96)

The problems left are, among others, these: what are the differences between 'doctrine' and 'view of life'? What exactly is the value to be given to the word 'mature'? (That Shelley is not 'the companion of age' (p. 89) may not be seen as a very telling objection by many readers.) And 'founded on the facts of experience' would seem to preclude many of the most important religious beliefs (e.g. the belief in the immortality of the soul).

But nevertheless the statement has a broad commonsense usefulness which answers many aspects of the general question. Applied to Eliot's own poetry, for instance, we might say that even for a reader who could not accept Eliot's belief in God the poet's attitudes towards many aspects of moral experience might still be found coherent and persuasive. A writer may, as Eliot put it later in an address on Goethe, have a quality of 'wisdom' which can be to a certain degree separated from his actual beliefs and can benefit the reader who holds very different beliefs (*On Poetry and Poets*, pp. 220–1).

There are other reasons for continuing to distinguish between the attitudes proper to assessing belief as expressed in poetry and assessing it as expressed in other forms such as philosophic argument and religious doctrine. We may, for example, be prepared to tolerate the explicit doctrine for the sake of insights and intimations that lie buried in it. Eliot, for instance, was completely antipathetic to Whitman's ideas about democracy and equality, and his general romantic optimism about the capabilities of the human soul. But Eliot could also write:

Beneath all the declamation there is another tone, and behind the illusions there is another vision. When Whitman speaks of the lilacs or the rocking bird, his theories and beliefs drop away like a needless pretext.

('Whitman and Tennyson', *Nation and Athenaeum*, 40, 11, 1926)

Poetry as a form can allow a vision to emerge which is not exactly the same as its explicit argument or structure of beliefs, and so many speak to the reader for whom the explicit beliefs are antipathetic. One might add to this the idea that poetry may also awaken sympathy in the reader for beliefs for which he had hitherto had none. In the words of George Herbert:

> A verse may finde him, who a sermon flies,
> And turn delight into a sacrifice.

('Perirrhanterium')

This is not, I think, simply an argument for poetry as a superior kind of covert propaganda. It appeals to the idea that the pleasures of poetry may be a means of extending our experience, including our sympathy and openness towards certain beliefs.

Eliot's repeated returns, throughout his critical writing, to the problem of poetry and belief in one form and another testify to its variety and complexity (and probable insolubility). And in reading Eliot's poetry we should try to maintain an equally open approach. His poems must be read for the intensity with which they realize certain experiences, for their varied music, their vivid imagery of physical, mental and spiritual sensation, and also for whatever 'wisdom' their discursive ideas (where the poetry employs these) may have. But we cannot, in the end, preclude the question of our assent or dissent from the beliefs embodied in many individual poems and in the complete *oeuvre* which they form. Neither assent nor dissent will necessarily make us more, or less, responsive readers of the poetry, but indifference to the problem surely will. In a passage from the discussion of Shelley, Eliot asks whether 'culture' requires that we exclude from our minds all our convictions and beliefs when we read poetry. His reply is: 'If so, so much the worse for culture'; and he admires D. H. Lawrence for refusing to make the separation. Nor does Eliot allow an easy distinction between the times when a poet is 'being a poet' and those when he is 'being a preacher': in the cases of, for instance, Shelley or Wordsworth or Goethe, an exclusion of the latter element would leave one merely with beautiful poetic fragments but not the substance of the poetry. 'By using, or abusing, this principle of isolation, you are in danger of seeking from poetry some illusory *pure* enjoyment, of separating poetry from everything else in the world, and cheating yourself out of a great deal that poetry has to give to your development' (*The Use of Poetry and the Use of Criticism*, pp. 97–8). Here, as in many other places, Eliot belongs to a central tradition of criticism which runs through Sidney, Johnson, Wordsworth and Arnold.

It may also be, however, that in an age of 'ideology' and totalitarian philosophies of both Right and Left, we need particularly to remember the power of poetry to subvert or circumvent uniform (or what are sometimes barbarously called 'totalizing') views of the world, as well as its power to bring home to us comprehensive visions of life. So our emphasis will be on the ability of poetry not so much to embody a complete view of the world as to remind us continually of those areas of experience which lie outside the area of conscious belief, and beyond any ideological scheme – its ability to express not so much the nature of belief as the nature of a reality larger than anything which can be encompassed by belief. In this way poetry can both show us the possibility of a belief 'being lived', and also show how belief can be open to the developments of further awareness. In this way, too, a religious poetry like that of Eliot may be an even greater necessity for a predominantly secular age than for a religious one.

9

From *Coriolan* (1931) to 'Burnt Norton' (1936)

After 'Marina' Eliot turned briefly to a quite different mode, that of the *Coriolan* poems (1931). These ('Triumphal March' and 'Difficulties of a Statesman') seem to have been an attempt to revive an element of social criticism or satire in his poetry. The 'eagles' and the 'trumpets' of 'Triumphal March', and the way the whole display of imperial might modulates at the end of the poem to the bathos of Cyril and the 'crumpets', recalls this comic deflation in 'A Cooking Egg':

> Where are the eagles and the trumpets?
>
> > Buried beneath some snow-deep Alps.
> > Over buttered scones and crumpets
> > Weeping, weeping multitudes
> > Droop in a hundred A.B.C.'s.

But instead of the crisp concision of that, we get a prose-like free verse, and at one point a deliberately flat listing of armaments (taken almost directly from a book about the Treaty of Versailles of 1918). The prosaic style is appropriate for the speaker — standing (one infers) with the ordinary people lining the way of the military procession, for whom 'The natural wakeful life of our Ego is a perceiving', a mere noting of outward phenomena without any awareness of consciousness itself. They await the leader, but when he comes he is passive and enigmatic:

> There is no interrogation in his eyes
> Or in the hands, quiet over the horse's neck,
> And the eyes watchful, waiting, perceiving, indifferent.

It is difficult to see what attitude the speaker means us to take towards this leader. One commentator finds a feeling of 'revulsion' in the word 'indifferent',[1] but that surely seems too strong. There may be an implied criticism of his indifference, and he too is only 'perceiving', but the watchful, waiting attitude might be a kind of wisdom. And do the next lines apply to something in the leader, or are they an intimation of a reality quite apart from him and outside the frame of reference of the rest of the poem? Certainly the utterance is that of a speaker suddenly possessed with a new depth of feeling and insight:

> O hidden under the dove's wing, hidden in the turtle's breast,
> Under the palmtree at noon, under the running water
> At the still point of the turning world. O hidden.

That phrase in the last line is our first intimation of the consciousness of 'Burnt Norton' and *Four Quartets* in general (although the idea is already implicit in the opening of Part V of *Ash-Wednesday*). But for the moment this poem reverts to the world of imperial nullity, the 'sacrifice' which is merely 'Dust of dust', and the martial grandeur, collapsing finally into the bathos of Cyril and 'Don't throw away that sausage'. The tone of the last line is surely difficult to gauge as it stands (translated: 'And the soldiers lined the streets? THEY LINED THEM'). The capital letters might suggest a shouted anger, a repudiation of the whole military show: but it seems a failure of realization in the poem itself that the appropriate tone only becomes apparent when we are aware of the source, a passage from Charles Maurras's *L'Avenir de l'Intelligence* in which a writer is ironically presented as talking excitedly about a procession in honour of some mediocre writer.[2] The story is received incredulously: 'Et les soldats faisaient la haie? – Ils la faisaient.' There is also a further possibility: if Eliot also thought of his leader as a writer, the poem takes on a new and ironic meaning; it becomes partly a confession of a feeling of personal emptiness. By 1931 Eliot was an acknowledged leader in the literary world, but this hint would suggest that there is a feeling of emptiness within, and that the life of real feeling and significance is 'hidden' from the public world. The poem then becomes a satire on the modern state, but one in which the self is implicated.

This reading leads directly to the next *Coriolan* poem, 'Difficulties of a Statesman', which is a lament of the statesman (the leader of the previous poem?) himself. It begins with the words from Isaiah 6 ('The voice said, Cry. And he said, What shall I cry? All flesh is grass, and all the goodliness thereof is as the flower of the field'), and then, after a list of various classes of dignitary, takes on the accents of the bureaucrat ('The first thing to do is to form the committees') in a way that recalls moments of satire in Matthew Arnold.[3] Cyril reappears as an example of the hapless populace whom the statesman has to rule and whose life reflects the emptiness of the statesman's own. Money, and what Carlyle and Arnold called 'machinery', are society's only values. As in earlier poems, this is a vision of a synthesis of historical periods – the 'telephone operator' co-exists with the 'Volscian commission' (Eliot may also have learned something from Pound's 'Homage to Sextus Propertius' here). And this last group recalls the hero of the Roman empire, the enemies and allies of that particular Coriolanus, who gives the work its overall title.

Coriolanus (essentially, that is, Shakespeare's Coriolanus) had already figured in Eliot's earlier poems – as one of the heroes of the speaker of 'A Cooking Egg', and in the reply to the Thunder's first utterance in Part V of *The Waste Land*, where he is associated with the self-locked enclosure of egotism:

> We think of the key, each in his prison
> Thinking of the key, each confirms a prison
> Only at nightfall, aethereal rumours
> Revive for a moment a broken Coriolanus

And it is this enclosure that he again represents here, the enclosure of someone locked in an empty world of public life, cut off from the roots of real feeling and human relationship.

> What shall I cry?
> Mother mother

The appeal 'O mother', repeated twice later in the poem, recalls Coriolanus's outburst at the climactic moment of Shakespeare's tragedy, when his iron will finally breaks and his humanity reasserts itself, as he responds to his mother's silent appeal:

> O mother, mother!
> What have you done? Behold the heavens do ope,
> The gods look down, and this unnatural scene
> They laugh at. (V.iii. 182–4)

The statesman in Eliot's poem also appeals to a mother, for some kind of meeting or reconciliation after the observation of (to gloss Eliot's deliberately heavy and pedantic Roman words) sacrifices, burials, offerings and entombments. It is surely not irrelevant here that Eliot's own mother, from whom he had in some ways felt unhappily estranged, had died two years before, in 1929. In the poem, at any rate, the speaker relates himself and his mother to those images of delicate life which seem to come from some other world of feeling.

> O hidden under the . . . Hidden under the . . . Where the dove's
>   foot rested and locked for a moment,
> A still moment, repose of noon, set under the upper branches of
>   noon's widest tree
> Under the breast feather stirred by the small wind after noon

These images and others which echo them are the heart of the poem, the feelings of the heart 'hidden' from the imperial public world. The tentative approach to significance of the opening phrase is strengthened by the momentary firmness of 'locked'. And once again lines anticipate, faintly but distinctly, in the 'still moment' and 'the dove's foot', and in the 'clematis' and the suggestion of children in 'the small creatures' of the subsequent lines, the imagery of profound inner life in 'Burnt Norton'.

Coriolan is one of the *Unfinished Poems* in *The Complete Poems and Plays*: Eliot said that the first two parts had been meant to begin 'a sequence of the life of the character who appears in the first part as Young Cyril'.[4] It has been suggested that this points in the direction of drama, and that Eliot broke off the work when he was offered the chance to exercise his dramatic powers by writing a text for *The Rock*.[5] But the elements of the poem point as much, I think, towards *Four Quartets*, not only in the imagery that has just been examined, but also in its combination of lyric passages and 'social' criticism. Just as here the prophetic note –

> All flesh is grass: comprehending
> The Companions of the Bath, the Knights of the British Empire,
>   the Cavaliers,

– is replaced first by the picture of Cyril and banal ordinary life and then by the glimpses of natural beauty and intimations of hidden significance, so the prophecy-like opening of Part III of 'East Coker' –

> O dark dark dark. They all go into the dark,
> The vacant interstellar spaces, the vacant into the vacant,
> The captains, merchant bankers, eminent men of letters.

modulates through the tube train passage to the lyrical natural beauty of

> Whisper of running streams, and winter lightning.
> The wild thyme unseen and the wild strawberry . . .

But *Four Quartets* is also very different in its variety of styles and its predominant mode of meditation and inner exploration. The element of (sometimes rather heavy-handed) humour represented by young Cyril is left behind, and the satire on the banalities of public and private life is also largely abandoned together with the more strident note of moral condemnation (both of which strains were allowed fuller play in *The Rock*). What is developed is the exploration of those intimations of the 'hidden' which break in on the critical and prophetic tone. In responding to the life of his times Eliot has again discovered the exploration of the inner life which is at the centre of his poetry.

II

It is not surprising that most of the *Minor Poems* in the *Complete Poems and Plays* date from around the period 1933–4, a time when, as Eliot later said when talking of the commissioning of *The Rock*, 'I seemed to myself to have exhausted my meagre poetic gifts, and to have nothing more to say' (*On Poetry and Poets*, p. 91). The *Five-Finger Exercises* are well named, being essentially little light-verse practisings in rhyme and rhythm, mixing snatches of serious preoccupations which Eliot was to develop later ('*When* will Time flow away') with comic and nonsense verse reminiscent of Edward Lear. There is a nice self-portrait in V which hits off one side of the poet (perhaps in particular his later prose style and part of *Four Quartets*) rather well:

> How unpleasant to meet Mr. Eliot!
> With his features of clerical cut,
> And his brow so grim
> And his mouth so prim
> And his conversation, so nicely
> Restricted to What Precisely
> And If and Perhaps and But.

But the poems are rarely quite relaxed or ebullient enough to be really successful comic light verse, and one feels that in this context the familiar literary references (to Shakespeare, Tennyson, Marvell and Conan Doyle) have a touch of pedantry or archness about them.

The sequence *Landscapes* (1934–5) is more significant and successful, and indicates the movement of Eliot's sensibility toward memories of his American past and a response to the natural world which were to play an important part in *Four Quartets*. 'New Hampshire' is lyrically simple, light and delicate in movement, and achieves a quality (faintly reminiscent of Hopkins's 'Spring and Fall') which, indeed, Eliot scarcely attempted elsewhere. Its evocation of childhood also anticipates that element in 'Burnt Norton' I and 'Little Gidding' V ('the children in the apple-tree') which plays such an important part in the larger whole. 'Virginia' catches a heavy dreaminess of atmosphere, and also has its anticipations, this time of the (different) river in the opening passage of 'East Coker', and although the passage there has a quite different function it is fair to observe that as an evocation of a *river* this earlier poem is more successful. 'Cape Ann' (also, though not explicitly, based on childhood memories) evokes the quick, darting, singing life of the birds of the New England coast. It recalls the keen memory in *Ash-Wednesday* VI of 'the cry of the quail and the whirling plover' – one of those memories which cause the 'time of tension' between renunciation and the life of the senses. Its 'quick quick quick' is a foretaste of the excitement of 'Burnt Norton' I ('Quick, said the bird, find them, find them'); and the 'resignation' of the land at the end 'To its true owner, the tough one, the seagull' is like a detail from the sea-piece in 'The Dry Salvages' I, where the rhythm of the sea comes to represent a perception of eternity, something below the rhythms of ordinary life, 'a time / Older than the time of chronometers'.

The two landscapes from the British Isles introduce elements of more distant history. 'Rannoch, by Glencoe' has again a subtle feeling of place, 'the soft moor / And the soft sky' (although 'moon hot' seems an awkward and inexplicable phrase), and its memories of history suggest a tendency of thought which reappears in the meditations on the Civil War in 'Little Gidding' III, though here there is a stress on the persistence of the old rivalries ('Shadow of the pride is long') rather than the essentially religious perspective of the later poem, which sees the rivalries subsumed, 'folded in a single party': here, there is 'No concurrence of bone'.

Finally, 'Usk' is a slight and tentative but distinct pointer to Eliot's changing religious and poetic sensibility. 'Do not spell / Old enchantments.' The mysteries, one might say, of fertility rituals, Grail legends and medieval emblems (the 'lance' and the 'white heart') are to be abandoned for a more active spiritual journey which looks out towards the actual world 'Where the roads dip and where the roads rise'. And the poem gains its vitality from its sense of actual exploration of old places, its tentative approach to the past: ' "Gently dip, but not too deep" '. (The line is from Peele's beautiful song,[6] which is, intentionally or not, especially appropriate because of the song's mysterious suggestion of folk rituals.) *Landscapes*, therefore, are more than minor: they are suggestive sketches, perfectly sufficient in themselves as painters' sketches often are, of scenes and perceptions which were deeply significant in the 'growth of a poet's mind', and which received fuller (but not always more evocative) treatment in *Four Quartets*.

III

In 1933 Eliot was commissioned to write dialogue and choruses for *The Rock*, a pageant to raise money for the building of forty-five churches in the 'New London' area, which was performed in the subsequent year. Soon afterwards he was asked to write a poetic drama for the Canterbury Festival, and this request resulted in *Murder in the Cathedral*, performed in 1935. Since these works are both dramas (as was the unfinished *Sweeney Agonistes*, which Eliot had begun writing in 1923 and which was published in full in 1932 and performed in 1934), this study is not directly concerned with them. But the choruses from *The Rock* are preserved as separate poems in the *Complete Poems and Plays*, and Eliot's decision to turn to drama prompts some comment in relation to the poems, and particularly in relation to 'Burnt Norton', published in 1936.

Eliot had talked about poetic drama in his last lecture at Harvard in 1933 (the Conclusion to the *Use of Poetry and the Use of Criticism*, 1933), and had suggested that 'the poet naturally prefers to write for as large and miscellaneous an audience as possible' and that 'the ideal medium for poetry . . . and the most direct means of social "usefulness" for poetry, is the theatre' (pp. 152–3). Eliot had always had a strong element of the dramatic in his poetry, a tendency to put his utterances into the mouths of *personae* like Prufrock or Gerontion, or into several figures, as in *The Waste Land* (the original draft title of which was 'He Do the Police in Different Voices', a quotation from *Our Mutual Friend*). But to transfer this element to the theatre is a very different matter; and it is probably true that Eliot can be described in the words he himself used of Browning, as a 'dramatic poet whose dramatic gifts are best exercised outside of the theatre' (*On Poetry and Poets*, p. 94). He does not seem to have the dramatist's power to project himself fully into characters completely different from himself: for the *personae* of the poems are of course versions of himself; and his greatest poetry, as I have already suggested, is never far from the poetry of the 'first voice', poetry in which the poet is not primarily 'concerned with making other people understand anything. He is not concerned, at this stage, with other people at all; only with finding the right words, or anyhow, the least wrong words . . . He is oppressed by a burden which he must bring to birth in order to obtain relief.'[7] If some such process is, as I suggest, at the heart of Eliot's greatest poetry, then the demands of poetic drama, in which, as he says in 'Poetry and Drama', 'the problem of communication presents itself immediately' (*On Poetry and Poets*, p. 79), may work counter to the natural bent of his genius. There is also something slightly ominous about the stress, in *The Use of Poetry*, on 'direct means of social "usefulness" ' (p. 153): Eliot hastened to say that he did not mean that the poet should 'meddle with the tasks of the theologian, the preacher . . . or anybody else', and added that the poet would like rather to be 'something of a popular entertainer'. But Eliot did also feel, around this time, that he had some obligation to the Church he had joined some five years before, and his first direct undertakings in staged drama, *The Rock* and *Murder in the Cathedral*, did have clear didactic and religious ends.

Sweeney Agonistes, however, published for the first time as a whole in 1932, was a dramatic experiment of another kind, with a flavour from the years between *The Waste Land* and *The Hollow Men*. Some of it at least had been written in draft form as early as 1923, and its first part, 'Fragment of a Prologue', appeared in *The Criterion* in 1926 and 'Fragment of an Agon' in 1927. The main characters, Sweeney, Dusty and Doris, and the social world of the drama obviously derive in part from the 'Sweeney' poems of 1920. Above all the combined sense of vitality and despair, the vigorous rendering of an arid and violent world, align the work with the consciousness that produced the tawdry and sinister settings of the 'Sweeney' poems and the black comedy of Madame Sosostris. But the fact that the work is a kind of drama (though Eliot included it under *Unfinished Poems* in the *Collected Poems, 1909–1962*), makes it appropriate for discussion here as much as in Chapter 8, for it provides a sharp and suggestive contrast to the solemn *Choruses from 'The Rock'*.

The two 'Fragments of an Aristophanic Melodrama' which make up *Sweeney Agonistes* have above all an imagistic spareness and a rhythmic life which remind one of the earlier poems rather than the later dramas. The dialogue between Dusty and Doris at the beginning of the play shows an extraordinary ability to combine the precise accents of conversation (and conversation appropriate to their world) with a kind of jazz rhythm. Arnold Bennett reported Eliot's saying in 1933 that he wanted to write 'a drama of modern life (furnished flat sort of people) in a rhythmic prose, "perhaps with certain things in it accentuated by drum beats" '.[8] (In 1965 this suggestion was brilliantly realized in a London production, with music by John Dankworth authentically setting the music-hall songs).[9] The rhythms and repetitions are at once conversational and incantatory, and convey a range of feeling, from uneasy boredom to urgent anxiety. Dusty and Doris, like Madame Sosostris, read the cards; and Doris cuts the two of spades:

> *Dusty*: The *two of spades*!
> THAT'S THE COFFIN!!
> *Doris*: THAT'S THE COFFIN?
> Oh good heavens what'll I do?
> Just before a party too!
> *Dusty*: Well it needn't be yours, it may mean a friend.
> *Doris*: No it's mine. I'm sure it's mine.
> I dreamt of weddings all last night.
> Yes it's mine. I know it's mine.
> Oh good heavens what'll I do.
> Well I'm not going to draw any more,
> You cut for luck. You cut for luck.
> It might break the spell. You cut for luck.

(There is also a nice macabre–comic touch in the association of the coffin with of 'I dreamt of weddings all last night').

What the melodrama is 'about' becomes clearer when we look back on it. The 'furnished flat sort of people' are more than a little louche (one wonders if furnished flats always had this connotation in the 1920s or if this was part of Eliot's slightly uncertain acquaintance with English social divisions). Who and

what is Pereira who 'pays the rent'? And what is the status of
the American visitors? This is presumably the world of what today would be punters and escort agencies. In the 'second act'
Sweeney appears with a story of a man he knew who 'did a girl
in' ('A woman runs a terrible risk' says Doris), whom he chillingly identifies with – or indeed sees as representative:

> Any man might do a girl in,
> Any man has to, needs to, wants to
> Once in a lifetime, do a girl in

But it is the man's state of mind after the murder which is the
moral centre of the piece (and the rhythm and repetition create
the sense of insistence):

> He didn't know if he was alive
>   and the girl was dead
> He didn't know if the girl was alive
>   and he was dead
> He didn't know if they both were alive
>   or both were dead
> If he was alive then the milkman wasn't
>   and the rent-collector wasn't
> And if they were alive then he was dead.

A passage from 'Eeldrop and Appleplex', a prose sketch which
Eliot published in *The Little Review* in 1917, provides an exact
gloss:

In Gopsum Street a man murders his mistress. The important fact is
that for the man the act is eternal, and that for the brief space he has
to live, he is already dead. He is already in a different world from ours.
He has crossed the frontier. The important fact is that something is
done which cannot be undone – a possibility which none of us realise
until we face it for ourselves. For the man's neighbours the important
fact is what the man killed her with? And at precisely what time? And
who found the body? . . . But the medieval world, insisting on the eternity of punishment, expressed something nearer the truth.

The last sentence suggests the connection between Eliot's interest in back-street crime and his interest in Dante. Along the
same lines, Sweeney's sexually aggressive teasing of Doris ('I'll
carry you off / To a cannibal isle.') might be seen as a parody–
reversal of the Dante–Beatrice relationship which was such an

important example for Eliot in *The Hollow Men* and *Ash-Wednesday*:

> *Sweeney*: I'll be the cannibal.
> *Doris*:   I'll be the missionary
>   I'll convert you!
> *Sweeney*:   I'll convert *you*!
>   Into a stew.
>   A nice little, white little, missionary stew.

But above all *Sweeney Agonistes* renders a vision of emptiness in life, 'the boredom and the horror', in the real language of men and women. There is a marked contrast with the stilted 'prophetic' mode of *Choruses from 'The Rock'* or the often flat and prosaic verse and involved sentences of the later plays.

> Birth, and copulation, and death.
> That's all the facts when you come to brass tacks:
> Birth, and copulation, and death.

The atavistic energies of 'average sensual man', brought up in bafflement against this central emptiness, are rendered in the modern accents of jazz and music-hall. The work has a claim to be called Eliot's best piece of poetry for the theatre. To borrow from Eliot's account of Tourneur: 'a horror of life, singular in his own or any age, finds exactly the right words and the right rhythms'.

III

One of the main interests of the *Choruses from 'The Rock'* (1934) is that it prefigures in places, in a completely different mode, a more public and strident form, some of the concerns of *Four Quartets* as a whole. The choruses take up a prophetic tone, which I have suggested already was not Eliot's *forte*, a tone of lament, exhortation and castigation relieved at times only by a rather heavy-handed irony and humour. The voices are divided between the voice of the Lord who speaks through the prophet–poet (as in III); the poet in an observer's role (as in I); the Chorus proper, with its different spokesmen; and in I the Rock himself, reminiscent of the figure of the leader in 'Triumphal March', but without the ambivalence which we saw in that figure. But despite these divisions the voices are monotonously the same. The ills of modern society are condemned, but in a banal and weary tone, at times with a kind of drone of pious indignation which suggests the gloomy murmurings of middle-class parishioners at coffee after the morning service, as near the end of Part II:

> And now you live dispersed on ribbon roads,
> And no man knows or cares who is his neighbour
> Unless his neighbour makes too much disturbance,
> But all dash to and fro in motor cars,
> Familiar with the roads and settled nowhere.
> Nor does the family even move about together,
> But every son would have his motor cycle,
> And daughters ride away on casual pillions.

Which then modulates suddenly to a would-be dignity and elevation:

> Much to cast down, much to build, much to restore;
> Let the work not delay, time and the arm not waste;

The anticipations of *Four Quartets* are, it must be quickly admitted, faint, a matter of half-grasped ideas (or notions) rather than any genuine poetic feeling. There is the sense of the 'perpetual recurrence of determined seasons' in I, which is to be taken up and expanded in 'East Coker'; and 'The Hunter with his dogs pursues his circuit', which finds expansion in 'Burnt Norton' II. The rather more striking line in I, 'The desert is squeezed in the tube-train next to you' (p. 149), anticipates the 'tube-train' passage in 'East Coker' III; and in VII there is a glimpse of the central idea of *Four Quartets*, the idea of the 'intersection of the timeless / With time' ('The Dry Salvages' V), in VII, here in the shape of its specifically Christian application:

Then came, at a predetermined moment, a moment in time and of time,
A moment not out of time, but in time, in what we call history:
> transecting, bisecting the world of time, a moment in time but not
> like a moment of time, [etc.]

There is also an anticipation of the reflections of writing in 'East Coker' V in IX (but cast in the form of the hoped-for ideal, rather than in the form of honest confession which, with the sense of failure and 'the fight to recover what has been lost / And found and lost again and again', predominates in the later poem):

Out of the slimy mud of words, out of the sleet and hail of verbal
> imprecisions,
Approximate thoughts and feelings, words that have taken the place of

thoughts and feelings,
There spring the perfect order of speech, and the beauty of incantation.

And one of the most successful Parts, Part X, with its concluding hymn to light, looks forward to those evocations of light
in 'Burnt Norton' and 'Little Gidding'. But despite the beauty
of one or two individual images –

> Moon light and star light, owl and moth light,
> Glow-worm glowlight on a grassblade.

or

> Our gaze is submarine, our eyes look upward
> And see the light that fractures through unquiet water.

– we feel that this is Eliotic 'Parnassian' (to use Hopkins's term
for that characteristic style which a poet can command without
much intensity of inspiration),[10] and that it is tailored rather
too conveniently to the didactic aims of the pageant ('And when
we have built an Altar to the Invisible Light . . .'). Certainly
these lights seem to pale when set beside the kingfisher's wing in
'Burnt Norton', or the winter sun of the opening of 'Little
Gidding'.

What the *Choruses from 'The Rock'* essentially lack is the
presence of personal experience and poetic personality. They
gather together the elements of modern society which Eliot
hates, and the elements of faith which he wishes to counteract
them, and simply set them down, both rather wearily. The satire
(such as it is) lacks the edge of wit and the element of self-
implication which made the Sweeney poems and drama bitingly
sardonic; and the celebrations lack the sense of personal exultation, or sudden release, the 'sudden relief from an intolerable
burden' (*The Use of Poetry*, p. 145).

The work fails to achieve genuine drama (though of course
there is slightly more in *The Rock* as a whole, and a 'Chorus'
is likely to repeat a limited range of tones). As Eliot confessed,
it was his own voice, 'that of myself addressing – indeed
haranguing – an audience, that was most distinctly audible'
(*On Poetry and Poets*, p. 91). *Four Quartets*, with its deliberately
varied styles and 'voices', though they remain those of a single
speaker, achieves a greater sense of drama, that of the mind in
conflict with itself.

Murder in the Cathedral is considerably more interesting and
successful partly because it centres on a figure (Thomas Becket)

who does undergo an internal struggle, and one which has parallels (though hardly equivalences, and this is a problem) with Eliot's own. But for our present purposes, the main interest of the play is that it also released poetic ideas which were to bear fuller fruit later. In an interview in 1953 Eliot said that he remembered feeling once again that he had 'written himself out' just before *The Rock* was commissioned. Having to write the latter led him to *Murder in the Cathedral*, and he thought that he would not write any more 'pure unapplied poetry'. But there were fragments which 'stayed in my mind', and he saw a poem 'shaping itself' around them which finally emerged as 'Burnt Norton'.[11] The main 'fragment' discarded from *Murder in the Cathedral* is a passage which appears, only slightly changed, as the opening lines (1–14) of 'Burnt Norton'. In the play the lines were to be given to the second Priest who was to comment on Thomas's rejection of the second Tempter: the latter had tempted Thomas with worldly power, particularly the Chancellorship which Thomas had resigned. It is the temptation of 'what might have been', the temptation to try and repeat the past, to go back and make a different choice in the same situation. Clearly this had a significance for Eliot which could not be fully realized within the confines of the drama: the pressure of personal experience needed a more personal poem.

10

'Burnt Norton' (1936) and the pattern for *Four Quartets*

'What a rum thing time is, ain't it, Neddy?'
(Mr Roker in *The Pickwick Papers*)[1]

I

'Burnt Norton' (1936) was conceived as a separate poem, with no thought of the three quartets which were to follow from 1940 to 1942. It is a meditation in varying moods on time and memory, and it attempts, with only occasional recourse to traditional religious language and imagery, to create an idea, and a sense, of absolute value which is outside time. It can be described as a philosophic poem, but it is not philosophy; rather it uses elements of philosophic language as part of a process of meditation which attempts to evoke the experience of consciousness rather than present a set of propositions. It contains propositions, but these are only a part of the whole. They are validated (if at all) not by argument or demonstration, but by the complete experience of the poem to which they contribute. The truth at which the poem and the later Quartets aims is that which Wordsworth described as the object of poetry in general, truth 'not standing upon external testimony, but carried alive into the heart by passion: truth which is its own testimony . . .'[2] Ultimately the poem will succeed just as far as, by responding to its feeling, we are led to accept its truth – though there may be many intermediate points of partial response and assent on this side of that acceptance.

Critics have been inclined to emphasize the differences between *Four Quartets* and Eliot's earlier poems, in particular *The Waste Land*, and of course these are many and radical. But in the matter of structure and general procedure there are also many continuities. It is interesting, for example, that in returning to the 'long poem' Eliot elaborates a five-part structure like that of *The Waste Land*. The parts of 'Burnt Norton' are in the main more clearly distinguished in mode than they are in the earlier poem; but in both poems the fourth part is a short lyric on the theme of mortality, and the first part contains in both cases what are arguably the most deeply personal and intense passages in the poems — on the hyacinth garden in the first and the rose garden in the second — both of which culminate in visions of a 'heart of light'. Part III in both consists of a presentation of social (and urban) desolation (though this, of course, is present in other Parts of *The Waste Land*); and Part V ends in both cases with a brief 'medley' of images which draws on the earlier parts of the poem. It would be a mistake to try and push these parallels too far, and Eliot may have been quite unconscious of them. But they would seem to be more than coincidental, and to offer another example of the organically developing nature, the repetition-within-change, of Eliot's poetic *oeuvre*.

Eliot's stylistic strategies in 'Burnt Norton' also have their parallels with earlier poems. In one way the poem is contrasted with the poetry before *The Hollow Men* by its much more markedly autobiographical elements — the place name in the title, the use of a direct first person pronoun, an 'I' who is the poet — although these elements are still only starting points for wider reflection. And these elements become even more marked in the later Quartets: in the direct autobiographical reflections ('So here I am, in the middle way, having had twenty years'), the memories of childhood ('the nursery bedroom', 'the April dooryard') the fire-watching scene in 'Little Gidding'. But within (or sometimes distinct from) this more directly 'personal' mode, there is a variety of 'voices' and styles which are in their way equivalents of the various *personae* of *The Waste Land*. There is the voice of discursive meditation and personal 'memory' in Part I; the 'Symbolist' lyric at the opening of Part II, followed by a style of conceptual abstraction; the dreamlike vision of London, the 'place of disaffection', followed by spiritual injunction in Part III. And in the later Quartets the voices are more varied still with the addition of a casual conversational voice, as in 'East Coker' II ('That was a way of putting it — not very satisfactory'), or a self-ironic voice, as in 'East Coker' III ('You say I am repeating / Something I have said before. I shall say it again. / Shall I say it again?'), the style of the metaphysical lyric ('East Coker' IV), the highly-wrought sestina ('The Dry Salvages' II), and the Dantean 'Canto', with its attempt at an equivalent for *terza rima*, in the meeting with the 'familiar compound ghost' in 'Little Gidding' II. More will be said about these in the next chapter, but for the moment my purpose is simply to point out that Eliot's method of 'different voices', though changed, did not disappear after *The Waste Land* — and indeed that *Four Quartets* shows itself closer to that poem in this respect than it is to *Ash-Wednesday*, which is closer to it in time. 'You cannot create a very large poem without introducing a more impersonal point of view, or splitting it up into various personalities,' Eliot wrote in his 1920 essay on Blake (*Selected Essays*, p. 321). In *The Waste Land* Eliot did mainly the latter (though there is the use of the former in the utterances of the Thunder). In *Four Quartets* he did both: the 'impersonal point of view' comes partly from the use of Christian language at certain points; and the 'splitting' is not into 'different personalities' but into different facets of the same personality.

The different voices, styles and verse forms enable Eliot to encompass a wider range of experience: to draw on different aspects of private and public life, to 'come at' certain fundamental preoccupations from various angles and in various moods. As well as the analogy of different voices, a musical analogy is possible, and Eliot drew it himself in his essay 'The Music of Poetry' (1942), written close in time to the Quartets, and suggesting clearly why he gave the poems the title he did. The analogy of 'the development of a theme by different groups of instruments' is most relevant to what I have been saying about different styles and voices, but the passage (*On Poetry and Poets*, p. 38) is also interesting in its remarks on rhythm, structure, theme and 'movement'. Eliot disclaims any technical knowledge of music, but says that the elements of music which are most important to the poet are the sense of rhythm and the sense of structure. He repeats the idea, which we have encountered before, of a poem or a passage realizing itself first in the poet's mind as a particular rhythm before it reaches expression in words. He speaks of music's use of recurrent themes being also natural to poetry; of the analogy in poetic style with the use of different instruments in a musical piece; and of the possibilities of transitions in a poem comparable to those in the movements of a symphony or quartet.[3] 'It is in the concert room, rather than in the opera house, that the germ of a poem may be quickened' — just as, one feels, a Chopinesque music may have helped to quicken the music of 'Portrait of a Lady'. There are also themes or motifs in *The Waste Land*, and motifs in 'Burnt Norton' ('the moment in the rose-garden' with its 'hidden laughter / Of children', the theme of stillness in movement, the various uses of light and dark, the idea of time and timelessness), which recur throughout the other Quartets. The different groups of instruments are analogous to tones of voice; and the 'transitions' or 'movements' are there in the different Parts, and sometimes in the transitions within a single part, like the transitions from the *allegro* rhythm of the lyric at the beginning of Part II (lines 1–15) to the slower *largo* of the longer-lines continuation beginning 'At the still point of the turning world. Neither flesh nor fleshless'.

A longer poem needs variety if it is to succeed, since it is impossible that the verse should remain at the same level of intensity throughout. Another element of variety which Eliot introduces is the use of more prosaic kinds of language, in terms of both rhythm and discursive content, which we have already seen him defending in his remarks on poetry and prose. In 'Burnt Norton' we have the quietly meditative opening lines, the more concentrated and intent effort to 'create' an abstract concept in the latter section of Part II, the exploratory analysis of Part V. One might say, in fact, that a kind of free verse often not far from prose, but with a clearly identifiable rhythm usually of four or five stresses to the line, is the foundation of the *Four Quartets* style, which at significant moments rises to a higher intensity, as in the formal lyrics at the beginning of Part II and in Part IV of each poem, and in the passages within other parts when the verse takes on a stronger pulse of incantation or lyric dance (like Part III of 'East Coker', which begins with the former and breaks for a moment into the latter, 'So the darkness shall be the light, and the stillness the dancing'). One of the striking things about the 'foundational' rhythm is the fact that it very largely avoids the iambic measure even as an underlying pattern. William Carlos Williams accused Eliot of being a conformist in metre as well as other things: 'He wanted to go back to the iambic pentameter; and he did go back to it very well; but he didn't acknowledge it.'[4] But in fact, in *Four Quartets*, the iambic pentameter line is very rare, and where it is used it is for particular and distinguishing effect, as in the 'compound ghost' passage in 'Little Gidding' II, where it is the basis of the metre.

Some parts of *Four Quartets* are even so prosaic as to be flat, and this presents a critical problem: how flat can the flat parts

of a long poem afford to be? And yet, though the problem remains, it appears at least that in such parts, like the opening of
'The Dry Salvages', Eliot was calculating his effects. He was
aiming at a poem which could incorporate a wide range of his
own experience in relation to certain predominant concerns, and
this included the casual and even — in one or two places — the
banal. The poem aims at the embodiment of the whole man.
And although we may still feel that there are important aspects
of human nature, even of Eliot's own nature, which it leaves
out, we can still recognize the range of experience it manages to
get in. On the problem of the long poem and its necessarily varying intensity, and responding to Poe's assertion that the long
poem was an impossibility because a poem had to be the expression of a single mood, Eliot defined his attitude in an interesting
passage in an essay of 1948, 'From Poe to Valéry', reprinted in
To Criticize the Critic (p. 34). He writes of how only a long
poem can express a variety of moods, which require 'a number
of different themes or subjects'. The parts can form a whole
which is more than the sum of those parts; and the long poem
can also afford passages which are less intense and less 'poetic'
than others: 'A long poem may gain by the widest possible variations of intensity.' The present study will consider these variations of intensity and their degree of success in particular
passages, and this relation of the parts to the whole, in more
detail in relation to individual poems.

II

Burnt Norton is the name of a manor house with gardens, near
Chipping Campden in Gloucestershire, which Eliot visited in
1934. Like the later Quartets, the poem starts from a particular
place from which its meditations radiate outwards into other experiences, and on which they touch again at the close. The
epigraphs from Heraclitus at the head of the poem can be
rendered in English thus: 'Although the Word (Logos) is common to all, most people live as if each of them had a private intelligence of his own'; and 'The way up and the way down are
one and the same'.[5] The first points towards the aspiration to
universal truth in the poem; the second will become clearer in the
light of the poem as a whole. The poem itself begins with a
meditative, philosophic passage which sceptically entertains propositions rather than asserting them:

Time present and time past
Are both perhaps present in time future
And time future contained in time past.
If all time is eternally present
All time is unredeemable.

'Perhaps . . .' and 'If . . .': these propositions are being mooted, turned over in the mind. And the possibility entertained is primarily a pessimistic one (though there may be an ambiguity): it is the possibility that human life in time is determined. If all time is present, then our destiny is fixed and unalterable. If the future is 'contained in time past' then, in one way of seeing that idea, we have no power over the future since it is already determined. Above all we have no power to rectify or 'redeem' the past: 'All time is unredeemable'. It is a kind of retort to the admonition of *Ash-Wednesday* IV: 'Redeem / The time': time cannot be redeemed, nothing can be saved.

What might have been is an abstraction
Remaining a perpetual possibility
Only in a world of speculation.

'What might have been': it is a preoccupation that runs through the whole of Eliot's poetry, from 'Prufrock's 'And would it have been worth it, after all', through 'Portrait of a Lady's 'things that other people have desired', 'I wonder how they should have been together' in 'La Figlia' and above all in Part V of *The Waste Land*:

The sea was calm, your heart would have responded
Gaily, when invited, beating obedient
To controlling hands

But the sense of possibility, of unfulfilled potentiality, which is still there in the very feeling, is now negated to a mere 'abstraction', a possibility for mere 'speculation'. And yet all this is only 'Perhaps . . .' and 'If . . .': and the next lines begin a new sequence of feeling:

Footfalls echo in the memory
Down the passage which we did not take
Towards the door we never opened
Into the rose-garden. My words echo
Thus, in your mind.

'Echo in the memory / Down the passage': but what is the status of those echoes? And where do they sound? If 'in the memory' then the footsteps must once have sounded in actuality. But 'Down the passage *which we did not take*': of what, then, are these echoes? Is the passage *only* 'in the memory' – and yet memory implies something remembered. The ambiguities of syntax and sense nevertheless do not negate our feeling that there *are* echoes and that the 'footfalls' have a reality. And the concluding lines strengthen this feeling: the speaker's words 'echo' in our minds; but how, since we have not actually *heard* them spoken? And yet the words of the poem are 'heard' within our minds; and the memory of those words, the hearing of them again in our minds, is perhaps no different from remembering and hearing again words actually spoken. What is the 'reality' of what is remembered? And what is the 'reality' of what is imagined? Subtly and unobtrusively the lines shift our minds from the mode of conceptual understanding ('What might have been is an abstraction') into a mode of imagination. The 'abstraction' begins to turn into something 'concrete', something actually being experienced. The words, and the footfalls, begin to echo.

'But to what purpose . . . ': there is a momentary doubt of the value of this imagining. Are words simply air, 'Disturbing the dust . . .'? Or is this toying with memories of the past, fragments of what once was ('a bowl of rose-leaves'), merely futile? The answer is not given; but the life of imagination cannot be checked now it has begun its course:

> Other echoes
> Inhabit the garden. Shall we follow?
> Quick, said the bird, find them, find them,
> Round the corner. Through the first gate,
> Into our first world, shall we follow
> The deception of the thrush? Into our first world.

The echoes gain a new substantiality: they 'inhabit'. And the rhythm of the bird's calls marvellously evokes the excitement of children's hide-and-seek, of running down the garden path, 'Round the corner. Through the first gate'. The feeling of excitement begins to take over; we are scarcely detained by the cautionary question 'shall we follow / The deception of the thrush?' and the answer is simply a confirmation of the movement as the rhythm slows emphatically: 'Into our first world'. The slower tempo continues in the passage that follows:

> There they were, dignified, invisible,
> Moving without pressure, over the dead leaves,

> In the autumn heat, through the vibrant air,
> And the bird called, in response to
> The unheard music hidden in the shrubbery,
> And the unseen eyebeam crossed, for the roses
> Had the look of flowers that are looked at.

We do not, at first, stop to ask who 'they' are: their presence is made palpable by the measured pressure of the rhythm in the first three lines, a paradoxical pressure for beings 'moving without pressure', but one which sorts with the 'unheard music', and the telling effect of the whole passage in making felt things beyond sense. The autumn heat has its own pressure and the 'vibrant' air has a double quality, a tremor that is physical and psychological. The music is 'hidden' (as if it were potentially visible) and the 'eyebeam' which 'crossed' is given a kind of substance, and by these effects of synaesthesia (or the use of one sense impression to give the mental effect of another) a kind of sixth sense or awareness beyond the senses is created – an awareness beyond the normal, like the idea of the self-consciousness of the roses.

'There they were as our guests, accepted and accepting.' The presences (already 'dignified') are made more human, more intimate, related to the onlookers or visitors by the paradox or reversal of 'as our guests', which, with 'accepted and accepting', implies perhaps some potential barrier overcome. The 'formal pattern' in which both parties move towards the box circle is also felt in the syntax ('So we moved, and they . . .'). And the syntax of the culminating movement also helps create the sense of visionary beauty arising from the most ordinary, even banal, of objects, as the features of the pool are neutrally itemized (a lesser poet would have made the pool stone, if not marble), followed immediately by the vision:

> Dry the pool, dry concrete, brown edged,
> And the pool was filled with water out of sunlight,
> And the lotos rose, quietly, quietly,
> The surface glittered out of heart of light,

The mysterious mingling of elements (substance arising out of light), the lotos with its mystical associations, the movement ('quietly, quietly'), the relation of 'surface' to 'heart of light' (the surface 'intimate with the depths'): we can begin to analyse this moment into its constituent elements, but its perfection, or something as close to perfection as poetry has reached in our century, is in the end beyond explanation. It is a vision, and it is also music; and it uses the simplest and clearest language. 'Heart of light' echoes — but I think quite fortuitously, as an unwilled, added grace — the moment in the hyacinth garden in *The Waste Land*, 'Looking into the heart of light, the silence', but transfigures it from a vision of sublime emptiness to one of plenitude. But the moment is not in need of 'interpretation': it can be presented, and dwelt upon, but in the end it simply needs to be read.

And this means, of course, that to linger on 'heart of light' is to distort slightly the full effect of the lines, since in reading we move on without more than a brief pause to

> And they were behind us, reflected in the pool.
> Then a cloud passed, and the pool was empty.

We do not lose ourselves entirely in the trance of the lotos rose and the heart of light, since the presences are also there — benignly guarding, or admonitory, as well as 'accepted and accepting' (and what was it that needed acceptance?) — and they disappear with the rest of the vision. The bird's voice is urgent again:

> Go, said the bird, for the leaves were full of children,
> Hidden excitedly, containing laughter.
> Go, go, go, said the bird: human kind
> Cannot bear very much reality.

This is 'our first world', in one sense the world of childhood, and this sense is confirmed by the hidden children. There is a possible note of mockery in their laughter, as well as happiness: their innocence mocks the time-ridden consciousness of the adult visitors. The adults cannot stay in this paradisal world for long. They 'cannot bear very much reality' — neither the reality, one takes it, of the vision of light, nor that of its swift passing.[6]

One might ask the question, who are 'they' in this passage? One response might be that the question is pedantic and that 'they' are defined quite clearly enough in the passage. They are 'dignified, invisible'; they are like guests 'accepted and accepting' — implying perhaps some barrier to intimacy removed, some alienation overcome, since each party is said to accept and be accepted by the other. They move in a formal pattern with the speaker and his companion or companions, again implying harmony, and they are mysteriously 'reflected in the pool' as the lotos rose and the surface glittered 'out of heart of light', and they disappear with the rest of the vision. (That they are both 'invisible' and 'reflected in the pool' is part of the general paradox of the seen and the unseen in the passage.) They are presences, then, who preside over the garden. But in relation to the children whose laughter is heard one might associate them with parental figures or guardians. Some critics have gone further and associated them with Adam and Eve, 'our first parents', since this is 'our first world' and has affinities with the idea of the 'golden world' and the garden of Eden, though this seems to me unnecessarily theological for this point in the poem.[7]

The passage ends with a return to the reflections of earlier in Part I: the 'reality' of the rose-garden is outside time: it lay 'Down the passage which we did not take', but it has been taken now, in the poem, and the door 'never opened' has been entered. The abstraction of 'What might have been' has, in the poem, become more than abstraction, it has become a reality. So the last lines can be read in two ways: either as a return to the world of time in which past, present, future and 'What might have been' point only to one end, which is the untranscendent present and, in effect, death, which is the one 'end' of time; or as an affirmation of an eternal present, glimpsed in a rose-garden, present outside time, and 'end' in the sense of 'goal', to which all time points. Given that the lines follow 'human kind / Cannot bear very much reality' and take their tone and cadence from that, it would seem that at *this* point in the poem it is the first reading which is uppermost and that the ending of this part is a falling back into an untranscendent, despairing sense of reality, as the mind ebbs back from the visionary to the actual.

Part II begins with a fifteen-line 'Symbolist' lyric. It is a quite different mode from the previous part, less intense, more provisional and experimental, and its significance is not to be pondered in the same way. The opening lines,

> Garlic and sapphires in the mud
> Clot the bedded axle-tree.

are not a code to be broken: they evoke, in an image derived from Mallarmé[8] (but with a closer approximation to prose sense), the thick palpability and texture of the physical world (the 'axle-tree' being the imaginary axis on which the world revolves). 'The trilling wire in the blood' etc. suggests a compression of the network of veins and that of a telegraph system in a single image: an analogy between the physical and social body. And 'The dance along the artery / The circulation of the lymph' has a similar parallel in 'the drift of stars'. The touch of a childhood world ('Ascend to summer in the tree') becomes an image of looking down on the leaves and hearing a hunt (a hint of the medieval too, perhaps, in line with the astrological image that follows) which is caught in the pattern of the stars. The 'boarhound and the boar' are not actual names of constellations, but they sound like them. The passage is a kind of emblem of life in the world, and of the pagan heavens which merely reflected the world.

The longer-lined, conceptual passage which follows attempts in a different way to 'create the concept' (to adapt D. W. Harding's phrase) of eternity,[9] of a state outside time. It attempts, that is, to evoke through conceptual terms what was evoked through a particular imagined event in the rose-garden in Part I. 'The still point of the turning world', for instance, is a mathematical fiction of the static point at the centre of a revolving circle (which contrasts directly with the solidly physical image of the centre of the world, the 'bedded axle-tree' of line 2). Otherwise, the passage employs a series of paradoxes or contradictions ('neither flesh nor fleshless', etc.), and images of the dance (a pattern − therefore in a sense static − of beautiful but purposeless movement, 'neither from nor towards'), of light, and ideas of freedom, completion and resolution (*Erhebung* means elevation or exultation). The passage is made up of largely abstract words, and taken by itself might seem not to convey more than a series of abstract paradoxes and mystical propositions. But the presence of the meditating voice adds a tone of intentness and effort, the pathos of thought ('I can only say, *there* we have been: but I cannot say where'); and there is a sense of 'language thrown out' (to use Matthew Arnold's terms for religious language) 'at certain great objects of consciousness'.[10] And some of the definitions of the state aimed at also involve terms which relate it to a moral state ('The inner freedom from the practical desire'), which helps us to place it in relation to what we know or can more easily begin to imagine. But perhaps the most directly clarifying part of the passage is in the conclusion of the first verse-paragraph and the paragraph that follows, which provide a discursive gloss on the experience of the rose-garden. That experience was necessarily brief because, as we were told, 'human kind / Cannot bear very much reality'; and here the 'enchainment' of past and future (woven aptly in sound with the word 'changing' in 'changing body') 'Protects mankind from heaven and damnation'. 'Consciousness' is a state outside time and only in time can it be remembered; the moments adduced include not only that in the rose-garden but also 'The moment in the arbour where the rain beat, / The moment in the draughty church at smokefall' — typically English places, one might think; at any rate, scenes as if from some unrevealed biography.

Part III takes us into a kind of limbo, a place of 'disaffection', a state of neither love nor genuine renunciation (probably to be associated, as Grover Smith suggests, with the idea of 'indifference' in 'Little Gidding' III, the state between 'attachment' and 'detachment'). It is a place of 'Time before and time after' merely, because it knows only the successive moments of linear time, thinks only of past and future and has no consciousness of the present. The 'dim light' and the 'flicker / Over the strained time-ridden faces' suggests an urban scene with artificial light, a scene like the London Underground (Eliot himself mentioned this association with the later lines beginning 'Descend lower').[11] There is that epigrammatic force that makes so many of Eliot's phrases memorable, in the word-play of 'Distracted from distraction by distraction'. And in general this passage is effective particularly in its power to combine a kind of abstract limbo with a particular place. The last six lines of the verse-paragraph, with their sudden expansiveness, achieve a fine modulation from the previous generalized setting to one rooted in a particular place. 'Eructation' is strange, but apt rather than pedantic: its literal sense of 'belching' gives us the appropriate unpleasantness and morbidity, and its latinity helps to give the scene at the same time the grandeur of some classical underworld:

> Eructation of unhealthy souls
> Into the faded air, the torpid
> Driven on the wind that sweeps the gloomy hills of London,
> Hampstead and Clerkenwell, Campden and Putney,
> Highgate, Primrose and Ludgate. Not here
> Not here the darkness, in this twittering world.

The sudden change of perspective, the lengthening of the lines with their sweeping rhythm, seems suddenly to transport us to a vision of the whole of London. Similarly in 'this twittering world' the exactly chosen adjective both suggests the sound of starling-filled London and is reminiscent of the classical ghosts of Hades:[12] it is a thrilling compression into a single phrase of present actuality and classical imagination.

'Descend lower': the darkness necessary for the soul is of another kind. And the command and the passage that follows emphasizes how extreme is the element of asceticism in Eliot's vision of spiritual progress:

> Desiccation of the world of sense,
> Evacuation of the world of fancy,
> Inoperancy of the world of spirit;

This for most people would seem to be a living death indeed. And it forces one to ask: do we want to follow the commands of the poet? It is possible to read the lines as directed simply at the poet himself, to see the commands as part of a spiritual method; and to suspend belief and disbelief so that we simply identify for the moment with the dramatic self-command. We need, I think, to be able to do that in order to be able to enter into the poem and to understand a range of experience which may be in many ways very alien. But in the end it would seem to be avoiding the challenge of the poem to deny that these lines can be read as directed at us too, and that we need to make up our minds about the path they direct us towards. We need to be able to distinguish between our imaginative identification with the process of experience being undergone and our actual assent or dissent from its injunctions. 'This is the one way'; what the other is is not very clear: 'the same, not in movement / But in abstention from movement' does not, I think, convey very much.[13] The commentators direct us to the writings of St John of the Cross, particularly to *The Ascent of Mount Carmel* whose teaching the passage is said to summarize.[14] But drawing on a source does not exempt the poet from making as clear as possible his own meaning when meaning is an important element, as it surely is here. It would seem that the 'other' way also involves desiccation, evacuation, etc., but instead of active 'descent' it requires a passive waiting like that in 'East Coker' III: 'while the world moves / In appetency, on its metalled ways / Of time past and time future' — an image as of metal rails, an image of the mechanical following of desire (and one which also strengthens the suggestions of a setting which is on one level that of the London Underground).

Part IV is a short lyric on mortality and a kind of immortality. The first two lines strike an emphatic music with a regular rhythm and end-stopped lines with rhymes, and then the third very effectively changes it to a wistful intonation that runs on to the fourth, fifth and sixth, the lines getting shorter as the voice becomes more longing and uncertain in its combined hope and fear. The 'black cloud carries the sun away' recalls the rose-garden: 'Then a cloud passed, and the pool was empty'. The sunflower has associations, from Blake, with a pining after immortality;[15] but the clematis and the yew are cold and sinister in clutching, clinging and curling (round the tomb?). However, the feeling is not simply of mortality. The light from the kingfisher's wing evokes another possibility, a brief flash of beauty which is not lost but is 'still / At the still point of the turning world'.

Part V is in its first paragraph a reflection on the nature of art, particularly the arts of language in relation to the question of time and timelessness; and, to anticipate for a moment, it is one of several points in the Quartets where Eliot reflects on the processes of poetry and often of the present poem itself. The general drift of the argument is clear: poetry moves, as we read it, through time, but in its finished state it constitutes a pattern which is timeless. It is form which gives language its power to reach a timeless centre of value (and also, in a possible secondary implication, to speak beyond the time of its composition). But there are one or two problems. 'Words, after speech, reach / Into the silence': does this mean that any kind of utterance is ultimately incomplete and reaches beyond itself to some unspoken meaning (a sense that would be in line with Prufrock's 'It is impossible to say just what I mean')? Or does it (as I think more likely from the context) mean that mere *speech* can only reach (weakly) into the silence, whereas the form of art can apprehend meaning (or 'reach / The stillness'), and, indeed, go on speaking, be a perpetual source of utterance? The example of music is less precise: words can exist without pattern, but music cannot, or it would not be music. The paradox of the violin is better: strictly, the violin is not 'still' while the note lasts (neither while the note is being played nor during its reverberation), but the single held note has a kind of stillness, since it does not change. The image is anyway rejected ('not that only'), for Eliot wants an image that more exactly captures the 'co-existence' of stillness and movement, as the Chinese jar, with its fluid yet static shape and pattern, captures it. In the end, of course, the paradox breaks down into sheer contradiction ('or say that the end precedes the beginning'). The effort at a logical statement of what the poem is trying to express collapses because it is aiming to describe a state beyond logical categories.

'Words strain, / Crack and sometimes break, under the burden': this is not just a statement about words in general but about the activity of thought the speaker is presently engaged in; and the amplification of the idea ('Under the tension, slip, slide, perish') reinforces the dramatic nature of the thought, the sense of present struggle. 'Shrieking voices / Scolding, mocking, or merely chattering' (respectively: the moralists, the cynics and the press or the 'social' world?), 'Always assail them.' The last lines introduce a religious note, 'the Word in the desert': but one might ask how justified this shift to the religious, from the 'word' to the 'Word', is. Was it merely an association of ideas arising from the 'shrieking voices'? At any rate, after a passage dealing wholly with the struggle of the artistic 'word', this is a shift to a new realm of experience. One can see that for Eliot the two areas were contiguous or even, perhaps, the same. For the reader there may be more of a division. But at the very least we are challenged to ponder the relations between the nature of artistic and of religious language: both are creative and are often called 'inspired'; both involve a solitary struggle; but a belief in the latter involves some belief in a sacred or transcendent realm, and belief in the former perhaps does not.

The concluding paragraph of Part V begins with discursive language and ends with a moment of direct 'presentation' and (it should be said, in spite of Eliot's reminders about prose-virtues in poetry) of more directly poetic embodiment. The discursive lines clarify the idea of pattern with

> The detail of pattern is movement,
> As in the figure of the ten stairs.

Primarily this is a straightforwardly pictorial idea: the pattern of the whole figure in a drawing of stairs is static, but if we move from detail to detail, stair to stair, we are aware of movement. There may also be an allusion here to the 'mystical ladder' with ten stairs in *The Dark Night of the Soul* of St John of the Cross, which would relate this passage to the end of Part III and the end of 'East Coker' III, and the idea of spiritual ascent and descent. This association would prepare for the transition to the language of 'Desire' and 'Love' in the next lines: and here is an appeal to an idea which is psychological as much as religious and hence perhaps does not involve questions of belief, as did the passage on the 'Word'. 'Desire' is movement because it drives one towards the object of desire; but 'Love' is 'unmoving', the cause of movement (or desire) but also the final perfect goal of desire. But perhaps the idea *is* inescapably 'religious' because it speaks of perfection, which is not to be had on earth (as both believers and non-believers may be prepared to agree). In this world love is inevitably involved with desire, because it is in a state 'Between un-being and being' and tries to move from the first towards the second.

The lines are not obscure, and I offer the above paraphrase with apology for its probable redundancy. But the idea is such a central one in the poem (and *Four Quartets* as a whole) that it seems worth bringing before the reader (even at the risk of tediousness) in a slightly different and elaborated form. The idea of a 'pattern' which gathers up all past experience and places it *sub specie aeternitatis*, in a perspective of eternity, is one which Eliot had already elaborated in many places in his prose works, particularly the essays on Dante.[16] Dante was able to integrate his youthful, idealistic and unfulfilled love for Beatrice into a pattern of both poetry and belief which gave it a new, wider and more permanent significance. In the Clark Lectures Eliot had written that whereas Laforgue was trapped in his adolescence, Dante in the 'Vita Nuova' placed his adolescent experience in the perspective of a mature philosophy. And in his poetry Eliot had almost from the first been returning again and again to certain central experiences and recasting them in new artistic forms and by means of new *personae*, working out patterns for experience which changed from poem to poem — a process one can see most clearly in the continual return to the image of the weeping girl and its avatars, but which one could follow in the changing use of other images too, like those of the desert or the garden. The motivating force behind every poem, that force, literally, which causes its movement, is desire (to revert to the terms of 'Burnt Norton'), but the state of perfection, the form or pattern to which every poem aspires, is love. No poem, of course, reaches this perfection: just as in *The Hollow Men* 'Between the potency / And the existence / . . . Falls the shadow', so in 'Burnt Norton' there is an awareness of being

> Caught in the form of limitation
> Between un-being and being.

But that last passage (and even more, of course, my clumsy paraphrase and attempts at 'explanation') is discursive language which is in the end particularly limited in trying to express these experiences. What gives most life to 'Burnt Norton' and constitutes its high poetic moments are those passages of direct vision which rise out of, or break in on, the lower register of the meditative reflections, passages like that which ends:

> Sudden in a shaft of sunlight
> Even while the dust moves
> There rises the hidden laughter
> Of children in the foliage
> Quick now, here, now always —

'Sudden': with that emphasis at the beginning of the line we are suddenly removed from reflection on experience to experience itself. The dust in the shaft of sunlight is an extraordinarily beautiful image of something that seems both still and moving. And 'there rises' — not 'there rose' (as in the past tense of the rose-garden passage in Part I), or only 'there often rises', but above all 'there rises' now, in the poem — the laughter of children which was there before in the rose-garden.

> Quick now, here, now, always —

The significance (which is also love, and happiness) is *here* in the poem. This effort of the poet to grasp, to hold on to something, is intensely moving. But the poem would be quite different if it ended with that line — its sense of reality demands the falling back into the sad admission of the inevitability of time and the nature of time.

> Ridiculous the waste sad time
> Stretching before and after.

And in the light of our examination of the discursive analytic passages in the poem might we not apply these closing lines to them too, and say that their effort is also, relatively, a 'waste sad time' stretching before and after these moments of intensity? Yet it is also true that the discipline of discursive meditation helps to make such moments possible.

11

The wartime Quartets (1940–2)

After the writing of 'Burnt Norton' Eliot turned back first to writing for the stage, and *The Family Reunion* appeared in 1939. It was the outbreak of war in September of that year that appears more than anything else to have impelled him to return to the more inward and searching exploration of experience which 'Burnt Norton' had represented. In the interview in 1953 already referred to in Chapter 9[1] Eliot recalled that it was the war which turned him away from his preoccupation with drama and towards the writing of 'East Coker', and that it was in writing that poem that he came to see the Quartets as a set of four. The three wartime Quartets, which take 'Burnt Norton' as their structural model, are essentially an attempt to explore the implications of that poem in relation to wider areas of personal experience, religion, culture and history: they establish a fuller relationship of the experience of the earlier poem to a public world at the same time as they continue the exploration of the self. It is difficult and probably not desirable to try and pin each of the remaining quartets down to a single 'subject':[2] as Eliot said in a letter, after suggesting that Part IV of 'East Coker' ('The wounded surgeon plies the steel') was 'in a way the heart of the matter', 'the poem as a whole – this five part form – is an attempt to weave several unrelated strands together in an emotional whole, so that really there isn't any heart of the matter'.[3] Each poem continues in varying ways the exploration of time and timelessness, the problems of writing, the conditions of spiritual life and the nullity of the merely mundane.

In relation to the last Quartets, A. D. Moody cites an important passage which concluded the lectures on *The Idea of a Christian Society*, which Eliot gave at Cambridge in 1939. Referring to the Munich Agreement (in which England and France ceded Czechoslavakian Sudetenland to Germany and Chamberlain proclaimed 'peace in our time') Eliot said that he was 'deeply shaken' by the events, in a way that involved a feeling of personal 'humiliation' and demanded 'an act of personal contrition, of humility, repentance and amendment'. It was a doubt, he wrote, of the 'validity of a civilization': a feeling that England and her allies had no firm ideas or beliefs to set against those which opposed them; a doubt about the whole nature of the materialistic bases of his own society.[4] The connection with the last three Quartets is not, of course, that such a realization is the sole explanation of why Eliot wrote them. But this feeling of personal humiliation and doubt surely contributed to the need to re-explore his own deepest experiences and convictions in a more inward medium than the drama. It also helps to suggest why the last three Quartets are in a number of places particularly concerned to relate the exploration of personal experience, even more than in 'Burnt Norton', to a consideration of religious belief, society and history.

I

'East Coker' (1940)

'East Coker' meditates variously on cyclical time and the tradition of marriage (Part I); the experience of middle and old age (II and V); the darkness of death and the 'darkness of God' (III); and Christian redemption (IV). These different preoccupations interpenetrate and appear in more than one Part, and the whole is also held together by the repetition of certain phrases and motifs; other motifs link the poem with its forerunner, 'Burnt Norton'. There is also the beginning of a preoccupation with history, the past not only of personal memory (as in 'Burnt Norton') but of society as well. East Coker in Somerset was the birthplace of Eliot's ancestor Andrew Eliot, who left England for Massachusetts in search of religious freedom in 1669, and thus the title links the personal and the historical. In addition, Sir Thomas Elyot, whose *The Boke of the Governour* (1531) is quoted in the passage on the marriage dance in Part I, was also an ancestor, and grandson of Simon Elyot of East Coker.

But this is in one way to anticipate; we should begin with the poem itself. 'In my beginning is my end' suggests initially, in the context of the first verse-paragraph, the *cycle* of time. The following lines, with their patterns of syntactic and verbal repetition, suggest the repetitiveness of time seen from a certain point of view. The point of view is partly that of Ecclesiastes 3, which the passage echoes, but without (at this point) the placing of the cycle of time in relation to God. Time is seen as repetitive, and apportioned to different activities, but without any overriding *telos* or goal other than death, then life, then death in an endless cycle. The rhythm is satisfying in its repetitions and yet also limited, relentless. Only the last line ('And to shake the tattered arras woven with a silent motto'), with its beautiful play of sounds, opens up a new perspective by looking back to a distant historical past.

The repeated 'In my beginning is my end' at the beginning of the second verse-paragraph this time has a specifically human and even personal direction of meaning: for what follows is concerned with human procreation and perhaps the poet's own past. His birth implies his death in the cycle of generation; and perhaps too there is a remoter sense of his having come back to his ancestral roots (remoter because we are aware of this only by way of our knowledge of East Coker's biographical connection with the poet). But the first sense is the important one. And the passage that follows evokes a feeling of pressure of the cycle of nature, once again (as in the equivalent past in 'Burnt Norton') through the evocation of a particular place. The 'pressure' is initially not just a general but a very particular one. The world of physical life is insistent and hypnotic here and now. The feeling of that insistence is marvellously evoked:

> Now the light falls
> Across the open field, leaving the deep lane
> Shuttered with branches, dark in the afternoon,
> Where you lean against a bank while a van passes,
> And the deep lane insists on the direction
> Into the village, in the electric heat
> Hypnotised. In a warm haze the sultry light
> Is absorbed, not refracted, by grey stone.
> The dahlias sleep in the empty silence.
> Wait for the early owl.

The light 'absorbed, not refracted', the soft light of a summer evening, suggests warmth, appealing to the sense of touch (a more purely physical sense) as much as to sight, evoking a world of physical sensation. (One might contrast the *reflected* light at the beginning of 'Little Gidding', which leads the imagination in the direction of a spiritual reality.)

In the passage on the marriage dance that follows, the fairy-tale scene of figures dancing to 'the weak pipe and the little drum', there are echoes of an ancient tradition, signalled also in the phrases in old spelling (of the sixteenth century, from Sir Thomas

Elyot writing on marriage). The rhythm of the dance is 'Dignified and commodious', but becomes heavier as the passage goes on. Marriage, in the end, is seen not so much as a 'sacrament' but as a part of that endless cycle of procreation which man shares with the animals, a cycle that for each generation ends only in death:

> The time of the coupling of man and woman
> And that of beasts. Feet rising and falling.
> Eating and drinking. Dung and death.

It has often been pointed out that Eliot's sense of marriage in his poetry is a limited one: the limits are imposed by those attending on his sense of sexuality. The preoccupation, in his poetry, with the failures of sexual love, up to and including *The Hollow Men* (1925), is not thereafter replaced by a more positive view. Rather, Eliot turns to the awareness of other kinds of love, the love of a maternal figure in *Ash-Wednesday* or of a daughter in 'Marina', the first of which (at least) is characterized as a kind of religious love, pointing towards the love of God. In *Four Quartets* this process is deepened and complicated, but not reversed. Unlike D. H. Lawrence, whose novels explore sexual love with a genius that led F. R. Leavis to call him a 'necessary opposite' to Eliot, Eliot's awareness of love in his writing moves away from the sexual after *The Waste Land*. In that poem sexuality, though a source of disgust in many places, is still a mystery that informs its moments of deepest passion (the hyacinth garden, the reply to Thunder's second admonition). Thereafter it is still a mystery, but one in the face of which the poet, for the purpose of his deepest insights, has to confess defeat; and he relegates it to the world of time and generation, which his poetry seeks to transcend in its moments of greatest intensity.

But in the concluding lines of Part I we get one of those moments of poetic vitality which makes *Four Quartets* a living poem and not just a disquisition.

> Dawn points, and another day
> Prepares for heat and silence. Out at sea the dawn wind
> Wrinkles and slides. I am here
> Or there, or elsewhere. In my beginning.

This sudden transition to another time of day, another place and another element, and the sense of expectancy in 'Dawn points' and the feel of the shifting wind, is exhilarating. The speaker is

217

not trapped in one mood (that of the preceding passage): imagination liberates him; he is 'here / Or there, or elsewhere'. And the repeated half of the opening phrase of the poem gives the change from the heavy cadence and sense of the whole phrase. 'In my beginning': he is beginning again.

But that new beginning is disturbing. The opening sequence in Part II repeats the Symbolist style of the same point in 'Burnt Norton', and evokes a sense of confusion attendant on the stirring of new life in middle or old age, 'the disturbance of the spring' in 'late November'. In contrast to the cosmic 'pattern' in the 'Burnt Norton' lyric ('reconciled among the stars') there is now a sense of 'vortex' and 'destructive fire', not a Last Judgement but simply a return to original chaos. We feel the lyric is something of an exercise in the style already tried (which itself had a slightly 'conventional' feeling, the convention being that of French Symbolism). So the disclaimer that follows is not entirely surprising ('That was a way of putting it — not very satisfactory / A periphrastic study in a worn-out poetical fashion'). And the passage that follows tries to approach the question of old age in a different mode.

The style here is discursive, not particularly abstract or philosophic, but a general language of ratiocination. One does not find powerful poetry in such passages in *Four Quartets*, but one often finds precise and cogent sense and wisdom in a measured and effective verse, a wisdom that questions conventional notions of wisdom. Is a knowledge of the past, for instance (of history, philosophy, literature), simply a knowledge of 'dead secrets'? And there is also an implicit challenge here to one of Eliot's own favourite ideas, the idea of a 'pattern' of experience which we have seen in his prose ('Not our feelings but the pattern we may make of our feelings is the centre of value')[5] and which informs so much of the practice of his verse. Now this idea is questioned, in questioning 'the knowledge derived from experience':

> The knowledge imposes a pattern, and falsifies,
> For the pattern is new in every moment
> And every moment is a new and shocking
> Valuation of all we have been.

No pattern can be adequate to developing experience — which is one of the reasons we need poetry, to bring pattern and belief into fresh contact with experience, and to show how (or whether) it can be 'lived'.[6] The 'wisdom of old men' is an illusion: this is a recurring theme throughout the Quartets, and one might almost say their central moral subject, to be reinforced more powerfully still in 'Little Gidding'. In 'the middle of the way' there is an echo of Dante's famous opening ('Nel mezzo del cammin di nostra vita'); but in the 'bramble', the 'grimpen', the 'monsters' and the 'fancy light' we have touches of the fantasies of second childhood. The final affirmation, that of 'the wisdom of humility', is a difficult one, difficult because of the problem of knowing what it consists of (and perhaps because of its associations with Uriah Heep). But the final touch of poetry, recalling the opening passage, guides our feelings. Humility is partly a recognition of transience:

> The houses are all gone under the sea.
>
> The dancers are all gone under the hill.

The prophetic and Miltonic note[7] of the opening of Part III is tempered by Eliot's strain of satiric wit ('the vacant into the vacant', 'the Directory of Directors'). But perhaps the similes for religious transformation and 'the darkness of God' are not very telling. The theatrical one has inevitably dated, and runs the risk of bathos; and the image of the Underground perhaps tells us more about Eliot's nervous state of mind than about human nature (people in such a situation usually go on talking or think about getting home to cook the dinner).[8] But the telling moment in that Part comes in the following lines, in the transition from the incantatory rhythm of the spiritual injunctions —

> I said to my soul, be still, and wait without hope
> For hope would be hope for the wrong thing; . . .

— to the dance-like rhythm and beautiful imagery of

> So the darkness shall be the light, and the stillness the dancing.
> Whisper of running streams, and winter lightning.
> The wild thyme unseen and the wild strawberry,
> The laughter in the garden, echoed ecstasy
> Not lost, but requiring, pointing to the agony
> Of death and birth.

It is one of several places where poetic life of a greater intensity breaks in on a quieter, less emphatic, meditative movement or an effort at disciplined discursive thought, to show the very process of the mind and feelings; and then at the end the moments of ecstasy are themselves related back to the spiritual effort which they 'require' and 'point to'.

The passage that concludes Part III is almost directly from *The Ascent of Mount Carmel* of St John of the Cross,[9] and one might feel the reliance on this traditional mystical source was too easy, did it not fit so closely with what Eliot has been saying already in 'Burnt Norton' III. Its radical asceticism, its 'negative way', will strain the comprehension and sympathy of many readers in a secular age: but that is its point. And it may not be the least of the functions of the poem to keep alive at least some awareness of and perhaps even an ability to enter imaginatively into this extreme of religious consciousness. The kind of religous poetry represented by Part IV, however, is another matter. It is a concise, clever, formal, 'metaphysical' poem in the seventeenth-century style, on Christ's sacrifice for man. Christian belief is its *donnée*: it does not seek to lead us into a state of mind or record the poet's personal journey, but simply presents in a striking analogy the Christian view of fallen man and his redemption. The 'wounded surgeon', the 'dying nurse' and the 'ruined millionaire' are all types of Christ (the latter because he gave up heaven for a life of poverty and suffering on earth, and underwent 'ruin' on the cross).[10] The polished formality of the poem reminds one oddly of the 1920 quatrain poems, as if their caustic satire on mankind has led to this caustic (in a stricter, medical sense) and sanative allegory of the Christian remedy. There is trenchancy but there is also something chilling about it (literally so, in 'freeze / And quake in frigid purgatorial fires'). The allegory anticipates the even more clinical embodiment of the divine idea in *The Cocktail Party*, an embodiment, one may feel, which gives up too much to the modern secular consciousness (Christianity seen as a kind of 'higher psychology'), though in 'East Coker' the sanative image is strictly a metaphor. The touch of sensationalism in the last stanza is perhaps overdone and verges on religious melodrama; the paradox of a spiritual food which is embodied in 'dripping blood' and 'bloody flesh' is strictly orthodox but one feels that the poet may be slightly bullying the reader with it, and the paradox of the last line is a little obvious.

Part V begins with one of the reflections on writing which recur throughout the Quartets. There is a frankness (and humility) about this personal confession which impressed Eliot's close associate, John Hayward, who found it 'poignantly self-revealing', but one cannot help feeling that some of it is rather laboured. 'Every attempt / Is a wholly new start' is a salutary reminder, but it is simply repeated in 'And so each venture / Is a new beginning'. And the military metaphor, although apt for a wartime poem, seems a shade banal and not very exact (a 'raid' might destroy 'the inarticulate' rather than make it articulate, and disciplined 'squads' would not seem to be a very attractive form of emotional organization). But the ending is a true thought despite its prosaic form:

> There is only the fight to recover what has been lost
> And found and lost again and again . . .
> For us there is only the trying. The rest is not our business.

The concluding verse-paragraph sums up the poem and ends with a stirring change of key which leads us into 'The Dry Salvages'. 'Home is where one starts from' is an affirmation of 'roots' *and* an affirmation of exploration: starts *out* from. 'Not the intense moment / Isolated,': the moment in the rose-garden, and others, are not entirely significant alone, but need to be involved with time, and the rest of life and a society and history ('old stones that cannot be deciphered'):[11] Eliot is here reaffirming that belief in a living tradition found in the early essay 'Tradition and the Individual Talent'. 'Love is most nearly itself / When here and now cease to matter': this says again, in a new way, what Eliot said in *Ash-Wednesday* I ('And what is actual is actual only for one time / And only for one place') and 'Burnt Norton' ('Love is itself unmoving, / . . . Timeless, and undesiring'). And in the concluding lines Eliot shifts to a brief recapitulation and recreation of Tennyson's 'Ulysses' ('Old men ought to be explorers') and the sudden imagination of a world elsewhere which touches the conclusion with the shiver of poetry:

> We must be still and still moving
> Into another intensity
> For a further union, a deeper communion
> Through the dark cold and the empty desolation,
> The wave cry, the wind cry, the vast waters
> Of the petrel and the porpoise. In my end is my beginning.

The poem has come full circle, but to a new awareness: in the sudden bracingness of that marine exploration, in that final reversal of the opening phrase of the poem, we complete the movement from a sense of a natural cycle to the sense of a spiritual journey in which the awareness of death is a 'beginning'.

II

'The Dry Salvages'(1941)[12]

There is a fairly widespread agreement that 'The Dry Salvages' is the least satisfactory of the four Quartets, though it contains some fine things. Part of the problem with it is the frequent use (whether advertent or not) of a slightly stiff or pedantic tone. 'I do not know much about gods': as Donald Davie has pointed out,[13] this sounds like the awkward opening gambit of a conversational poseur, and we shall come to other examples in due course. The rest of the opening verse-paragraph conveys a clear idea, but is a little too close to journalistic cliché (again, Davie's term): 'dwellers in cities'; 'unpropitiated / By worshippers of the machine'; 'waiting, watching and waiting'. The river does accumulate some significance as the image of a physical energy which is both in nature and within each individual (a life force like that represented by primitive gods), but we have to take it merely as an idea: the verse does not embody it in its own vitality. The most vivid lines are perhaps the last four, where the poet's personal memory of the river (the Mississippi, if one is to think of Eliot's own life) is specifically treated: there is a satisfying particularity and a satisfying sound in 'the rank ailanthus of the April dooryard'.

The image of the sea which follows is an effective symbolic contrast: the river represents the personal life and a personal sense of time, and the sea an idea of prehistoric time and ultimately eternity. Prehistory is there in the 'hints of earlier and other creation', approached with fastidious delicacy of tone and sound in

> The pools where it offers to our curiosity
> The more delicate algae and the sea anemone.

and the idea of eternity in the 'time not our time, rung by the unhurried / Ground swell'. Again the sound of the language is evocative in this passage (as it generally is in the best parts of the poem − where Eliot is employing the full resources of verse): the lilt, assonance and dissonance in

> It tosses up our losses, the torn seine,
> The shattered lobsterpot, the broken oar
> And the gear of foreign dead men. . . .

or still more in

> The menace and caress of wave that breaks on water,
> The distant rote in the granite teeth.

And the change of rhythm in the shorter lines catches the new rhythm of which the words speak, as

> The tolling bell
> Measures time not our time, rung by the unhurried
> Ground swell, a time
> Older than the time of chronometers, . . .

Finally there is the use of fleeting, as if parenthetic, imagery (as at the end of 'East Coker' II) which touches the passage with a mysterious sense of the mingling of two worlds and faintly recalls other passages and other poems ('Burnt Norton' I, 'East Coker' IV, 'Marina'):

> The salt is on the briar rose,
> The fog is in the fir trees.

The sestina lyric (six-line rhyming stanzas) in Part II impresses us perhaps rather more with its form than with its content (whereas in Part I the two are inextricable); and yet the difficult form is handled expertly, and it does have a certain rightness in conveying the sense of repeated action, the feminine (unstressed) endings to the lines catching a 'gerundive' mood of continual action, and the rhythm a sense of dying and fading. The sense of work and communal action in the passage is a weary one, and one might agree with F. R. Leavis that Eliot's view of this traditional community life of the new England coast seems to deny it any creative purpose).[14] But it is an embodiment of the poet's vision of life ('one has to think of them . . .'), of course, with the undeniable limits of that vision, not an objective social analysis: we think as much of the man looking as of the scene perceived. And for him, the world of work is merely a kind of treadmill process without the illumination of a religious consciousness. Without that, the 'Clamour of the bell of the last annunciation' is merely the bell announcing death, and the 'Prayer at the calamitous annunciation' is the 'unprayable' prayer on the point of death. The only end to the process is the transformation of this 'annunciation' into

> the hardly, barely prayable
> Prayer of the one Annunciation.

– the Annunciation by the angel Gabriel to Mary, of the coming of Christ.

In the discursive reflections on the past in the passage that follows there is perhaps a problem about the tone. The opening ('It seems, as one becomes older') strikes the predominant note of elderly expatiation; and there is something of the lordly accent of the 'superior person' in some of the qualifications ('in the popular mind') and asides. The phrase 'not forgetting / Something that is probably quite ineffable' is a conversational urbanity which is the danger of sounding almost fatuous as an introduction to 'The backward look behind the assurance / Of recorded history . . .', etc. Its advance apology for the vagueness of what follows tends to weaken further what are already uncertain lines which gesture towards things not really grasped ('the backward half-look / Over the shoulder, towards the primitive terror'). The irony of the earlier parenthesis about what happiness is not ('Or even a very good dinner') is feeble. Worse, it casts doubt on whether Eliot has any real grasp of the genuine values which precede it ('Fruition, fulfilment, security or affection'), without which what he is affirming ('the sudden illumination') becomes less impressive.

But in spite of this the ideas in the passage are worth pondering. Eliot is countering a common notion of time as sequence or development, and asserting a view of it which makes us look at the values of the past — both our own individual past (in particular its moments of happiness) and that of society — with as much respect and attention as we do those of the present.

> We had the experience but missed the meaning,
> And approach to the meaning restores the experience
> In a different form, beyond any meaning
> We can assign to happiness . . .

That in many ways sums up the whole of Eliot's poetic progress: in his later poetry certain fundamental experiences are restored 'in a different form' (as we have seen in *Ash-Wednesday* and 'Marina'). And the assertion that

> . . . the past experience revived in the meaning
> Is not the experience of one life only
> But of many generations . . .

links these individual experiences to a tradition which substantiates and deepens them — the tradition of literature, for example, which Eliot explores in his prose essays. The rest of the passage talks of 'the moments of agony' which are also permanent; and the image of the rock (recalling the title of this

Quartet), despite an unfortunate hint of the jingle of 'the ragged rascals' in its alliterative line, is an effective one for an underlying unhappiness preserved through time and uncovered in times of stress.

Part III opens with one of the most awkward of Eliot's casual urbanities:

> I sometimes wonder if that is what Krishna meant –

That is bad enough in its tone of pretentious off-handedness, but to add 'Among other things' approaches the ludicrous. (It is slightly reminiscent of the anticipatory qualifications and circumlocutions of Henry James's later style.) The images that follow seem to be a rather random clutch of metaphors for the idea (which we have encountered before) of the identity of past and future – though they do add the interesting notion of a kind of nostalgia for the future (where dwelling wistfully on the future is as fruitless as dwelling on the past). But the main problem of this Part seems to be a confusion of meaning, or a hovering between two meanings. The central idea would seem to be that of the value of action in the present moment without regard to the future or the 'fruit of action'. It is this idea which Eliot takes from Krishna in the Hindu *Bhagavad Gita* (2.47–8), and to this is added the idea that what the mind is intent on 'at the time of death' is what shall 'fructify in the lives of others' (which adapts 8.6 of the *Gita*). So far the idea is clear enough. But to this Eliot adds the repeated injunction 'Fare forward' (which is not in the *Gita*, though Eliot gives the words to Krishna). 'Fare forward', with the images of travel which accompany it, suggests the spirit of the end of 'East Coker': 'Old men ought to be explorers'. But to fare forward is to aim at the future and a destination in time and place, and would seem to suggest a different spirit from the concentration on the present moment in the idea that it is what the mind is intent on at the time of death – '(And the time of death is every moment)' – which is the one important 'action'. The image of being aboard ship, suspended in time, is appropriate to the idea of a consciousness of a present moment as if 'outside time'. But the injunction 'Fare forward' seems to suggest another set of values. We have already been told (in line 6) that 'the way forward is the way back' so this insistence on a particular direction seems (in this context) perplexing. The passage ends 'Not fare well, / But fare forward, voyagers': but leaving aside the play on 'farewell' it is not entirely clear why 'fare well' (in the sense of 'virtuously') would not fit the logic of the ideas with equal appropriateness. It may be that there is some way of reconciling these ideas; and it could be objected that it is wrong to subject the passage to this kind of logical scrutiny. But it is a passage which employs a mode of discursive argument, and so objections to its logic would seem to be permissible; and beyond this one might still say there is an obscurity of feeling.[15]

The lyric prayer in Part IV recalls the addresses to the 'Lady' of *Ash-Wednesday*, though here she is specifically the Virgin Mary. As a lyric poem it is not very distinguished. As a prayer it has a certain dignity, though the phrase 'those / Whose business has to do with fish' seems stilted (why not just 'fishermen'?). In the light of its personal association with the New England coast one can see it as a part of Eliot's renewed awareness of his own past. And more broadly it suggests his widening sympathy towards a larger community of different classes, in this case of those who work on the sea as opposed to those like the poet who simply contemplate it, and those family relations of women, sons and husbands which hitherto – at least up until *The Family Reunion* – Eliot's poetry has largely ignored. The Virgin Mary represents both mothers and daughters, as 'Figlia del tuo figlio', 'daughter of thy son' (in the mystical phrase of Dante's *Paradiso* XXXIII, 1). And the 'perpetual angelus' refers to the Angelus service celebrating the angel Gabriel's Annunciation to Mary – which takes up the motif of Annunciation in Part II.

It is refreshing, at the beginning of Part V, to get a glimpse of the wry, satirical Eliot and to catch an echo of the world of Madame Sosostris, the fortune teller in *The Waste Land*; and irony is reinforced satisfyingly in the dry music of individual lines and the (here appropriate) pedantry of their diction ('Describe the horoscope, haruspicate or scry'; 'riddle the inevitable / With playing cards, fiddle with pentagrams'). It is a nicely concentrated conspectus of superstition across time and space ('Whether on the shores of Asia, or in the Edgware Road') which in its ironic bathos also recalls, more generally, the earlier poem. A genuine religious sense abandons the searching of past or future (say, through psychoanalysis or prophesy) 'to apprehend / The point of intersection of the timeless / With time' – but this is 'an occupation for the saint'. And Eliot returns then to 'the unattended / Moment' which 'for most of us' is the closest we get to such reality — to those images from the earlier poems (the wild thyme, the winter lightning, etc.) which now need merely to be mentioned to recall those earlier moments (and to them is added 'the waterfall', which is to recur at the end of Little Gidding'): [16]

> These are only hints and guesses,
> Hints followed by guesses; and the rest
> Is prayer, observance, discipline, thought and action.
> The hint half guessed, the gift half understood, is Incarnation

The 'prayer, observance' and the rest are, in fact, represented in the poem by those parts which are not primarily intense or lyrical but discursive, reflective or liturgical (like Part IV of 'The Dry Salvages'): they represent the more habitual activities of the mind which are more in control of the will, and by means of which the significance of the 'unattended moments' can be related to the rest of life. The fourth line is the most daring leap in the poem: the 'hint' and 'gift' of the 'unattended moments' *are* 'Incarnation': they are the Word (the Word of God, the Word that is God) made flesh, the spirit given body. The tentativeness of the line ('*half* guessed', '*half* understood') makes all the more striking its last word. Eliot would not be drawn to comment when the capital 'I' of 'Incarnation' was questioned by a reader of an early draft: was this simply the embodiment of the spirit or the full Christian sense of the word?[17] One must surely say that for Eliot it was the latter, since for him Christianity was the only possible way of giving final significance to the idea of incarnation. But the reader must make of it what sense he can: a non-doctrinal meaning may be open to him, but he needs also to be aware that the meaning would not have satisfied the author.

'Here the impossible union / Of spheres of existence is actual': 'here' that is, in the 'moments' fleetingly, and in Christian doctrine permanently. The rest of the closing lines summarize again many of the issues with which we have been made familiar (of time, movement, action) and echo the language of 'Burnt Norton' ('the past and future / Are conquered', 'that which is only movement / And has in it no source of movement') and recall the 'earthy' images of 'East Coker' ('Driven by daemonic, chthonic powers'). The summing-up is perhaps (as Helen Gardner suggests) a little perfunctory in comparison with the other expressions of similar ideas, but there is a satisfying concentration of meaning in the last four lines, where the limited but real creative achievements of life are wryly and soberly given their due:

> We, content at the last
> If our temporal reversion nourish
> (Not too far from the yew-tree)
> The life of significant soil.

The 'temporal reversion' is both our return to time after the 'unattended moments' and our reversion to earth in death; and the 'significant soil' is both the social 'bed' out of which art and civilization grow, and the literal earth of the grave.

III

'Little Gidding' (1942)

'East Coker' and 'The Dry Salvages' are on the whole the Quartets with the fewest moments of high intensity, and ones where the discursive element is most marked, and in the case of the latter, often awkward in form. 'Little Gidding' at times achieves an intensity equal to that in 'Burnt Norton' and some of its discursive passages have a new clarity and precision. The last Quartet treats much the same areas of experience that we have already encountered, but in places gives a deeper account of them, and also constitutes a culmination and completion. 'Burnt Norton' was concerned with 'personal' time and memory and the moment of eternity perceptible through them, 'East Coker' with time as a recurring cycle of seasons and years, history and traditions (like those of marriage), 'The Dry Salvages' with the world of work, action, scientific curiosity, and the inner powers (the river) and the outer impersonal rhythms of time (the sea) which disrupt these or represent, in the latter case, a quite other order of time. 'Little Gidding' brings together the life of the individual and that of history: the moments of the former (insights into a timeless world) are completed and validated by their relation with those moments of insight achieved by others in the past: '... history is a pattern / Of timeless moments'. There is also a culmination of the specifically Christian element in the poems (seen most clearly in the progression of the fourth parts of each poem: in 'Burnt Norton' Part IV is about death and 'the still point'; in 'East Coker', Christ's redemption of man; in 'The Dry Salvages', it is a prayer to the Virgin to intercede for man), in a lyric on the fires of hell and purgatory.

It is probably true that, even after repeated readings, the reader is more conscious of individual passages in *Four Quartets*, and different attempts to come at the same truths of experience, than of any clear structure or progression.[18] The opening of 'Little Gidding' is one of the most memorable passages and one of the finest poetic moments in the work. What makes it so powerful is its fusion of physical sensation and spiritual apprehension (so that one needs a phrase like 'spiritual sensation' to sum up the effect).

> When the short day is brightest, with frost and fire,
> The brief sun flames the ice, on pond and ditches,
> In windless cold that is the heart's heat,
> Reflecting in a watery mirror
> A glare that is blindness in the early afternoon.
> And glow more intense than blaze of branch, or brazier,
> Stirs the dumb spirit: no wind, but pentecostal fire
> In the dark time of the year. Between melting and freezing
> The soul's sap quivers.

The sharp perception of the natural scene and the strong physical response to it is inseparable from the spiritual perception and response: the 'Windless cold that is the heart's heat' evokes both an inner physical warmth of resistance to cold, and by its syntax a mysterious heat that is paradoxical, beyond the realm of physical ('cold that *is* the heart's heat'). The 'glare that is blindness' is another instance: physically apprehensible, and yet strictly a paradox (and also recalling 'Burnt Norton's 'heart of light', and even more 'The Burial of the Dead' and its supreme moment and different kind of paradox: '. . . my eyes failed . . . / Looking into the heart of light'). And 'the soul's sap quivers' also concentrates the fusion of physical and spiritual. The passage is a triumph of that 'metaphysical' language of which Eliot had often written, in which word becomes flesh, or spirit body. And it makes possible the rise to the idea: 'This is the spring time / But not in time's covenant', to the symbolic 'blossom / Of snow' (where the break in the line also effects that slight, enlivening shock of surprise), and to the final metaphysical question:

> Where is the summer, the unimaginable
> Zero summer?

Without the fusion of physical and spiritual the symbolic snow 'not in the scheme of generation' would seem contrived, and the final question merely clever or 'Clevelandish' (as it seemed to John Hayward).[19] But arising out of the passage as a whole it achieves as well as the transcendental *idea* of a condition 'out of time', the embodying of that idea, and the illumination of poetry.

The conversational passage that follows relates the visionary evocation of the first verse-paragraph to common experience and the common processes of time (the actual spring, with its blossoms of 'voluptuary sweetness').[20] The seeming circumlocution ('Taking the route you would be likely to take', etc.) has in fact a necessary generalizing function, reminding us of the many possible individual routes to the meaning of which he is going to talk. The place which is the focus of significance for Eliot is Little Gidding, the home of the seventeenth-century religious community of Nicholas Ferrars which 'attempted to combine the values of monastic and family life'.[21] But the historical details are absent in the poem: the place is important as a place in the poem, somewhere local and actual, from which the meditations arise. There is a mingling of the historical with the present — 'If you came at night like a broken king' is a reference to an occasion on which Charles I took refuge at Little Gidding during the Civil War — but it is the fusion of past history with the present that matters, and the idea of reaching the same goal (of religious revelation) by different routes and at different times. The particularities of the scene ('when you leave the rough road / And turn behind the pig-sty to the dull façade / And the tombstone') combine with the generalizing instances to give it a 'personal' actuality — to make it personal as well as impersonal. There is a feeling (for the reader) of something 'both intimate and unidentifiable' (to borrow a phrase from Part II), or of arriving somewhere familiar, and 'knowing the place for the first time' (Part V). This embodies in feeling the idea that follows of a purpose 'beyond the end you figured': it is the fulfilment of a purpose and yet only now is the purpose discovered. The evocation of 'other places / Which also are the world's end' carries the imagination briefly out into the strange and the romantic which make more moving the assertion which follows, by contrast with its note of familiarity:

> But this is the nearest, in place and time,
> Now and in England.

The passage that follows specifies the action the reader would need to take 'If you come this way'. It is directly Christian teaching — 'You are here to kneel . . .' — but one should note the provisional opening: 'If you came this way'. Some readers object to what they see as elements of preaching in *Four Quartets*, and are inclined to cite Keats's remark about art which has 'a palpable design' on us.[22] Perhaps it would be misguided to deny entirely the existence of this element in the poem. But here at least, 'If you come . . .' suggests more the quietly deliberate report of a witness to a truth than the hectorings of a preacher. And in general it should be said that the 'doctrinal' element in the poem is rarely if ever nakedly pedagogic, but rather just one part of the record of a totality of experience. We are led along a route that seems familiar, we enter into an experience. Whether we follow the final direction in which that experience seems to lead us is left to us. The poem is not coercive. As much as being told 'You are here to kneel', we are told about the nature of prayer and its relation to tradition ('Where prayer has been valid'). And whether or not we follow or fully understand what is being said about prayer, we may more easily understand the general application of this in relation to the idea of tradition:

> the communication
> Of the dead is tongued with fire beyond the language of the living.

'Tongued with fire' has, of course, its specific religious meaning, relating to the Pentecostal imagery of the opening verse-paragraph and that in Part IV (drawn from the Pentecost in Acts 2, when the cloven tongues of fire rested on the Apostles and they began to speak 'with other tongues'), so that the 'communication' is that spiritual meaning of the actions of the dead. But it also — like Ferrars or Charles I — surely relates to the 'tradition' of which Eliot had written in 1920 and the 'presence' of the past: so that the communication is that of the great dead authors who can speak to us now in ways in which they could not speak to their own contemporaries. 'The intersection of the timeless moment' with time can be found in the great acts, and the great writings, of the dead. And it is 'England and nowhere. Never and always' because Eliot can only find it in his place, time and tradition, though it belongs to no place and no time.

The lyric at the opening of Part II is the most powerful of all the lyrics at the same point in the other Quartets, all of which contain a different idea of death (a pagan harmony 'among the stars' in 'Burnt Norton', 'destructive fire' in 'East Coker', and shipwreck in 'The Dry Salvages', with or without the prayer of Annunciation). It recapitulates and shows the end of the worlds of those Quartets and their related elements, in four stanzas of incisive double quatrains: 'Ash on an old man's sleeve / Is all the ash the burnt roses leave', recalling 'Burnt Norton'; 'Dust inbreathed was a house / The wall, the wainscot and the mouse', recalling 'East Coker'; 'Flood and drouth' and 'water', recalling 'The Dry Salvages'; and 'fire', being the element of 'Little Gidding'. Life as a merely natural process leads only to death, death 'by' as well as 'of' air, earth, water and fire. Once again the quatrain form provides Eliot with an ideal form for a poetry of sombre 'satire' in the broadest sense, resembling the satire of the old medieval '*contemptu mundi*' lyrics and the Johnson of 'The Vanity of Human Wishes' in its Latinate (and tersely Anglo-Saxon) language:

> The parched eviscerate soil
> Gapes at the vanity of toil,
> Laughs without mirth.
> This is the death of earth.

What followed the lyrics on life and death in Part II of the other three Quartets were largely abstract passages on time and timelessness, experience and meaning. In 'Little Gidding' there is instead a short episode of encounter and recognition, a dialogue that reveals in pointed terms the poet's final attitude to a merely humanistic wisdom, what he had earlier called 'the wisdom of age' and 'the knowledge to be derived from experience'. The change is undoubtedly a gain in poetic power and this section stands out as one of the finest achievements of the poems. The meeting with a 'familiar compound ghost' is strongly influenced, as Eliot has indicated,[23] by Dante, and has the lineaments of one of Dante's encounters in the underworld: the choice of metre (a basic iambic pattern with alternating ten- and eleven-syllable lines with strong and weak endings respectively) was an attempt to find an equivalent for English of the effect of Dante's *terza rima*. But what is most important for the reader is that the form achieves a combination of ease and control, embodying perfectly both the narrative and a revelatory wisdom which is at once spontaneous and deeply pondered.

The scene is at once some placeless underworld and, we become gradually aware, a London street in the early morning after an air raid. This mysterious double location constitutes a large part of the scene's atmosphere and mystery. 'The dark dove with a flickering tongue' is both some mysterious spiritual agent (the dove is the traditional symbol of the Holy Ghost, as we see in Part IV, so that here the 'dark dove' is a kind of Evil Spirit), and also an enemy bomber. The 'asphalt' and 'between three districts whence the smoke arose' reinforce the urban connotations, and 'the blowing of the horn' at the end is both romantic or medieval and, specifically, the sounding of the 'all clear'. The 'metal leaves' that 'rattled on like tin' are autumn leaves, and yet there is a slightly surreal quality about the images. And 'We trod the pavement in a dead patrol' has the connotations of a patrol of wardens or fire-watchers[24] as well as a kind of pun on 'dead', suggesting a strange synchronization between the two figures, and an underworld of death.

This double or composed identity of the scene is echoed in the identities of the actors. The ghost is 'compound', a mingling of many figures, 'some dead master', 'both intimate and unidentifiable'. It recalls many 'masters':[25] Yeats, who died abroad in Paris and whose poem on old age, 'The Spur' ('You think it horrible that lust and rage / Should dance attendance upon my old age'), Eliot had discussed in his essay on Yeats (1940); Mallarmé in the line from 'Le Tombeau de Charles Baudelaire', 'To purify the dialect of the tribe'; Brunetto Latini, the humanist poet in Dante's *Inferno* XV, condemned to the seventh circle for his sexual perversion, and whose 'cotto aspetto' is almost literally translated in Eliot's 'brown baked features' and Dante's ' "Siete voi qui, ser Brunetto?" ' in ' "What are *you* here?" ' There are also echoes of Dr Johnson in the style of the ghost's homily with its trenchant general truths (compare ' "Then fools' approval stings and honour stains" ' with Johnson's 'Grief aids disease, remembered folly stings' in 'The Vanity in Human Wishes') and of the ghost of Hamlet's father in 'And faded on the blowing of the horn', which echoes Marcellus's 'And faded on the crowing of the cock').[26] But there is no precise identity, and these echoes are only important in so far as they give dimension to the general idea of a compound 'dead master' in the art of poetry, who comes to tell the narrator of the limitations of a merely human and poetic wisdom. The narrator too assumes 'a double part': it is Eliot's final and crowning use of that poetic 'doubling of the personality' which he observed in Laforgue − here not a symptom of a fragmented self as it had been before, but an active technique to compose the mind and confirm a new identity in a newly discovered faith.

> So I assumed a double part, and cried
> And heard another's voice cry: 'What! are *you* here?'
> Although we were not. I was still the same,
> Knowing myself yet being someone other –
> And he a face still forming; yet the words sufficed
> To compel the recognition they preceded.

In his 'double part' the narrator is his old self and a new one, and his effort of projection also helps to conjure the compound figure of the ghost.

The dramatic vividness of the passage is caught in the details which are either simply and precisely familiar ('That pointed scrutiny with which we challenge / The first-met stranger in the waning dusk'), or combine with extraordinary effectiveness the familiar and the unfamiliar: the 'metal leaves', the movement of the ghost 'loitering and hurried', the being 'Too strange to each other for misunderstanding', the 'easy' wonder (' "Yet ease is cause of wonder" '). And this prepares us for the point of the passage, in the ghost's utterance. First he dismisses his own 'thought and theory' and bids the narrator dismiss his: the human wisdom of poetry and poetic theory is of no use at the point which they have both reached. But poetry will have one last function in revealing ' "The gifts reserved for age" '. And in the passage which follows we have the full power of a trenchant 'Augustan' poetry of general truth, a sombre irony which sums up the 'gifts' in phrases of measured disenchantment: ' "the cold friction of expiring sense" ', ' "the laceration / Of laughter at what ceases to amuse" ', ' "Then fools' approval stings, and honour stains" '.

> From wrong to wrong the exasperated spirit
> Proceeds, unless restored by that refining fire
> Where you must move in measure, like a dancer.

The ghost ends with the remedy of the refining fire of purgatorial suffering and the 'measure' of the 'dancer', which takes up again the predominant image of fire in 'Little Gidding' and the image of the dance from 'Burnt Norton' ('there the dance is') and 'East Coker' ('So the darkness shall be the light and the stillness the dancing'). The passage ends swiftly with a daylight which confirms the inner illumination of the teaching, and an 'all clear' which signals the end of the air raid, and the end of the vision.

After the intensity of Part II, the relaxation to general reflection in Part III is satisfying, as if the mind has gained a new ease of discursive thought. But the metaphor for the 'three conditions' is perplexing. Eliot would seem to mean that attachment and detachment are both, in their way, good (though we know from the rest of the poem that detachment is better), whereas 'indifference' is not. The idea is complicated by the metaphor which relies (as Eliot commented in a letter) on the fact that the 'live' nettle and 'the dead nettle' are different kinds of plants, of which the first stings and the second flowers, not live and dead versions of the same plant.[27] This is likely to elude most readers; and in any case the argument is still obscure. Indifference is 'unflowering', but otherwise it is not clear enough that it is the least desirable member of the trio (it resembles the others 'as death resembles life', but one cannot be quite sure how Eliot means us to value 'death' here).[28] The passage continues, 'This is the use of memory: / For liberation . . .', but while this is clear enough in itself it is not clear how it relates to what has just gone before: 'liberation' is presumably to be associated with 'detachment', but the syntax seems to associate it with 'indifference'. The passage would only have been slightly clearer if Eliot had left out the nettles, as he did in his first draft. But the ideas get clearer as we go on, and the negative view of 'indifference' seems to be confirmed in the idea 'not less of love but expanding / Of love beyond desire', and the idea of love of country beginning with our love of 'our own field of action' and coming 'to find that action of little importance / Though never indifferent'. As a parallel case to 'love of country', 'History may be servitude' because it may impose dead conventions or 'a pattern which falsifies' ('East Coker' II), and 'History may be freedom' because it can be 'a pattern of timeless moments' ('Little Gidding' V) and reveal to us (through great literature and great actions) the nature of the real.

The ideas of this passage, and others like it in the Quartets, are worth thinking about and lend themselves (all too easily, some might say) to exposition. But we may regret the absence of poetry and even, at times, of the clearest possible prose sense which this kind of verse should aim at. So it is a moment of relief when a more urgent voice breaks in, as it had done before in the discursive passages, with some lines that remind us of Eliot's earlier experience.

> See, now they vanish,
> The faces and places, with the self which, as it could, loved them,
> To become renewed, transfigured, in another pattern.

'See, now they vanish': it is as if the poet catches a final glimpse of them before they disappear, and we are reminded of the 'faces' of the earlier poems, the eyes' 'fugitive resentment', the 'Eyes I dare not meet in dreams', 'the blessèd face', the 'face, less clear and clearer' and 'the self, which *as it could*, loved them'. One effort of *Four Quartets* is, one might say, summed up here: the effort to convey a new sense of love in which these partial loves are renewed and transfigured. Nevertheless one might reflect on how small a part personal relationships play in this poem and wonder whether this new 'pattern' of them is more than gestured at. If religious Love is to be shown to be the crowning and 'transfiguration' of ordinary human love then one might feel that human love needs to be shown contained within it, as it is, for instance, in the New Testament, not simply 'vanished'. And the importation of Julian of Norwich at this point ('sin is Behovely . . .')[29] seems a little too abrupt, and too easy in its assurance of ultimate salvation (and for whom?).

The return at this point to reflections arising out of the place Little Gidding ('If I think, again . . .') is again slightly abrupt: one wonders if Eliot is completely in control of the sequence of thought here. The lines are now shorter and more controlled and deliberate, the tone is quietly understated (as in 'not wholly commendable') but firm. There are a few problems: what is the 'common genius' which touched both sides in the Civil War ('the strife which divided them') − that of dedication to a cause? And is not the line 'And those whom they opposed' an unnecessary prolixity? But the main idea is clear: that *both* sides can now be seen to be exemplary. The lines

> Accept the constitution of silence
> And are folded in a single party

gloss the common fate of death with political metaphors of fine and sombre irony ('folded' is particularly good). And it is the defeated who leave the most salutary example, 'A symbol perfected in death' − a symbol of self-sacrifice. One thinks perhaps (because of the Civil War context) of Marvell's Charles I:

> *He* nothing common did or mean
> Upon that memorable scene . . .
> But bowed his comely head,
> Down as upon a bed.

In the final lines of this Part, the 'purification of the motive' is the purification from any hope of worldly gain.

The lyric in Part IV is the final concentrated expression of the purgatorial idea of redeeming love. It is powerful in its directness and concentration of metaphor, unlike the more elaborate and 'conceited' allegory of Christ's redemption in 'The Dry Salvages' IV (it is interesting to learn that Eliot originally drafted a lyric in a similarly 'metaphysical' manner and then decided, after advice, to abandon it).[30] The 'dove descending' is the Holy Ghost or the enemy bomber (as in Part II): the double sense becomes clear in the division of 'hope, or else despair' and the division of 'pyre or pyre' (the conflagration of the Spirit or of literal flame), and in 'To be redeemed from fire by fire' (from the fire of sin and hell by the fire of love and purgatory). Similarly 'the one discharge from sin and error' has two possible meanings: the discharge into mere death if the 'flame of incandescent terror' is merely that of the enemy bomber, or the discharge into redemption if the flame is that of the Holy Ghost; which of the two we take depends on 'the choice of pyre or pyre'. The 'intolerable shirt of flame' in the second stanza derives from the fate of Hercules poisoned by the contaminated shirt of Nessus (as in Sophocles's *Women of Trachis* or Seneca's *Hercules Oetaeus*), adapted as an image of Christian purgatory. 'Love' is certainly an 'unfamiliar name' for the power behind such suffering: one has to say that it is not much like 'love' as most people understand it. But then, Eliot would agree.

The opening of Part V, the last part of the last Quartet, recalls the 'beginning' and 'end' of 'East Coker', and in particular here the idea 'In my end is my beginning'. The end of *Four Quartets* 'is where we start from' − or at least where Eliot starts from in the sense that in the end 'The poetry does not matter' ('Burnt Norton' II), being merely the prelude to an isolated spiritual quest. Every poem is 'an epitaph' in that it closes an experience, leaves the mind and spirit free for a new departure. The parenthetic description of the 'phrase / And sentence that is right' might prompt one to ask at this point how far in *Four Quartets* Eliot achieves this ideal style, with

> The word neither diffident nor ostentatious,
> An easy commerce of the old and the new,
> The common word exact without vulgarity,
> The formal word precise but not pedantic,

(Is 'Those whose business has to do with fish' not slightly pedantic? And 'sempiternal'? Or can that be justified by its touch of grandeur, appropriate at that point? Or *'Erhebung'*? Or 'hebetude'? But nevertheless, to cite these exceptions makes one aware that as a rule Eliot's style comes remarkably close to meeting this ideal.) Every poem can be seen as an epitaph also because it can at its fullest epitomize a life and place it in relation to death. An action, too, is a step towards death, literally (in terms of time: we are always moving towards death) and morally, in that action is finally to be judged in the light of death, *sub specie aeternitatis*. Eliot wrote that he did not understand the idea of 'faith in life': 'faith in death is what matters'.[31] 'We die with the dying . . .': the statement is somewhat gnomic and intended perhaps to carry various suggestions. We see others die, and grieve over them; and we are dying too. 'We are born with the dead': we discover our real lives in the significance of the actions of the great dead, which 'return', survive. The 'rose' in the following lines is, by way of the symbolism the poems have gradually accumulated for it, love: the love glimpsed in the rose-garden, the love expressed in political sacrifice (the 'Royal Rose' of 'The Dry Salvages' and 'the spectre of a Rose', 'Little Gidding' III, the English royal emblem associated here with Charles I), and divine love (as in the 'roses' of purgatorial fire in 'East Coker' IV, and at the end of 'Little Gidding'). And the 'yew-tree' is of course the emblem of death; both love and death are, under the aspect of time, 'of equal duration'. In the concluding lines of this part there is a fusion of the personal experience of the poet with the historical experience of society: if 'History is a pattern of timeless moments' – moments of insight into eternity – the poet's moments of insight become a part of History, including, with a moving touch of poetic immediacy, this particular moment in the chapel at Little Gidding:

> So, while the light fails
> On a winter's afternoon, in a secluded chapel
> History is now and England.

The concluding passage of 'Little Gidding' begins with a phrase ('With the drawing of this Love and the voice of this

Calling')[32] that hangs suspended typographically, so that although it is part of a new sentence it seems to refer back as much as forward: that 'History is now and England' depends on this Love and this Calling, as well as the exploration which follows. The phrase is a moment of pause, as if 'suspended in time', an intimation as if perceived out of the corner of the mind's eye. Amid the poetry of statement which predominates in this Part it is one of those moments which keep alive another kind of poetry; and it also adds the indispensable predicate of Grace to the idea of exploration, of individual effort which follows. The images of exploration and of 'the unknown remembered gate', the source of the river, the waterfall, the children in the apple-tree, all gather up those images which have been charged with significance at earlier points in the Quartets and sometimes in earlier poems (the 'children in the apple-tree' are from 'New Hampshire'). Is is notable that the images are once again mainly from childhood, 'the beginning', and that it is the supreme and fleeting 'moments' which are called up again, with the phrase from the end of 'Burnt Norton': 'Quick now, here, now, always – '. But by now they have been involved with the processes of adult life, the effort of 'exploration' and the effort at simplicity '(Costing not less than everything)' (recalling the many passages of renunciation in the Quartets, like the end of Part III in 'Burnt Norton' and 'East Coker').

The last five lines draw the more explicitly religious imagery of the poems into this final coda and recapitulation: the lines from Julian of Norwich ('And all shall be well . . .') and the image of the fire and the rose, which together recall so many images in the poems of suffering and love. It is a final attempt at a mode which combines the technique of French Symbolism with the visionary allegory, the 'higher dream' of Dante. How successful we feel it is will depend on how far we feel that these religious emblems have really been given new life in the poem, or how far they are still only literary and traditional religious emblems giving a merely nominal conclusion to the religious themes of the poem. It is possible to feel that the images of childhood and returning to the source have an emotional power in themselves, echoing as they do some of the most intensely poetic passages of the Quartets, which the religious symbols dissipate and 'mystify' rather than complete. In the end, a lot must surely depend here (despite what Eliot himself often said about the difference between poetic assent and philosophic assent) on the beliefs of the reader. The concluding symbols can be seen by any reader to be a masterly drawing together of various images of fire and rose throughout the poems, but for the lines to have a feeling of final poetic conviction the reader needs perhaps to have made a step which the poetry alone cannot lead him to take. But it is difficult to be sure: the Christian reader who assents to the doctrine might still feel less moved by this kind of religious language than by other kinds of language in the poem. One thing is certain: it is impossible to restrict one's judgement of these lines, and ultimately of the whole poem, to *purely* 'literary' criteria.

Is *Four Quartets* the crowning achievement of Eliot's poetry (as Eliot himself and many others have considered), or is it a fall into prosaism, *longueurs* and mere doctrine, enlivened by all too few moments of poetic power? Is Eliot at his best essentially an imagist or symbolist poet of intense fragments and short poems, and is his effort at a more Augustan style of poetry of statement a misguided one? Probably most of his readers have seen it as a culmination, but there have always been dissenting voices. George Orwell wrote in 1942: 'it is clear that something has departed, some kind of current has been switched off, the later verse does not contain the earlier'; Stephen Spender in 1954: 'nothing of Eliot is so good as "Preludes" and "The Waste Land" . . . the naked, isolated, raw material has disappeared. The imagery and the rhythm have ceased to be uniquely personal and have become responsible in a way of which I am suspicious – responsible to publishers and a public'; Herbert Read in 1965: ' "In my end is my beginning" – yes, but it is the end of the earthly poet and the beginning of the redeemed sinner'; C. H. Sisson in 1971: 'Of course it is the writing of a man of immense accomplishment, but it is not the writing of a man impelled. The words come from a region where half-forgotten reasonings settle, not from profounder depths.'[33] And in a recent book C. K. Stead (who cites the above testimonies) has spoken of an 'inner failure of spirit' and 'the dark treadmill verse' of much of the work, which he associates with Eliot's failure 'to overcome a reluctance to look upon the body of a fallen world' and also his tendency (springing from the same causes) towards the external structures of established religion and right-wing politics.[34]

It is difficult to deny entirely the justice of some of these criticisms. *Four Quartets* is a work which lacks the kind of intensity of 'Prufrock' and *The Waste Land*. And yet it is a work which has its own intensities, and which attempts to show their place in relation to other kinds of life and thought, even when the thought is 'prosaic'. It is impossible to dismiss it with the completeness which declares that 'it is not for the health of the literature of the English-speaking countries that attention should be deflected from *The Waste Land*, *Sweeney Agonistes*, *and Prufrock*'.[35] There would seem to be a closer analogy with Wordsworth's *Prelude* than with the *Excursion* (or the Duddon Sonnets which Sisson proposes): there is an element in it of poetic biography and a similar method in which moments of illumination rise out of or break in on general reflection. Stead admits the power of the rose-garden episode in 'Burnt Norton'; and can one not add to that the sharply actual *and* visionary passage on the 'mid-winter spring' in Part I and the intensely imagined meeting with the 'compound ghost' in Part II of 'Little Gidding', as well as, to a lesser extent, the finely evocative passages like that on the sea in Part I of 'The Dry Salvages', or the mysteriously familiar and yet timeless passage on the urban limbo in Part II of 'Burnt Norton'? There is also the way in which briefer flashes of poetic intensity break in on passages that are primarily discursive or incantatory: 'Dawn points, and another day / Prepares for heat and silence' at the end of 'East Coker' I; 'So the darkness shall be the light and the stillness the dancing' in 'East Coker' III; the stirring transition to 'The wave cry, the wind cry, the vast waters' at the end of 'East Coker'; and the gleams of recollected images at the end of 'Burnt Norton' and 'Little Gidding'. There are also the beautiful touches in the lyrical Parts IV − 'After the kingfisher's wing / Has answered light to light, and is silent', 'The silent withering of autumn flowers / Dropping their petals and remaining motionless' − or the power of 'The parched eviscerate soil / Gapes at the vanity of toil'. It is difficult to see such lines coming from a poet who has suffered 'poetic bankruptcy'.[36] Rather, the poems are those of a man who is undergoing a drama of the middle of life, the 'middle way' in which prosaic thought and doctrine contend with lyricism and moments of regained intensity, and in which the mind needs to see the relation of those moments to ideas, and to the more prosaic virtues of 'prayer, observance, discipline, thought and action'. One suspects that many of the objections to the poems arise, by a natural enough process, from a lack of sympathy for the religious beliefs (as in

Orwell's case and, it seems, in Stead's). But whether or not one shares Eliot's beliefs, one may still feel that *Four Quartets* does more than any other literary work of this century to create what Tolstoy called the 'religious perception' of an age,[37] and that it is a vital matter that a society should continue to create forms of such a perception. Eliot's own words in an essay of 1945, 'The Social Function of Poetry', are apposite here. They are not unproblematic: one might ask whether it is possible, as the passage seems to imply, for men to feel towards God and man 'as they did' if they no longer believe as they did. And the phrase 'as they did' itself becomes a problem when we are told a few lines later that religious feeling varies 'from age to age'. But nevertheless, with its concern for keeping alive a continuity with past feeling, and for men's struggle with language and expression, it may perhaps serve as a fitting conclusion to this discussion of *Four Quartets* and this study of Eliot's poetry as a whole:

Much has been said everywhere about the decline of religious belief; not so much notice has been taken of the decline of religious sensibility. The trouble of the modern age is not merely the inability to believe certain things about God and man which our forefathers believed, but the inability to *feel* towards God and man as they did. A belief in which you no longer believe is something which to some extent you can still understand; but when religious feeling disappears, the words in which men have struggled to express it become meaningless. It is true that religious feeling varies naturally from country to country, and from age to age, just as poetic feeling does; the feeling varies, even when the belief, the doctrine, remains the same. But this is a condition of human life, and what I am apprehensive of is death.

(*On Poetry and Poets*, p. 25)

Notes

Dates of publication are those of editions used; dates of first editions are also given where appropriate.

Introduction

1 *Selected Essays* (London, 1966, first published 1932, revised and enlarged 1934). All subsequent references to this work are to this edition.
2 *The Use of Poetry and the Use of Criticism* (London, 1964; first published 1933). All subsequent references to this work are to this edition.
3 Leonard Woolf, *Downhill all the Way* (London, 1968), p. 109.
4 'Verse and Prose', *Chapbook* 22 (1921), p. 8.
5 All quotations from the poetry and plays are taken from *The Complete Poems and Plays* (London, 1982; first published 1966). Dates against poems in the text are those of first publication except where otherwise stated.
6 *On Poetry and Poets* (London, 1961; first published 1957), p. 84. All subsequent references to this work are to this edition.
7 *Cf.* C. H. Sisson, *English Poetry 1900–1950: An Assessment* (New York, 1971), p. 145.
8 Most recently for example by C. K. Stead in *Pound, Yeats, Eliot and the Modernist Movement* (London, 1986).
9 William Empson, 'The Style of the Master', in *T. S. Eliot*, compiled by Tambimuttu and Richard March (London, 1965; first published 1948), p. 35.
10 Donald Davie, 'Eliot in One Poet's Life', in *'The Waste Land' in Different Voices*, ed. A. D. Moody (London, 1974), pp. 221–37.

1. Aspects of the life of the poet

1 For the biographical facts in this chapter, I have drawn mainly on Lyndall Gordon, *Eliot's Early Years* (Oxford and New York, 1977), and Peter Ackroyd, *T. S. Eliot* (London, 1984).
2 Edmund Wilson, *Axel's Castle* (London, 1969; first published 1931), p. 90.
3 *Eliot's Early Years*, p. 12, for this and other quotations in this paragraph.
4 *Ibid.*, p. 27.
5 *Selected Essays*, p. 429.
6 *T. S. Eliot*, p. 23.

7 Letter to Ottoline Morrell, undated. Quoted in Ackroyd, *T. S. Eliot*.

8 *Ibid.*, p. 22.

9 *Ibid.*, p. 25.

10 Irving Babbitt, *Rousseau and Romanticism* (Boston, 1979; first published 1919), p. 51.

11 In *La Nouvelle Revue Francaise* 21 (1923), p. 122.

12 *Eliot's Early Years*, pp. 40–1.

13 *Ibid.*

14 Quoted, *ibid.*, p. 51.

15 *The Waste Land: A Facsimile and Transcript of the Original Drafts including the Annotations of Ezra Pound*, ed. Valerie Eliot (London, 1971), p. 21.

16 *T. S. Eliot*, p. 149.

17 William Empson, *Using Biography* (London, 1984), p. 199. I am grateful to Michael Grant for directing me to this reference.

18 'Poetry and Drama', *On Poetry and Poets*, p. 79.

19 'The Three Voices of Poetry', *On Poetry and Poets*, pp. 96–100.

20 *T. S. Eliot*, p. 160.

21 *Ibid.*, p. 163.

22 *Hommage à Charles Maurras*, 1948, cited in *T. S. Eliot*, p. 76.

23 *The Criterion* 8: 31 (1928), pp. 280–90.

24 See the passage from *The Idea of a Christian Society*, cited below, pp. 214–15.

25 See Helen Gardner, *The Composition of 'Four Quartets'* (London and Boston, 1978), p. 55, note 51. There is a judicious discussion of the question of Eliot's anti-semitism in A. D. Moody, *Thomas Stearns Eliot: Poet* (Cambridge, 1980), p. 370, note 18.

26 Bonamy Dobrée, 'T. S. Eliot: A Personal Reminiscence', in *T. S. Eliot: The Man and his Works*, ed. Allen Tate (London, 1966), p. 81.

27 *T. S. Eliot*, p. 252.

28 *Ibid.*, p. 316.

29 'John Ford', *Selected Essays*, p. 203.

30 'Shakespeare and the Stoicism of Seneca', *ibid.*, p. 137.

2. Early poetic influences and criticism, and
Poems Written in Early Youth

1 'Dante' (1929), in *Selected Essays*, p. 276.

2 *Selected Essays*, p. 21. (For a fuller discussion see below, pp. 73–6.)

3 In 'Imperfect Critics', *The Sacred Wood* (London, 1966; first published 1920), p. 31; quoted in A. D. Moody, *Thomas Stearns Eliot: Poet* (Cambridge, 1980), p. 17.

4 Preface to *John Davidson: A Selection of his Poems*, ed. Maurice Lindsey, with an essay by Hugh McDiarmid (London, 1961).

5 Arthur Symons, *The Symbolist Movement in Literature* (New York, 1971; first published 1899), p. 115.

6 Hugh Kenner, *The Invisible Poet: T. S. Eliot* (London, 1965; first published 1959). For Eliot's approval of the title see W. T. Levy and Victor Scherle, *Affectionately, T. S. Eliot* (London, 1969), p. 105.

7 Quotations from Laforgue's poetry are taken from *Poésies Complètes*, ed. Pascal Pia (Paris, 1960), pp. 85, 257, 279.

8 *The Oxford Book of Twentieth Century English Verse*, chosen by Philip Larkin (Oxford, 1973), p. 497.

9 'Personal Choice', 30 December 1957, B.B.C. Sound Archives, Cited in Peter Ackroyd, *T. S. Eliot*, p. 27.

10 Letter to Conrad Aiken quoted by Aiken in *T. S. Eliot: A Symposium*, ed. March and Tambimuttu (London, 1948), p. 23. 'Hah! That was a bit brash, wasn't it?', Eliot commented in 1959 when asked about the remark. (*Writers at Work: The 'Paris Review' Interviews*, ed. C. Plimpton and Van Wyck Brooks (London and New York, 1982; first published 1963), p. 95).

11 'American Literature and American Language', in *To Criticize the Critic* (London, 1965), p. 58 (all subsequent references to this work are to this edition). See also Ronald Bush, *T. S. Eliot: A Study in Character and Style* (New York and Oxford, 1984), p. 124.

12 *Cf.* below, Chapter 5, note 1.

13 *The Criterion* 12: 48 (1933), p. 469.

14 Lyndall Gordon, *Eliot's Early Years*, p. 58.

3. *Prufrock and Other Observations* (1917)

1 For fuller information on the dates of publication of these and other poems see Donald Gallup, *T. S. Eliot: A Bibliography* (London, 1969), and Caroline Behr, *T. S. Eliot: A Chronology of his Life and Works* (London, 1983); and for discussion of the dates of composition, see Lyndall Gordon, *Eliot's Early Years*, and Piers Gray, *T. S. Eliot's Intellectual and Poetic Development, 1909–1922* (Sussex, 1982).

2 Jules Laforgue, *Derniers Vers* (Toronto, 1965), p. 7, quoted in Piers Gray, p. 9.

3 In *The Madwoman of Chaillot* (1945).

4 Quoted in F. O. Matthiessen, *The Achievement of T. S. Eliot* (New York and London, 1958; first published 1935), p. 9.

5 F. R. Leavis, 'Eliot's Classical Standing', *Lectures in America* (London, 1969), p. 42.

6 I have been helped in thinking about the ambiguities of this line by Piers Gray's discussion in *T. S. Eliot's Intellectual and Poetic Development*, pp. 85–6 (which also, however, finds further possibilities of meaning).

4. Poetic theory and poetic practice

1 E.g. by James Smith, in 'Notes on the Criticism of T. S. Eliot', *Essays in Criticism* 22 (1972), pp. 333ff. Cited in Brian Lee, *Theory and Personality: The Significance of T. S. Eliot's Criticism* (London, 1979), p. 11.

2 A thoughtful and questioning discussion of these issues can be found in Brian Lee, *ibid*.

3 E.g. in *The Sacred Wood* (London, 1966; first published 1920), p. xiv (all subsequent references to this volume are to this edition).

4 Cited in F. R. Leavis, 'Eliot's Classical Standing', *Lectures in America* (London, 1969), p. 31.

5 See Brian Lee, *Theory and Personality*, Chapter 2.

6 By F. R. Leavis, 'Eliot's Classical Standing', p. 30.

7 *Selected Essays*, p. 321.

8 *Fortnightly Review*, 1 September 1924, pp. 463–4; quoted in Michael Alexander, *The Poetic Achievement of Ezra Pound* (London, 1979), p. 51.

9 The typescript of Eliot's Clark Lectures is in the John Hayward Bequest in the library of King's College, Cambridge, where it may be read with the permission of the Modern Archivist.

10 'Donne in Our Time', *A Garland for John Donne*, ed. Theodore Spencer (Cambridge, Mass., 1931), p. 8.

5. *Poems* (1920)

1 *Poetry* 68 (1946), p. 335; quoted in Piers Gray, *T. S. Eliot's Intellectual and Poetic Development*, p. 209, n. 71.

2 Quoted in Herbert Howarth, *Notes on Some Figures behind T. S. Eliot* (London, 1965), p. 131.

3 For the identification of some of the allusions in this and other poems I am indebted to Grover Smith, *T. S. Eliot's Poetry and Plays* (Chicago, 1961; first published 1956). B. C. Southam's *A Student's Guide to the Selected Poems of T. S. Eliot* (London, 1972; first published 1968) is also useful in this respect.

4 Quoted in *The Waste Land Facsimile*, p. xxviii.

5 Lyndall Gordon, *Eliot's Early Years*, p. 70.

6 *Ibid*., p. 70.

7 Grover Smith, *T. S. Eliot's Poetry and Plays*, p. 41.

8 From The Clark Lectures, 1926; cited above, p. 86.

9 See 'A Commentary', in *The Criterion*, 12: 48 (1933), pp. 470–1.

10 See A. D. Moody, *Thomas Stearns Eliot: Poet*, pp. 76–8. As well as for its prompting the discussion here, I have found this study often valuable, particularly in its chapter on *Four Quartets* and in its concluding chapter.

11 Moody, *Thomas Stearns Eliot: Poet*, p. 78.

12 The passage is quoted in full above, pp. 36–7.

13 The phrase is also quoted and discussed by Eliot in his essay on Lancelot Andrewes of 1926; see *For Lancelot Andrewes* (London, 1970; first published 1928), pp. 22–3.

6. *The Waste Land* (1922)

1 William Empson, *Using Biography* (London, 1984), p. 190.
2 Southam, in his *Student's Guide*, suggests identification also with Ezra Pound, noted for his American style of dress and 'stetson' hat, though this is, I think, of secondary importance for the poem. The French phrase is from Baudelaire's poem 'Au Lecteur' (tr. 'Hypocrite reader – my double – my brother').
3 William Empson, *Seven Types of Ambiguity* (Harmondsworth, 1971; first published 1930), p. 78.
4 Ovid, *Metamorphoses*, tr. Mary M. Innes (Harmondsworth, 1983; first published 1955), Book VI. Philomela is raped by King Tereus, the husband of her sister Procne, and her tongue is cut out to prevent her telling of her shame. But she communicates the story of Procne by representing it in a tapestry. To revenge the crime against her sister, Procne kills the son she bore Theseus and serves the flesh of his body to the unwitting King at a great feast. When Theseus discovers what has happened he rushes at Philomela and Procne, but they escape, Philomela turning into a nightingale and Procne into a swallow.
5 See above, Chapter 3, note 4.
6 Southam, *Student's Guide*, draws attention to the echo of the description of the Thames in Conrad's *Heart of Darkness*: 'The tanned sails of the barges drifting up with the tide seemed to stand still in red clusters of canvas.' Kurtz's phrase from the same, 'The horror! the horror!', was part of the epigraph in the original draft of the poem; and the same story provides the epigraph to *The Hollow Men*: 'Mistah Kurtz – he dead.'
7 The Rhine-daughters are seductive sirens in *Das Rheingold*. But Eliot's note directs us to their role in *Die Götterdämmerung* (*The Twilight of the Gods*) III.i., where they are anticipating the return of the gold whose theft deprived the river of its beauty. (See B. C. Southam, *A Student's Guide*, p. 86.) So the associations are perhaps more with the lifting of a curse here.
8 Eliot's note draws attention to the echo of Dante's *Purgatorio*, V. 133:

> Ricorditi di me, che son La Pia
> 'Siena mi fe', disfecemi Maremma.'

('Remember me, who am La Pia; / Sienna made me, Maremma unmade me'.) La Pia was a lady of the thirteenth century, put to death by her husband either out of jealousy or because he wanted to marry again. She is therefore another example of a woman destroyed by a failure of love. It was doubtless the fine and dignified cadence of her words that caused the echo to stay in Eliot's mind.

9 *Writers at Work: The 'Paris Review' Interviews, Second Series*, ed. George Plimpton and Van Wyck Brooks, p. 96.

10 Hieronimo in Kyd's *The Spanish Tragedy* is driven mad by the murder of his son. He contrives a revenge on the murderers which takes place during a play which he writes for them – a play, written (like *The Waste Land*) in different languages. He says 'Why then I'll fit you' to the murderers before writing the play, meaning both 'I'll fix something up for you' and (with hidden dramatic irony) 'I'll fix you'. In Eliot's poem, the line refers perhaps both to the poet fixing something together ('to shore against my ruins') and to his closeness to mental breakdown.

11 Among the more suggestive associations in this closing passage, 'Le Prince d'Aquitaine . . .' is a line from 'El Desdichado', a poem by de Nerval, and evokes a lost romantic world. 'Quando fiam . . .' ('When may I become like the swallow') is from a Latin hymn and recalls the swallow of 'A Game of Chess' (line 100), but changes the association to a Christian one, an image the soul flying to God. For the line from Dante ('Poi s'ascose . . .') see below, p. 131.

12 *Writers at Work: 'The 'Paris Review' Interviews, Second Series*, p. 96.

13 F. O. Matthiessen (*The Achievement of T. S. Eliot*), for example, seems to overstate the case when he talks of Eliot 'grounding the structure of his . . . poem in something outside himself, in an objective pattern of myths' (p. 44). The myths seem to me to provide not so much a clear structure as a source of elusive but suggestive echoes. Cleanth Brooks has an interesting essay, 'The Waste Land: A Critique of the myth' (reprinted in *T. S. Eliot: 'The Waste Land'*, Casebook Series, ed. C. B. Cox and A. P. Hinchliffe (London, 1968), but he is inclined, I think, to regard the mythic element too much as a firm structure, as when he says that 'Eliot's theme is the rehabilitation of a system of beliefs' (p. 160).

14 Quoted in Hugh Kenner, *The Invisible Poet: T. S. Eliot* (London 1965; first published 1959), p. 156.

15 A review of Joyce's *Ulysses*, first published in *The Dial* 75:5 (1923), p. 480.

16 Southam, *A Student's Guide*, pp. 21–2.

17 *The Waste Land Facsimile*, pp. 125–6, note 1.

18 Grover Smith, *The Waste Land* (London, 1983), pp. 123–4.

19 *Inferno*, iii, 55–7.

20 The marriage between Elizabeth and Leicester, about which the Spanish courtier De Quadra speculates in the letter which Eliot quotes, never came about, despite much rumour, including the story that Leicester's first wife died in mysterious circumstances.

21 Quoted by A. D. Moody, 'To fill all the desert with inviolable

voice'; *'The Waste Land' in Different Voices*, ed. Moody (London, 1974), p. 48.

22 *Writers at Work*, p. 97.

23 Yvor Winters, *The Anatomy of Nonsense* (New York, 1943), reprinted in *In Defense of Reason* (Denver, n.d.), pp. 499–500; extract reprinted in *T. S. Eliot: 'The Waste Land'*, pp. 60–1.

7. From *The Hollow Men* (1925) to 'Marina' (1930)

1 Interview of 1959, reprinted in *Writers at Work*, p. 100.

2 See Southam, *A Student's Guide*, pp. 134–5.

3 Eliot accepted the suggestion that the phrase 'Falls the shadow' was derived from the phrase 'There falls thy shadow' in Ernest Dowson's best-known poem, 'Non sum qualis eram' ('I am not now as once I was'): 'The lines . . . have always run in my head.' The 'shadow' is also a repeated image in Conrad's *Heart of Darkness* (see Southam, *A Student's Guide*, pp. 106–7.) But these echoes do not, I think, play any essential part in our understanding of the poem.

4 See for example Southam, *A Student's Guide*, p. 104.

5 'From Poe to Valéry', in *To Criticize the Critic*, p. 34. For further discussion of this idea, see below, p. 201.

6 See Grover Smith, *T. S. Eliot's Poetry and Plays*, p. 130.

7 *For Lancelot Andrewes*, p. 17.

8 Conrad Aiken, *Selected Letters* (New Haven and London, 1978), p. 185; quoted in Ronald Bush, *T. S. Eliot: a Study in Character and Style* (New York and London, 1984), p. 250, note 56.

9 *The Bookman* 70 (1930), reprinted in *Literary Opinion in America*, ed. M. D. Zabel, Vol. 1 (New York, 1962), p. 106.

10 See Grover Smith, *T. S. Eliot's Poetry and Plays*, p. 157; also Southam, *A Student's Guide*, p. 116.

11 In a letter to John Hayward, Eliot wrote: 'Perhaps the yew does not mean as much as you suppose. It happened to occur in two or three dreams – one was a dream of the "boarhound between the yew trees"; and that's all I know about it.' Quoted in Helen Gardner, *The Composition of 'Four Quartets'* (London and Boston, 1978), p. 39, note 26.

12 See below, Chapter 10, note 9.

13 *The Prelude* (1805), Book XI, 11, 171–84.

14 Ronald Bush, *T. S. Eliot: A Study in Character and Style*, p. 167.

15 Cited in Bush, *ibid*.

16 For a suggestion that there is a 'correspondence between Seneca's two Hercules plays . . . and certain features of Eliot's own Christianity' in its development from the recognition of sin to the fire of purgatorial suffering, see A. D. Moody, *Thomas Stearns Eliot: Poet*, pp. 158–9. But as Moody admits, 'none of this is actually in "Marina" – it is simply what the epigraph can lead us to'.

8. Poetry, pattern and belief

1 'The Metaphysical Poets', in *Selected Essays*, p. 289.
2 See above, p. 39.
3 *La Nouvelle Revue Francaise* 14: 158 (1926), p. 525.
4 Hugh Kenner, *The Pound Era* (Berkeley and Los Angeles, 1971), p. 439; quoted in Ronald Bush, *T. S. Eliot: a Study in Character and Style*, p. 157.
5 This essay first appeared under the title 'Johnson's *London* and *The Vanity of Human Wishes*' as the Introduction to the Haslewood Books edition, 1930. It was reprinted in *The Pelican Guide to English Literature*, Vol. 4, *From Dryden to Johnson* (Harmondsworth, 1977; first published 1957).
6 *La Nouvelle Revue Francaise* 14: 158 (1926), pp. 525–6; my translation, italics in the original.
7 *Chapbook* 22 (1921), p. 9.
8 The third Turnbull Lecture, 1933, MS in the Houghton Library, Harvard University; cited in Bush, *T. S. Eliot: A Study in Character and Style*, pp. 175–6.
9 *The Bookman* 70 (1930), reprinted in *Literary Opinion in America*, ed. M. D. Zabel, Vol. 1 (New York, 1962), p. 106.
10 Valéry, *Le Serpent*, tr. Mark Wardle (London, 1924); cited in Bush, *T. S. Eliot: A Study in Character and Style*, pp. 82, 98.
11 'Charybde et Scylla: lourdeur et frivolité', *Annales du Centre Universitaire Meditérranien* 5: 71 (1951–2); cited in Bush, *ibid.*, p. 99. (There is also an English version of these lectures in the Hayward Collection, King's College Library, Cambridge.)
12 'A Note on Poetry and Belief', in *The Enemy* 1 (1927), pp. 15–17.

9. From *Coriolan* (1931) to 'Burnt Norton' (1936)

1 Ronald Bush, *T. S. Eliot: A Study in Character and Style*, p. 154.
2 See F. O. Matthiessen, *The Achievement of T. S. Eliot*, pp. 82–3.
3 For example, in 'The Function of Criticism at the Present Time', *Essays in Criticism* (Everyman Edition, London, 1964), p. 26: ' "Away with the notion of proceeding by any other course than the course dear to the Philistines; let us have a social movement, let us organise and combine a party to pursue truth and new thought, let us call it *the liberal party*, let us all stick to each other and back each other up . . ." In this way the pursuit of truth becomes really a special, practical, pleasurable affair, almost requiring a chairman, a secretary, and advertisements . . .'
4 From Eliot's Commentary when reading the poems on NBC radio; printed in University of Chicago Round Table, No. 659 (12 November, 1950). Cited in A. D. Moody, *Thomas Stearns Eliot: Poet*, p. 165.

5 *Ibid*.

6 *The Old Wives Tale*, ed. P. Binnie (Manchester, 1980), line 812; also to be found in *The Penguin Book of English Verse*, ed. John Hayward (Harmondsworth, 1981), p. 26.

7 *On Poetry and Poets*, p. 98. Quoted more fully above, p. 78.

8 Entry for 10 September 1926, *Journals of Arnold Bennett*, ed. Newton Flower (London, 1932–3). Cited in Peter Ackroyd, *T. S. Eliot*, p. 145.

9 Recorded on the Memorial Record of *Homage to T. S. Eliot* at the Globe Theatre, London, 13 June 1965, E.M.I. Records, CPL 1924.

10 Letter to A. W. M. Baillie, 10 September 1864. *Gerard Manley Hopkins: A Selection of his Poems and Prose*, ed. W. H. Gardner (London, 1964; first published 1953), pp. 154–9.

11 Interview in *The New York Times Book Review*, 29 November 1953; reprinted in *T. S. Eliot: Four Quartets*, Casebook Series, ed. Bernard Bergonzi (London, 1977), p. 23.

10. 'Burnt Norton' (1936) and the pattern for *Four Quartets*

1 *The Pickwick Papers*, Chapter 42. Mrs Valerie Eliot has related that Eliot thought of prefixing this quotation as an epigraph to *Four Quartets* as a whole. See Helen Gardner, *The Composition of 'Four Quartets'* (London, 1978), p. 28.

2 Preface to *Lyrical Ballads*, 1800.

3 Despite his remarks about musical analogies, it is not fully clear whether Eliot was influenced by any particular pieces of music. Beethoven's late quartets have been suggested as influences, and Eliot is reported to have said he was thinking of Bartok's quartets, nos. 2–6. Bernard Bergonzi (ed.) *T. S. Eliot: Four Quartets*, p. 182. See also Grover Smith, *T. S. Eliot's Poetry and Plays*, p. 253.

4 *Interviews with William Carlos Williams*, ed. L. Wagner (New York, 1976), p. 63.

5 Translation by Philip Wheelwright, *Heraclitus* (Princeton, 1959), pp. 19, 90.

6 Kipling's story 'They' (in *Traffics and Discoveries*, 1904), with its poetic and mysterious evocation of hidden children in the garden of a remote country house inhabited by a blind housekeeper, was mentioned by Eliot (see Gardner, *The Composition of 'Four Quartets'*, p. 39) as one of the influences on this Part, and the fineness of the story makes it genuinely illuminating in relation to the poem. Kevin Taylor has suggested to me that 'they' in Eliot's poem can also be seen as the children 'hidden excitedly' in the leaves. I still tend to see Eliot's presences as distinguished from his 'children' by the description 'dignified' and the sense of adult meeting in 'accepted and accepting' and 'So we moved, and they, in a formal pattern'. But it is also true that in Kipling's story much turns on the narrator's

'acceptance' by the children and his ability to see them, and at one point the children gather themselves 'in a roundel'. The encounter in Eliot's rose-garden would then be one with the ghosts of the adults' former selves or indeed with lost or unborn children of their own. But, of course, these are matters of atmosphere, association and suggestion; it is not a question of establishing one precise interpretation.

7 Ronald Bush (*T. S. Eliot: a Study in Character and Style*, pp. 189–92) has made an interesting connection between these presences and the Eumenides in *The Family Reunion*, written two years later. The Eumenides are the spirits or furies, derived from Aeschylus's *Oresteia*, who torment the conscience of the protagonist Harry with a sense of guilt about the death of his wife. There are several phrases and passages in Eliot's play that recall 'Burnt Norton'. In Part I, Scene I, Harry says to Mary, 'You bring me news / of a door that opens at the end of a corridor, / Sunlight and Singing' (p. 310), but then is struck with an apprehension of his tormentors:

> When I remember them
> They leave me alone: when I forget them
> Only for an instant of inattention
> They are roused again, the sleepless hunters
> That will not let me sleep.   (p. 311)

And in Part I, Scene I Harry had also talked of 'them':

> Can't you see them? *You* don't see them, but I see them,
> And they see me. This is the first time that I have seen them.
> . . . I knew they were coming
> They were always there but I did not see them
> Why should they wait until I came back to Wishwood?
> There were a thousand places where I might have met them!
> Why here? Why here?   (p. 292)

Wishwood, a place whose name suggests 'what might have been' or what is now desired, has certain affinities with the rose-garden in 'Burnt Norton' (and has a rose-garden itself). And the echo aroused by these images and others (e.g. in Agatha's speech in I.1, 'Yes, I mean that at Wishwood he will find another Harry', etc., pp. 288 and 334–5) suggest a connection between Harry's search for reconciliation and the harmonious relation with the presence in the rose-garden, 'accepted and accepting'. In the play too, there is in the end a reconciliation with the Eumenides (II.2, p. 336), and they become 'bright angels', or, as they do for Aeschylus's Orestes, 'the kindly ones'. It should be emphasized again that this identification is not, of course, explicit in 'Burnt Norton', and that it would distort the mysterious effect of the presences in their various associations to *equate* them with the figures in the play. One should not even claim,

I think, that a reader who does not make the association necessarily responds less well to the passage, and one might even argue that some of the associations aroused need to be kept out of our response, or at least held at a distance. But the association is nevertheless a real one: at the very least it shows something of the workings of Eliot's imagination and the complex inter-connectedness of his different works.

8 From 'Tonnerre et rubis aux moyeux' ('Thunder and rubies up to the axles') in 'M'introduire dans ton histoire'; and also perhaps 'la bouche / Sépulcrale d'égout bavant boue et rubis' ('The sewer's sepulchral mouth, slobbering mud and rubies') in 'Le Tombeau de Charles Baudelaire' (*Mallarmé*, ed. Anthony Hartley (London 1965), pp. 101 and 91). For Eliot's own comments on Mallarmé's lines, see above, p. 171.

9 'If our words "regret" and "eternity" were exact bits of mosaic with which to build patterns much of 'Burnt Norton' would not have had to be written . . . One could say, perhaps, that the poem takes the place of the ideas of "regret" and "eternity". Where in ordinary speech we should have to use those words, and hope by conversational trial-and-error to obviate the grosser misunderstandings, this poem is a newly created concept, equally abstract but vastly more exact and rich in meaning.' In this passage in Part II, Harding suggests, Eliot begins by making 'pseudo-statements', 'putting forward and immediately rejecting ready-made concepts that might have seemed to approximate to the concept he is creating'. D. W. Harding, 'Words and Meanings: A Note on Eliot's Poetry', in *Experience Into Words* (London, 1963), p. 109; extract reprinted in Bernard Bergonzi (ed.), *Four Quartets: A Selection of Critical Essays*, p. 29.

10 *Literature and Dogma* (Thomas Nelson and Sons, London, [1873]), p. 166 and *passim*.

11 See Helen Gardner, *The Composition of 'Four Quartets'*, p. 86: 'Eliot travelled daily from Gloucester Road Station, whose two means of descent, by the stairs or by the lift, suggested to him the movement down and the "abstention from movement", while being carried down . . . He gave this information in a letter to his brother.' It is clearly important, however, that the particular associations are hardly there in the verse itself, where they might detract from the generalizing force of the lines. Rather, the associations hover behind the lines as a ghostly particularity which, once pointed out, may become part of the experience of the poem.

12 E.g. in *The Odyssey*, XXIV, 4. The seven named hills of London also intensify the classical association by their echo of the seven hills of Rome.

13 But for a possible private association for Eliot, see above, note 11.

14 See Helen Gardner, *The Composition of 'Four Quartets'*, p. 89. The 'other' way may also suggest ascent, as in St John of the Cross: 'For on this road; to descend is to ascend, since he who humbles himself

is exalted, and he who exalts himself is humbled' (*The Dark Night of the Soul*, Book II, Chapter 18).

15 'The Sunflower', *Songs of Experience*, 1794.

16 See above, pp. 35 and 172–4.

11. The wartime Quartets (1940–2)

1 See above, Chapter 9, note 11.

2 The common critical observation that the four poems are related to the four seasons and the four elements is based on Eliot's own remarks. Eliot said in 1948 that it was 'during the writing of "East Coker" that the whole sequence began to emerge, with the symbolism of the four seasons and the four elements. "Burnt Norton" then has to stand for spring in the sequence, though its imagery was perhaps more summery.' (See Kristian Smidt, *The Importance of Recognition* (London, 1961, p. 34). In 1949 he wrote: 'By the time ['East Coker'] was finished I envisaged the whole work as having four parts which gradually began to assume, perhaps only for convenience sake, a relation to the four seasons and the four elements' (letter to Professor William Matchett, January 1949). Both sources are cited in Helen Gardner, *The Composition of Four Quartets*. But, as Eliot's qualifications suggest, the relation was perhaps only a convenient rough plan. It is not strictly adhered to, and one is not, I think, strongly conscious of the divisions in reading the poems. The pattern would go: 'Burnt Norton': Air and Spring; 'East Coker': Earth and Summer; 'The Dry Salvages': Water and Autumn; 'Little Gidding': Fire and Winter.

3 Quoted in Gardner, *ibid.*, p. 109.

4 See *The Idea of a Christian Society*: 1939, pp. 63–4; quoted in A. D. Moody, *Thomas Stearns Eliot: Poet*, pp. 203–4.

5 Introduction to *Le Serpent* by Valéry, tr. Mark Wardle, p. 12.

6 See above, p. 174.

7 See *Samson Agonistes*, line 80.

8 *Cf.* F. R. Leavis, *The Living Principle* (London, 1975), p. 204.

9 *The Ascent of Mount Carmel*, I xiii. 11.

10 The view that the 'ruined millionaire' represents Adam is not finally convincing in the light of the evidence. See Helen Gardner, *The Composition of 'Four Quartets'*, pp. 43–6.

11 John Hayward, in his Notes to a French translation of *Four Quartets*, says that there is a particular allusion here to the graveyard at East Coker. But while this may be so it does not seem to be very important for the understanding of the poem, in which the 'old stones' are memorials in general. It is another example of an 'allusion' which is not 'functional', being either private or incidental.

12 Eliot's head-note informs us: 'The Dry Salvages – presumably "les

Trois Sauvages'', is a small group of rocks . . . off the N.E. coast
of Cape Ann, Massachussetts. *Salvages* is pronounced to rhyme
with *assuages*.'

13 See 'T. S. Eliot: The End of an Era', reprinted in Bernard Bergonzi
(ed.), *T. S. Eliot, 'Four Quartets': A Casebook*, p. 154. Davie goes
on, however, to suggest that 'The Dry Salvages' as a whole stands
in a relation of parody to the rest of the Quartets.

14 F. R. Leavis, *The Living Principle*, p. 222.

15 It is worth mentioning that in his recent discussion of the poem,
A. D. Moody (*Thomas Stearns Eliot: Poet*) does not comment on
the significance of 'Fare forward', and Helen Gardner (*The Composition of 'Four Quartets'*) says she is unable to find a clear source
for the phrase despite Eliot's own suggestion that it is taken from
a saying of Alaric.

16 *Cf.* also *The Family Reunion*, Part I, Scene II, Harry's speech to
Mary:

> You have stayed in England, yet you seem
> Like someone who comes from a very long distance,
> Or the distant waterfall in the forest,
> Inaccessible, half-heard.
>
> (*Collected Poems and Plays*, p. 309)

17 See Helen Gardner, *The Composition of 'Four Quartets'*, p. 145.

18 For a contrary view, however, see A. D. Moody, *Thomas Stearns
Eliot: Poet*, pp. 237–42.

19 See Helen Gardner, *The Composition of 'Four Quartets'*, p. 160.
Hayward was a friend of Eliot's at the time of the writing of 'Little
Gidding' and made many detailed comments on Eliot's first drafts,
some of which Eliot accepted (e.g. the brilliant suggestion of 'laceration' in the phrase 'laceration / Of laughter' in Part II). John
Cleveland (1613–58) was one of the most fanciful of the
'metaphysical' poets.

20 The phrase recalls 'depraved May' in 'Gerontion', which suggests
that we have here one of those momentary echoes of earlier feeling
that frequently enliven Eliot's later poetry.

21 Helen Gardner, *The Composition of 'Four Quartets'*, p. 58.

22 Letter to J. H. Reynolds, 3 February 1818: 'We hate poetry that has
a palpable design upon us and when we do not agree, seems to put
its hand in its breeches' pocket' (*Letters of John Keats*, selected by
Frederick Page (London, 1965; first published 1954), p. 72).

23 See 'What Dante Means to Me', in *To Criticize the Critic*,
pp. 128–9.

24 Eliot did fire-watching duty at the offices of Faber and Faber during
the war.

25 Eliot himself acknowledged primary references to Yeats and Dante,
but the main point is that it is a *compound* ghost. Eliot wrote in

1943: 'Why the phrase "compound ghost" "Both one and many" should still leave people still convinced that the stranger was one particular person, I don't understand' (quoted in Gardner, *The Composition of 'Four Quartets'*, p. 67, note 77).

26 *Hamlet*, I.i.157.

27 See Helen Gardner, *The Composition of 'Four Quartets'*, p. 200.

28 The term 'death' in Eliot's poetry can clearly have a negative value, as in 'Marina' ('Those who sharpen the tooth of the dog, meaning / Death', etc.), or a positive one, as in the statement: 'What faith is life may be I know not . . . for the Christian, faith in death is what matters' (*The Criterion* 12: 47 (1933), p. 248; quoted in Moody, *Thomas Stearns Eliot: Poet*, p. 161).

29 *Revelations of Divine Love*; The Thirteenth Revelation, Chapter 27.

30 See Helen Gardner, *The Composition of 'Four Quartets'*, p. 212.

31 See note 28.

32 The phrase is from *The Cloud of Unknowing*, a fourteenth-century mystical work.

33 Orwell, 'T. S. Eliot' in *T. S. Eliot, Four Quartets: A Selection of Critical Essays*, ed. Bergonzi, London, 1969, p. 81; Spender, 'The Modernist Movement is Dead', in *Highlights of Modern Literature*, ed. F. Brown (New York, 1954); Read, 'T. S. E. – a Memoir', in *T. S. Eliot, The Man and his Work*, ed. A. Tate (London, 1967), p. 37; C. H. Sisson, *English Poetry, 1900–1950* (London, 1971), p. 151.

34 C. K. Stead, *Pound, Yeats, Eliot and the Modernist Movement* (London, 1986), pp. 194–5.

35 C. H. Sisson, *English Poetry, 1900–1950*, p. 154.

36 Robert Graves, *The Crowning Privilege* (London, 1955), p. 129; quoted in Stead, *Pound, Yeats, Eliot and the Modernist Movement*, p. 194.

37 Tolstoy, 'What is Art?', in *What is Art? and Essays on Art*, trans. Aylmer Maude (London, 1962; first published 1930), p.232.

Select bibliography

Editions of Eliot's work

The following is a selective chronological list of first editions of Eliot's poetry, criticism and plays from 1917 to 1965 with dates of publication. Unless otherwise indicated, the place of publication is London. For editions used in the present book, the reader is referred to the list in my Acknowledgements.

Prufrock and Other Observations, 1917
Poems, 1919
Ara Vos Prec, 1920 (published in New York as *Poems*)
The Sacred Wood (criticism), 1920
The Waste Land, New York, 1922; London, 1923
Poems 1909–1925 (including *The Hollow Men*), 1925
Journey of the Magi, 1927
A Song for Simeon, 1928
For Lancelot Andrewes (criticism), 1928
Animula, 1929
Ash-Wednesday, 1930
Marina, 1930
Triumphal March, 1931
Selected Essays 1917–1932 (criticism), 1932
John Dryden: The Poet, the Dramatist, the Critic (criticism), New York, 1932
Sweeney Agonistes (play), 1932
The Use of Poetry and The Use of Criticism (criticism), 1933
After Strange Gods (criticism), 1934
The Rock (play), 1934
Murder in the Cathedral (play), 1935
Collected Poems 1909–1935 (including 'Burnt Norton'), 1936
The Family Reunion (play), 1939
Old Possum's Book of Practical Cats, 1939
The Idea of a Christian Society (social criticism), 1939
East Coker, 1940
The Dry Salvages, 1941
Little Gidding, 1942
Four Quartets, New York, 1943; London, 1944
Notes Towards the Definition of Culture (social criticism), 1948
The Cocktail Party (play), 1950

Poems Written in Early Youth, 1950
The Confidential Clerk (play), 1954
On Poetry and Poets (criticism), 1957
The Elder Statesman (play), 1959
George Herbert (criticism), 1962
Knowledge and Experience in the Philosophy of F. H. Bradley (philosophy), 1964 (Eliot's doctoral dissertation of 1914–16)
To Criticize the Critic and Other Writings (criticism), 1965

Bibliography and textual studies

Gallup, Donald, *T. S. Eliot: A Bibliography* (London, 1969)
Eliot, Valerie (ed.), *The Waste Land: a Facsimile and Transcript of the Original Drafts including the Annotations of Ezra Pound*, London, 1971.
Gardner, Helen, *The Composition of 'Four Quartets'* (London, 1983)

Chronology

Behr, Caroline, *T. S. Eliot: A Chronology of his Life and Works* (London, 1983)

Biographical studies

Ackroyd, Peter, *T. S. Eliot* (London, 1984)
Gordon, Lyndall, *Eliot's Early Years* (Oxford, 1977)
Howarth, Herbert, *Notes on Some Figures behind T. S. Eliot* (London, 1965)

Criticism

Bergonzi, Bernard, *T. S. Eliot* (London, 1972)
    (ed.), *T. S. Eliot, A 'Four Quartets' Casebook* (London, 1969)
Braybrooke, Neville (ed.), *T. S. Eliot: A Symposium* (London, 1958)
Bush, Ronald, *T. S. Eliot: A Study in Character and Style* (New York and London, 1984)
Calder, Angus, *T. S. Eliot* (London, 1987); (this work appeared after completion of the present study)
Cox, C. B., and Hinchliffe, A. P. (eds.), *T. S. Eliot, 'The Waste Land': A Casebook* (London, 1968)
Gardner, Helen, *The Art of T. S. Eliot* (London, 1949)
Grant, Michael (ed.), *T. S. Eliot: The Critical Heritage* (London, 1982), 2 vols.
Gray, Piers, *T. S. Eliot's Intellectual and Poetic Development 1909–1922* (Sussex, 1982)
Kenner, Hugh, *The Invisible Poet* (London, 1960)
    ed.), *T. S. Eliot, a Collection of Critical Essays* (Englewood Cliffs, 1962)

Leavis, F. R., *New Bearings in English Poetry* (London, 1932)
　Lectures in America (London, 1969)
　English Literature in our Time and the University (London, 1969)
　The Living Principle (London, 1975)
Lee, Brian, *Theory and Personality: The Significance of T. S. Eliot's Criticism* (London, 1979)
Litz, A. W. (ed.), *Eliot in his Time* (London, 1973)
March, Richard and Tambimuttu (eds.), *T. S. Eliot: A Symposium* (London, 1948)
Margolis, J. D., *T. S. Eliot's Intellectual Development, 1922–1939* (London, 1972)
Martin, C. G. (ed.), *Eliot in Perspective: A Symposium* (London, 1979)
Matthiessen, F. O., *The Achievement of T. S. Eliot* (London, 1935)
Moody, A. D., *Thomas Stearns Eliot: Poet* (Cambridge, 1979)
　(ed.), *The Waste Land in Different Voices* (London, 1974)
Newton-de Molina, D. (ed.), *The Literary Criticism of T. S. Eliot* (London 1977)
Schneider, Elisabeth, *T. S. Eliot: The Pattern in the Carpet* (Berkeley, 1975)
Smidt, Kristian, *Poetry and Belief in the Work of T. S. Eliot* (London, 1961)
Smith, Grover, *T. S. Eliot's Poetry and Plays* (London, 1974)
　The Waste Land (London, 1984)
Southam, B. C., *A Student's Guide to the Selected Poems of T. S. Eliot* (London, 1968)
　(ed.), *T. S. Eliot, 'Prufrock', 'Gerontion', 'Ash-Wednesday' and other Shorter Poems: A Casebook* (London, 1978)
Spender, Stephen, *T. S. Eliot* (London, 1975)
Stead, C. K., *The New Poetic: Yeats to Eliot* (London, 1964)
　Pound, Yeats, Eliot and the Modernist Movement (London, 1986)
Tate, Allen (ed.), *T. S. Eliot: The Man and his Work* (London, 1967)

Index

Page numbers in bold type indicate the main discussion of an entry

INDEX